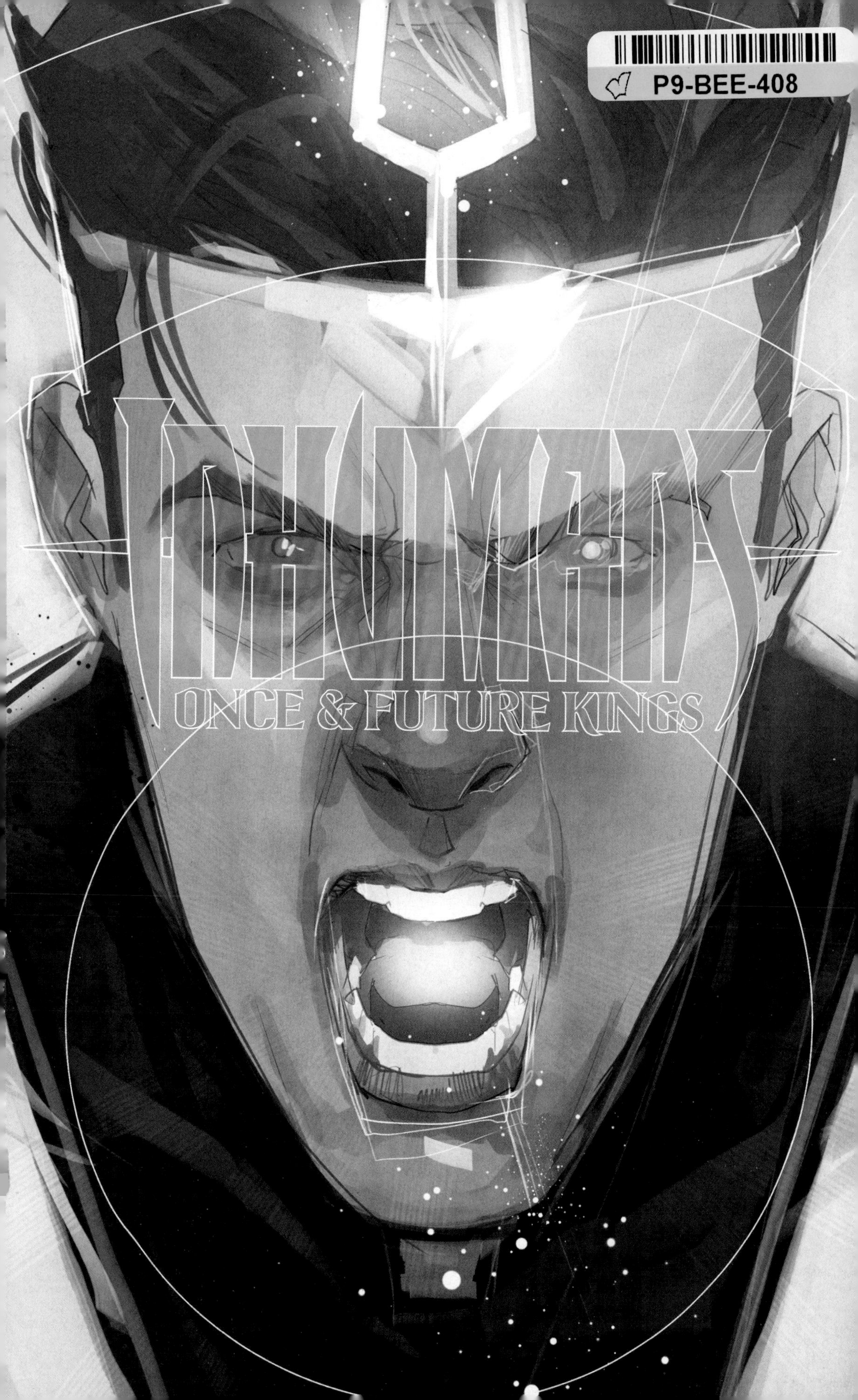
INHUMANS
ONCE & FUTURE KINGS

COLLECTION EDITOR **MARK D. BEAZLEY**
ASSISTANT EDITOR **CAITLIN O'CONNELL**
ASSOCIATE MANAGING EDITOR **KATERI WOODY**
SENIOR EDITOR, SPECIAL PROJECTS **JENNIFER GRÜNWALD**

VP PRODUCTION & SPECIAL PROJECTS **JEFF YOUNGQUIST**
SVP PRINT, SALES & MARKETING **DAVID GABRIEL**
BOOK DESIGNER **ADAM DEL RE**

EDITOR IN CHIEF **C.B. CEBULSKI**
CHIEF CREATIVE OFFICER **JOE QUESADA**
PRESIDENT **DAN BUCKLEY**
EXECUTIVE PRODUCER **ALAN FINE**

INHUMANS: ONCE AND FUTURE KINGS. Contains material originally published in magazine form as INHUMANS: ONCE AND FUTURE KINGS #1-5. First printing 2018. ISBN 978-1-302-90940-6. Published by MARVEL WORLDWIDE, INC., a subsidiary of MARVEL ENTERTAINMENT, LLC. OFFICE OF PUBLICATION: 135 West 50th Street, New York, NY 10020. Copyright © 2018 MARVEL No similarity between any of the names, characters, persons, and/or institutions in this magazine with those of any living or dead person or institution is intended, and any such similarity which may exist is purely coincidental. **Printed in Canada.** DAN BUCKLEY, President, Marvel Entertainment; JOE QUESADA, Chief Creative Officer; TOM BREVOORT, SVP of Publishing; DAVID BOGART, SVP of Business Affairs & Operations, Publishing & Partnership; DAVID GABRIEL, SVP of Sales & Marketing, Publishing; JEFF YOUNGQUIST, VP of Production & Special Projects; DAN CARR, Executive Director of Publishing Technology; ALEX MORALES, Director of Publishing Operations; SUSAN CRESPI, Production Manager; STAN LEE, Chairman Emeritus. For information regarding advertising in Marvel Comics or on Marvel.com, please contact Vit DeBellis, Custom Solutions & Integrated Advertising Manager, at vdebellis@marvel.com. For Marvel subscription inquiries, please call 888-511-5480. **Manufactured between 12/15/2017 and 1/15/2018 by by SOLISCO PRINTERS, SCOTT, QC, CANADA.**

10 9 8 7 6 5 4 3 2 1

THE INHUMANS are a race of beings genetically altered in the early days of humanity by the alien Kree. They lived isolated from human society until the reign of **BLACK BOLT** and his queen **MEDUSA**, who deposed the former king when they deemed him corrupt, and cast his name from their history books. He is called only **"THE UNSPOKEN."** Now, the Inhuman empire is known across the cosmos.

This is the story that comes before thrones and empires, when Black Bolt was only a prince and his brother Maximus not yet the Mad. When Medusa wore only the crown of youth. This is the story of the...

ONCE & FUTURE KINGS

WRITER
Christopher Priest

ARTIST
Phil Noto

LOCKJAW: CANINE MASTER OF TIME AND SPACE

WRITER
Ryan North

ARTIST
Gustavo Duarte

COVER ARTISTS
Nick Bradshaw & Jim Campbell

LETTERER
VC's Joe Sabino

ASSOCIATE EDITOR
Sarah Brunstad

EDITOR
Wil Moss

INHUMANS CREATED BY **STAN LEE** & **JACK KIRBY**

ONE

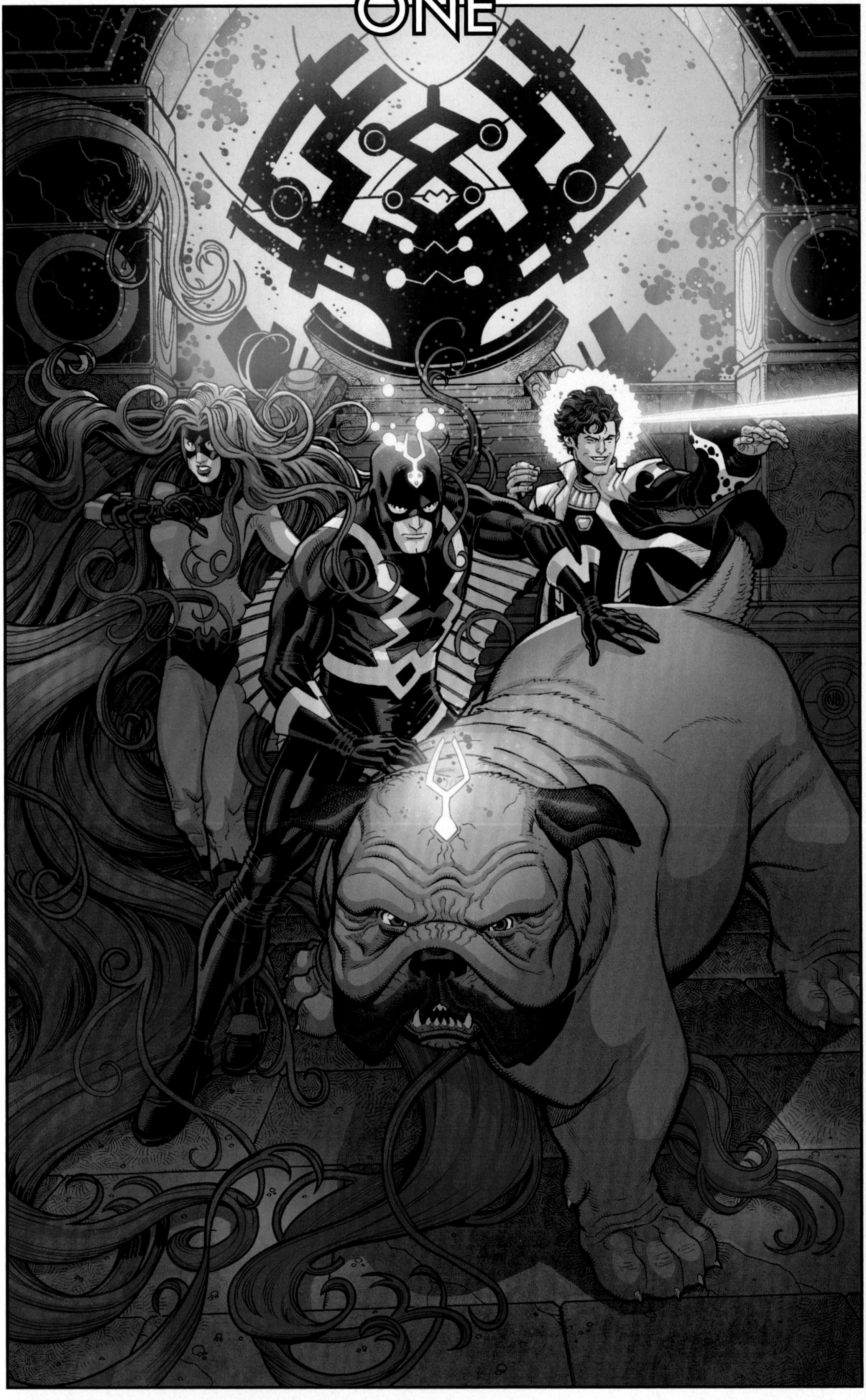

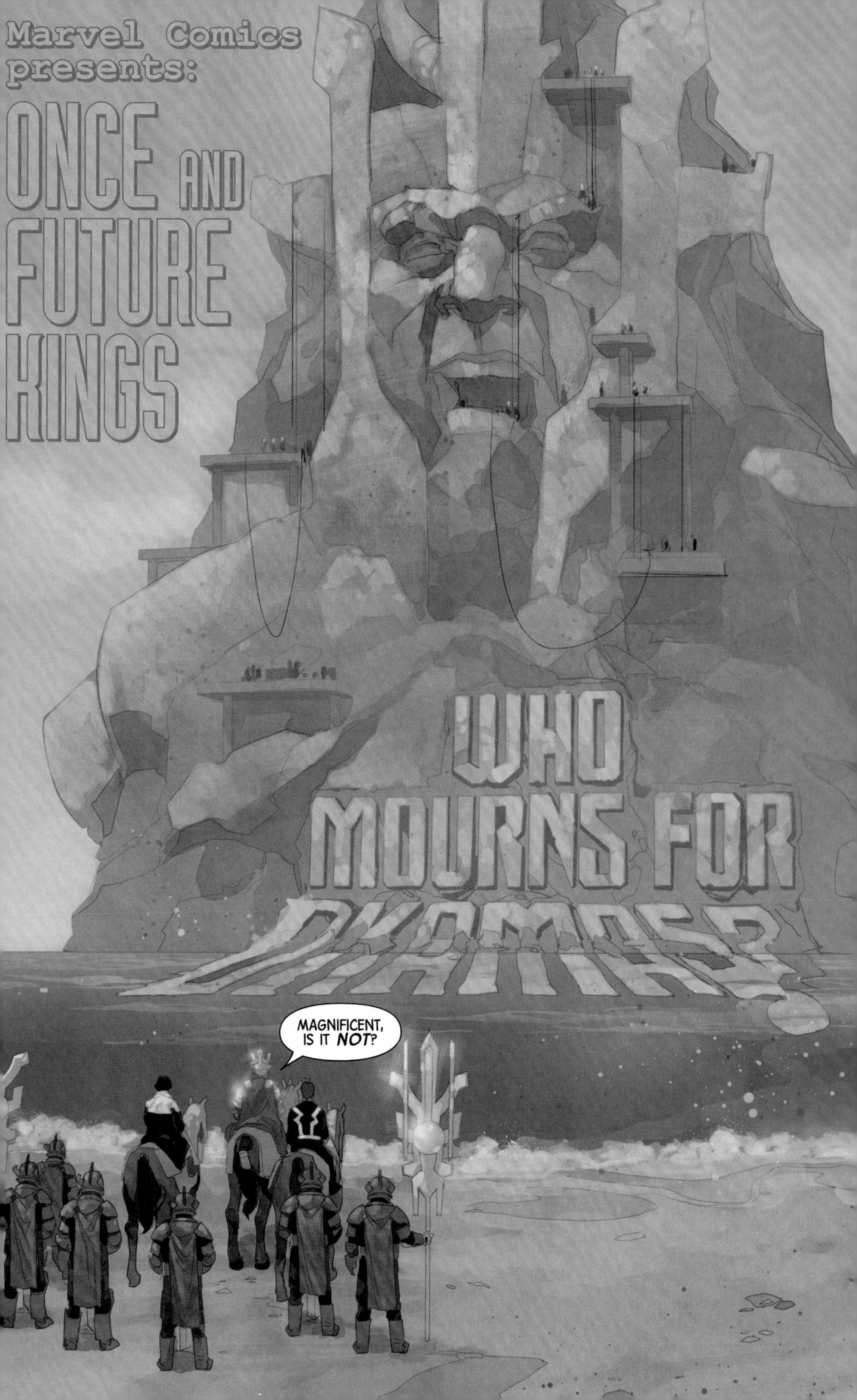
Marvel Comics presents:
ONCE AND FUTURE KINGS
WHO MOURNS FOR
MAGNIFICENT, IS IT NOT?

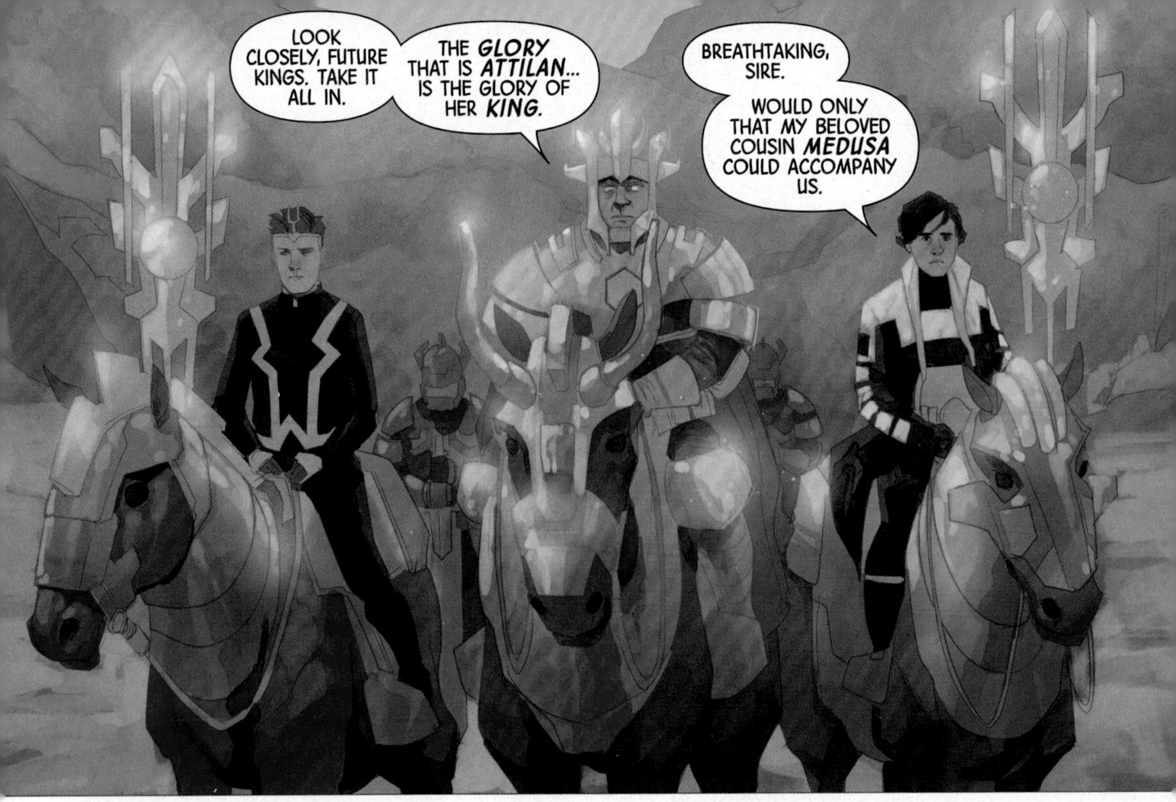
LOOK CLOSELY, FUTURE KINGS. TAKE IT ALL IN.
THE GLORY THAT IS ATTILAN... IS THE GLORY OF HER KING.
BREATHTAKING, SIRE.
WOULD ONLY THAT MY BELOVED COUSIN MEDUSA COULD ACCOMPANY US.

"Moral Theory"

THE ATTILAN SHORE

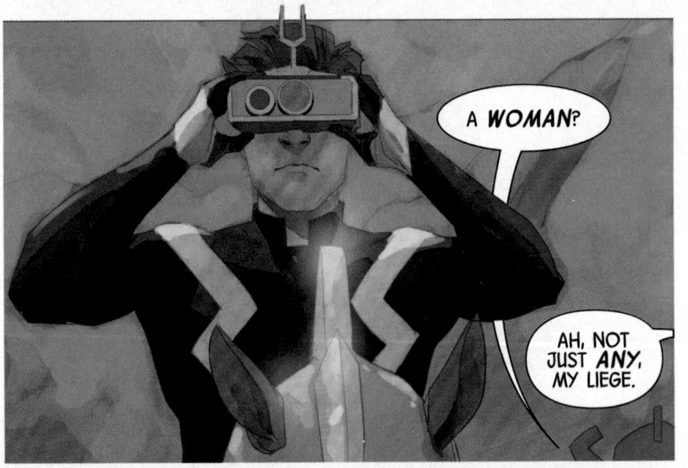
A WOMAN?
AH, NOT JUST ANY, MY LIEGE.

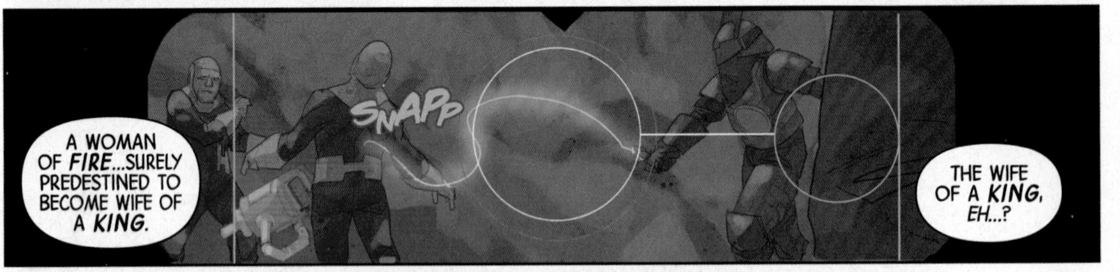
A WOMAN OF FIRE...SURELY PREDESTINED TO BECOME WIFE OF A KING.
SNAPP
THE WIFE OF A KING, EH...?

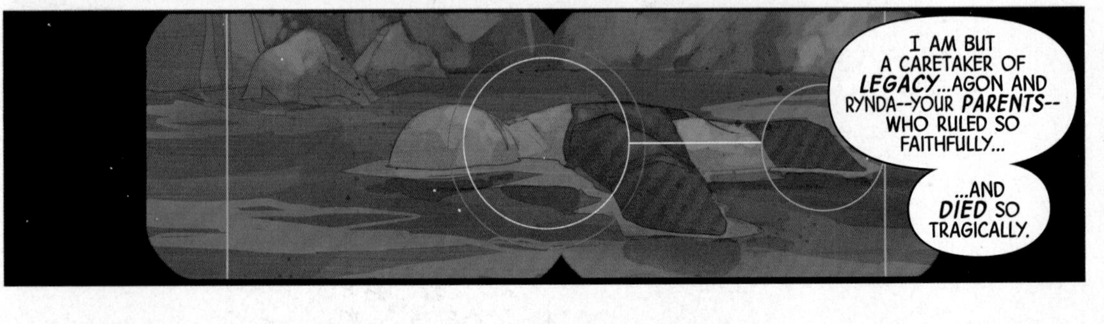
I AM BUT A CARETAKER OF LEGACY...AGON AND RYNDA--YOUR PARENTS--WHO RULED SO FAITHFULLY...
...AND DIED SO TRAGICALLY.

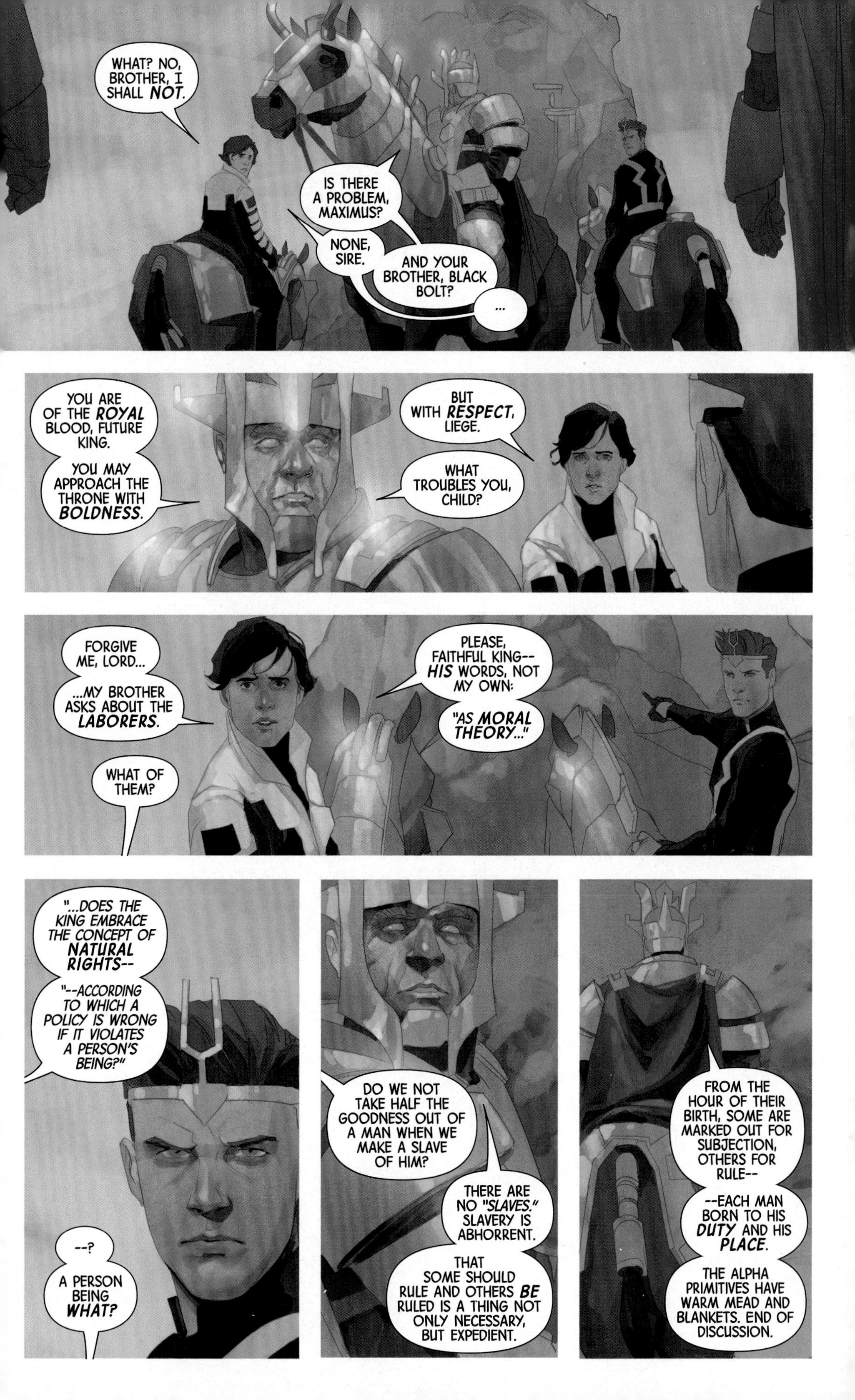
WHAT? NO, BROTHER, I SHALL NOT.
IS THERE A PROBLEM, MAXIMUS?
NONE, SIRE.
AND YOUR BROTHER, BLACK BOLT?
...
YOU ARE OF THE ROYAL BLOOD, FUTURE KING.
YOU MAY APPROACH THE THRONE WITH BOLDNESS.
BUT WITH RESPECT, LIEGE.
WHAT TROUBLES YOU, CHILD?
FORGIVE ME, LORD...
...MY BROTHER ASKS ABOUT THE LABORERS.
WHAT OF THEM?
PLEASE, FAITHFUL KING--HIS WORDS, NOT MY OWN:
"AS MORAL THEORY..."
"...DOES THE KING EMBRACE THE CONCEPT OF NATURAL RIGHTS--
"--ACCORDING TO WHICH A POLICY IS WRONG IF IT VIOLATES A PERSON'S BEING?"
--?
A PERSON BEING WHAT?
DO WE NOT TAKE HALF THE GOODNESS OUT OF A MAN WHEN WE MAKE A SLAVE OF HIM?
THERE ARE NO "SLAVES." SLAVERY IS ABHORRENT.
THAT SOME SHOULD RULE AND OTHERS BE RULED IS A THING NOT ONLY NECESSARY, BUT EXPEDIENT.
FROM THE HOUR OF THEIR BIRTH, SOME ARE MARKED OUT FOR SUBJECTION, OTHERS FOR RULE--
--EACH MAN BORN TO HIS DUTY AND HIS PLACE.
THE ALPHA PRIMITIVES HAVE WARM MEAD AND BLANKETS. END OF DISCUSSION.

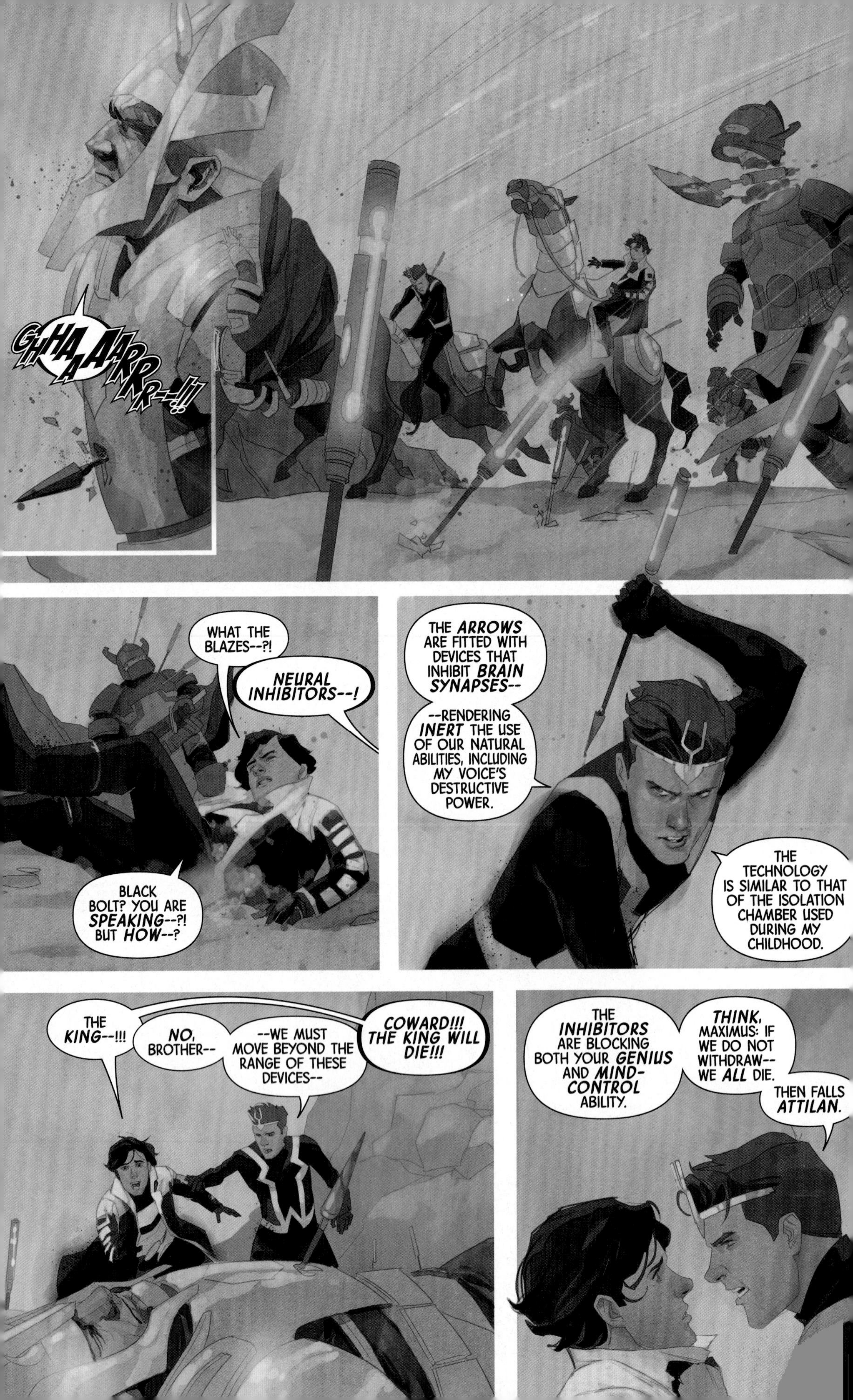
GHHAAAARRR--!!
WHAT THE BLAZES--?!
NEURAL INHIBITORS--!
BLACK BOLT? YOU ARE SPEAKING--?! BUT HOW--?
THE ARROWS ARE FITTED WITH DEVICES THAT INHIBIT BRAIN SYNAPSES--
--RENDERING INERT THE USE OF OUR NATURAL ABILITIES, INCLUDING MY VOICE'S DESTRUCTIVE POWER.
THE TECHNOLOGY IS SIMILAR TO THAT OF THE ISOLATION CHAMBER USED DURING MY CHILDHOOD.
THE KING--!!!
NO, BROTHER--
--WE MUST MOVE BEYOND THE RANGE OF THESE DEVICES--
COWARD!!! THE KING WILL DIE!!!
THE INHIBITORS ARE BLOCKING BOTH YOUR GENIUS AND MIND-CONTROL ABILITY.
THINK, MAXIMUS: IF WE DO NOT WITHDRAW-- WE ALL DIE.
THEN FALLS ATTILAN.

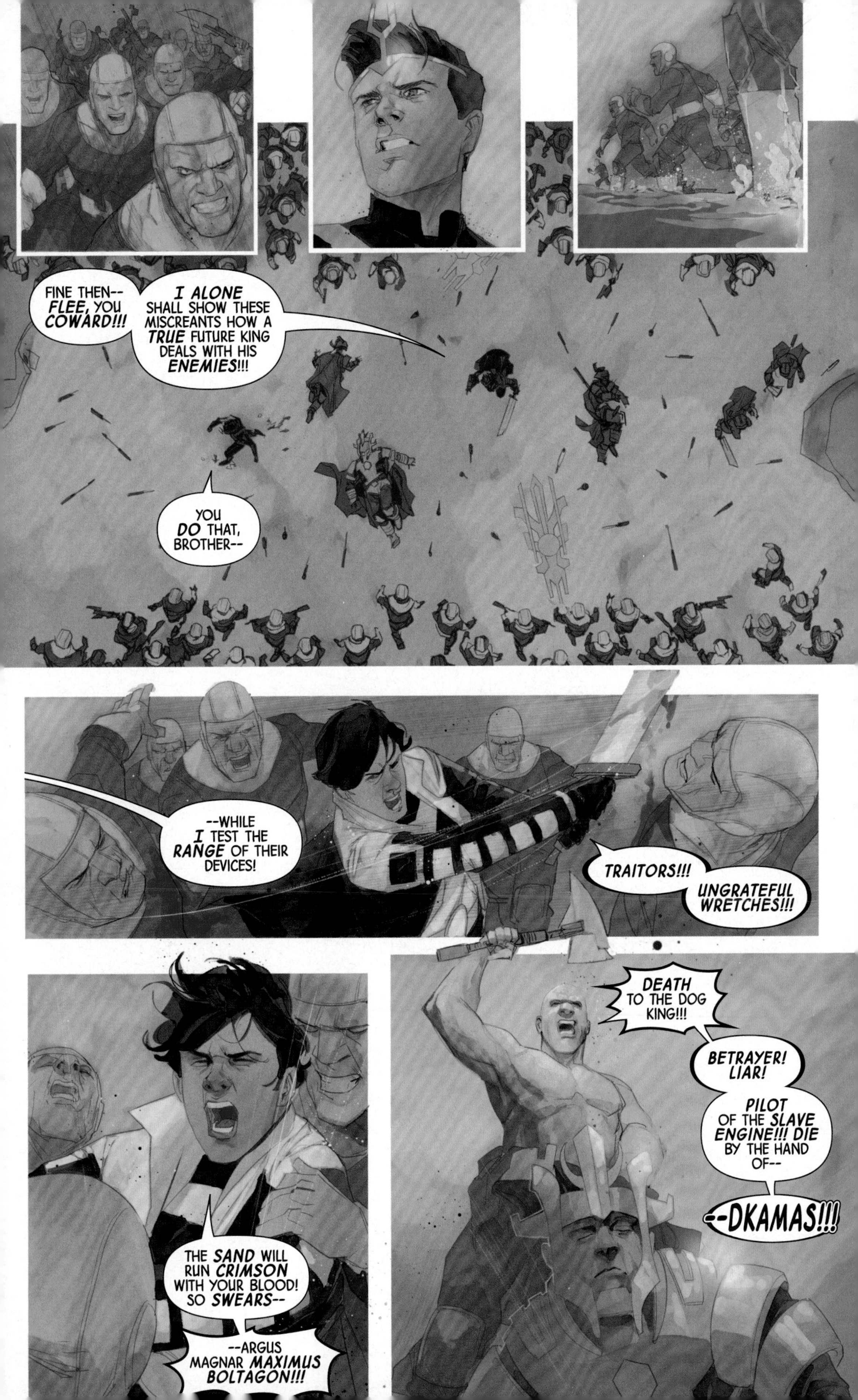
FINE THEN-- FLEE, YOU COWARD!!!
I ALONE SHALL SHOW THESE MISCREANTS HOW A TRUE FUTURE KING DEALS WITH HIS ENEMIES!!!
YOU DO THAT, BROTHER--
--WHILE I TEST THE RANGE OF THEIR DEVICES!
TRAITORS!!!
UNGRATEFUL WRETCHES!!!
THE SAND WILL RUN CRIMSON WITH YOUR BLOOD! SO SWEARS--
--ARGUS MAGNAR MAXIMUS BOLTAGON!!!
DEATH TO THE DOG KING!!!
BETRAYER! LIAR!
PILOT OF THE SLAVE ENGINE!!! DIE BY THE HAND OF--
--DKAMAS!!!

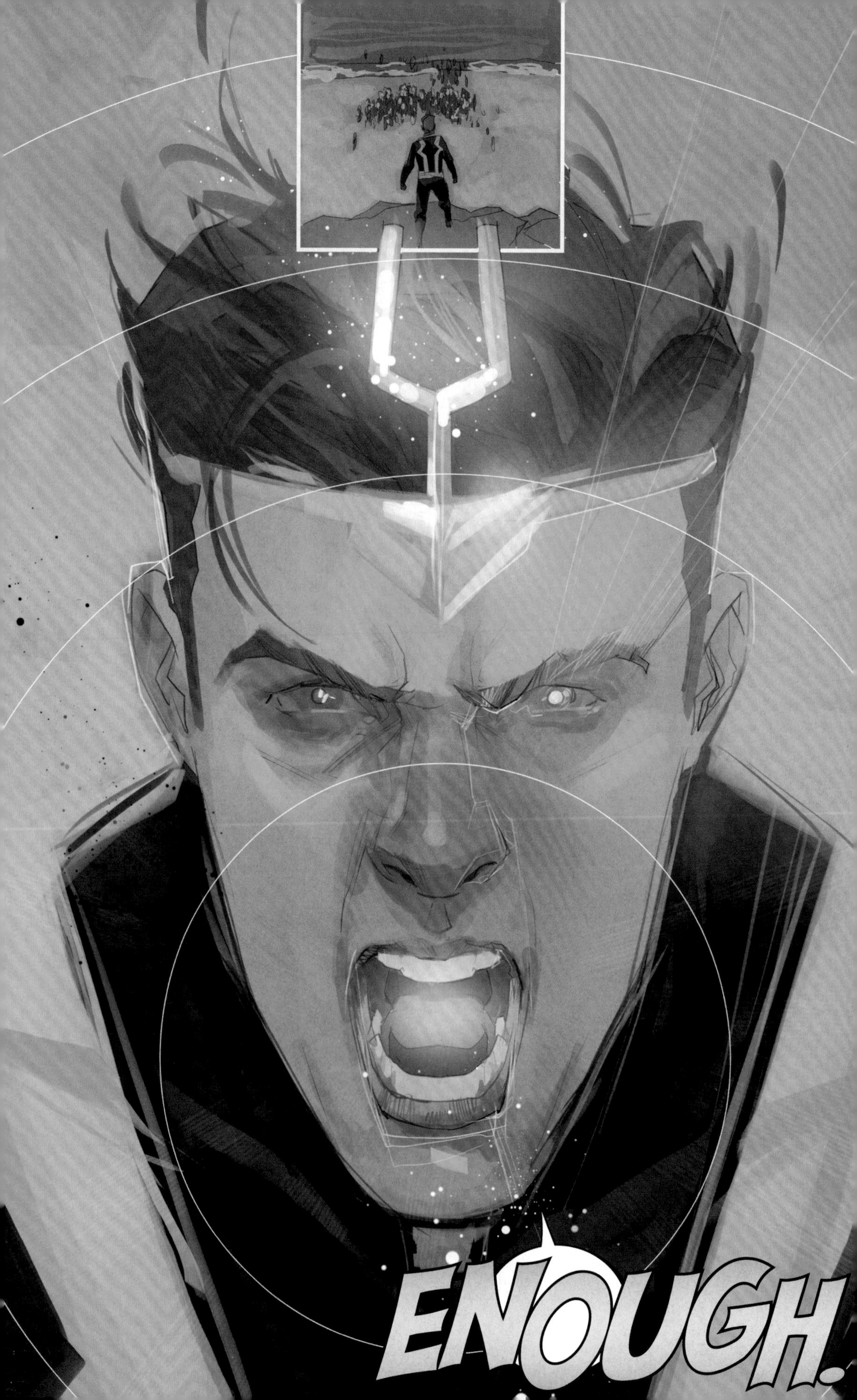
ENOUGH.

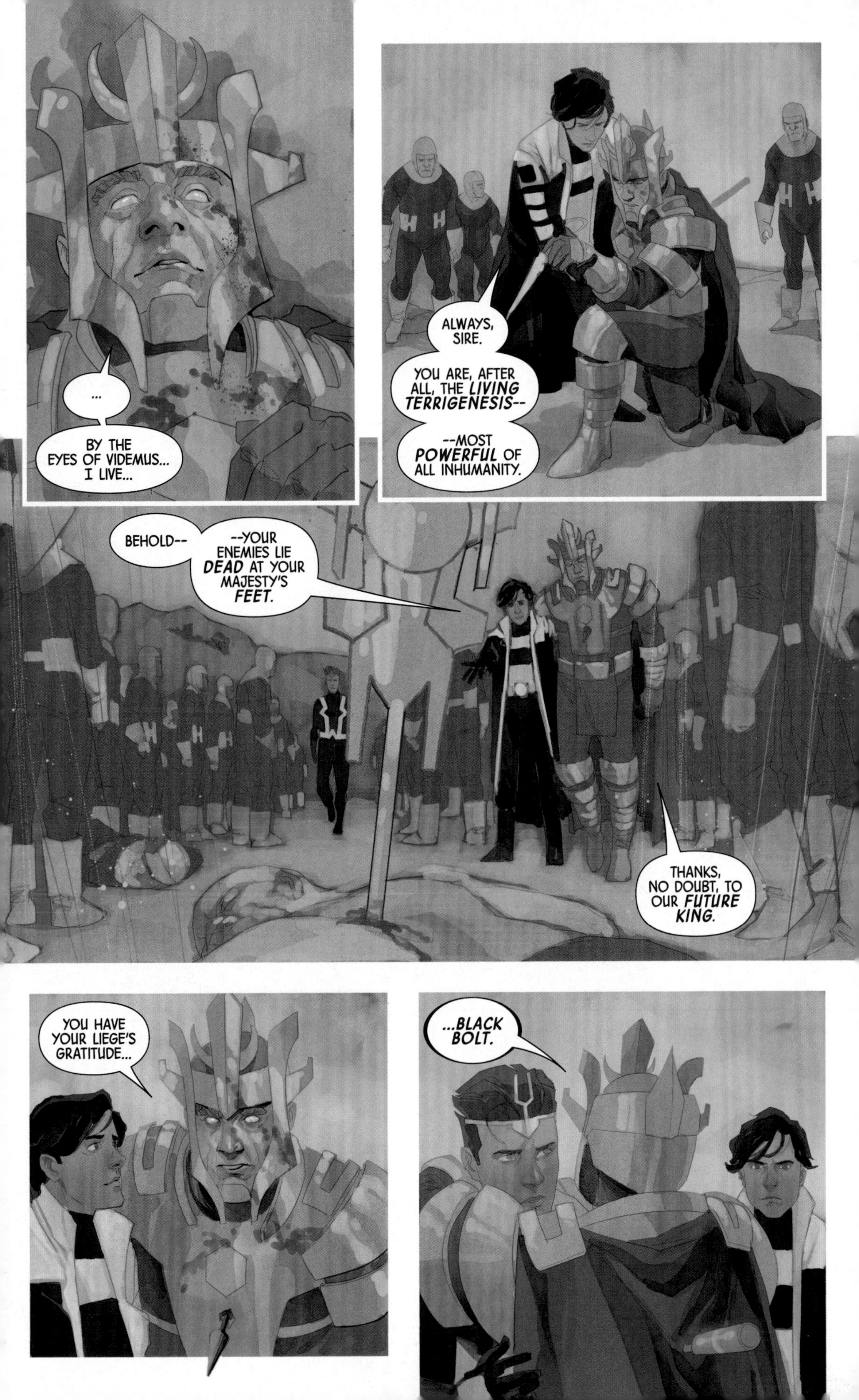
...
BY THE EYES OF VIDEMUS... I LIVE...
ALWAYS, SIRE.
YOU ARE, AFTER ALL, THE LIVING TERRIGENESIS--
--MOST POWERFUL OF ALL INHUMANITY.
BEHOLD--
--YOUR ENEMIES LIE DEAD AT YOUR MAJESTY'S FEET.
THANKS, NO DOUBT, TO OUR FUTURE KING.
YOU HAVE YOUR LIEGE'S GRATITUDE...
...BLACK BOLT.

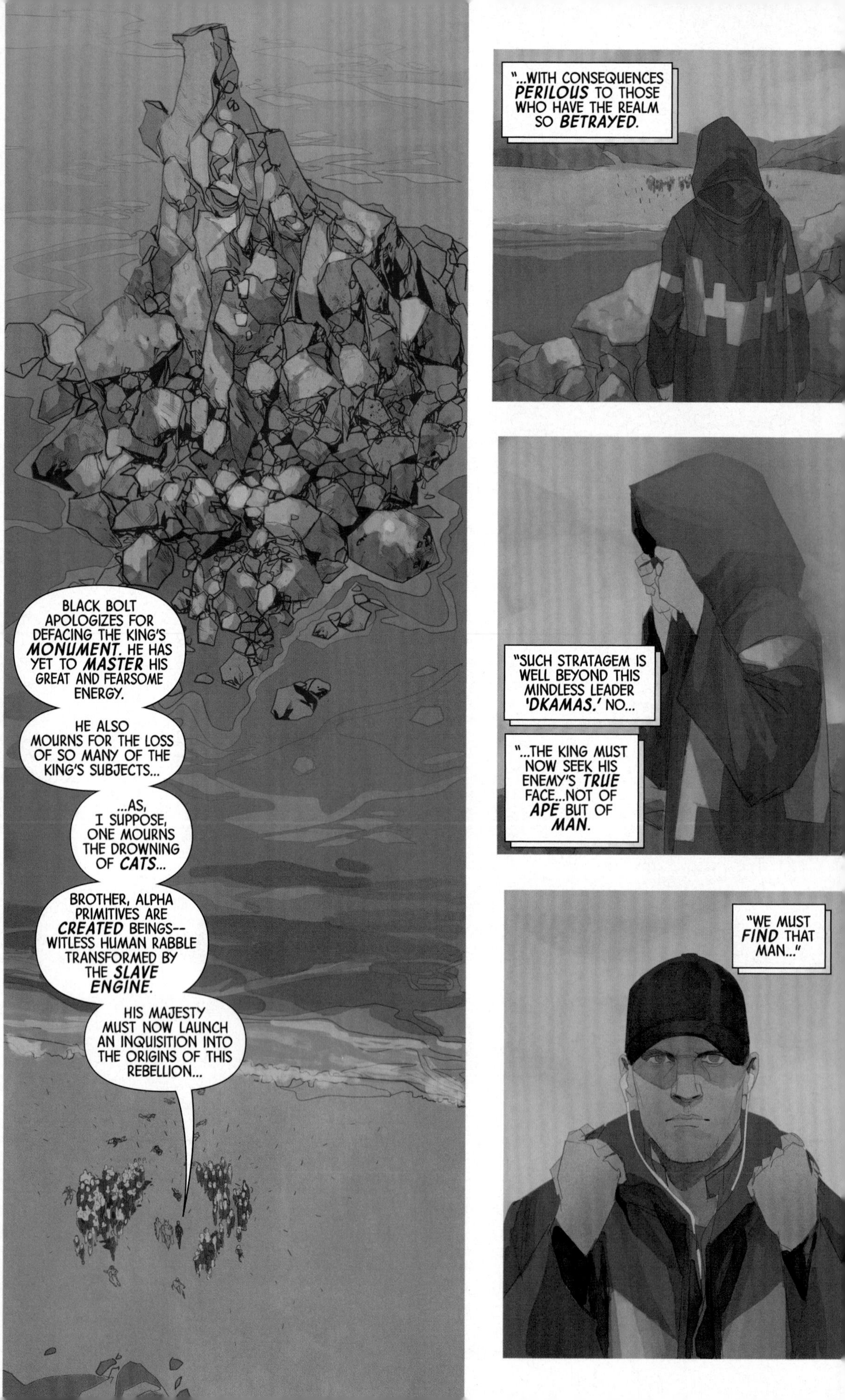
BLACK BOLT APOLOGIZES FOR DEFACING THE KING'S MONUMENT. HE HAS YET TO MASTER HIS GREAT AND FEARSOME ENERGY.
HE ALSO MOURNS FOR THE LOSS OF SO MANY OF THE KING'S SUBJECTS...
...AS, I SUPPOSE, ONE MOURNS THE DROWNING OF CATS...
BROTHER, ALPHA PRIMITIVES ARE CREATED BEINGS-- WITLESS HUMAN RABBLE TRANSFORMED BY THE SLAVE ENGINE.
HIS MAJESTY MUST NOW LAUNCH AN INQUISITION INTO THE ORIGINS OF THIS REBELLION...
"...WITH CONSEQUENCES PERILOUS TO THOSE WHO HAVE THE REALM SO BETRAYED.
"SUCH STRATAGEM IS WELL BEYOND THIS MINDLESS LEADER 'DKAMAS.' NO...
"...THE KING MUST NOW SEEK HIS ENEMY'S TRUE FACE...NOT OF APE BUT OF MAN.
"WE MUST FIND THAT MAN..."

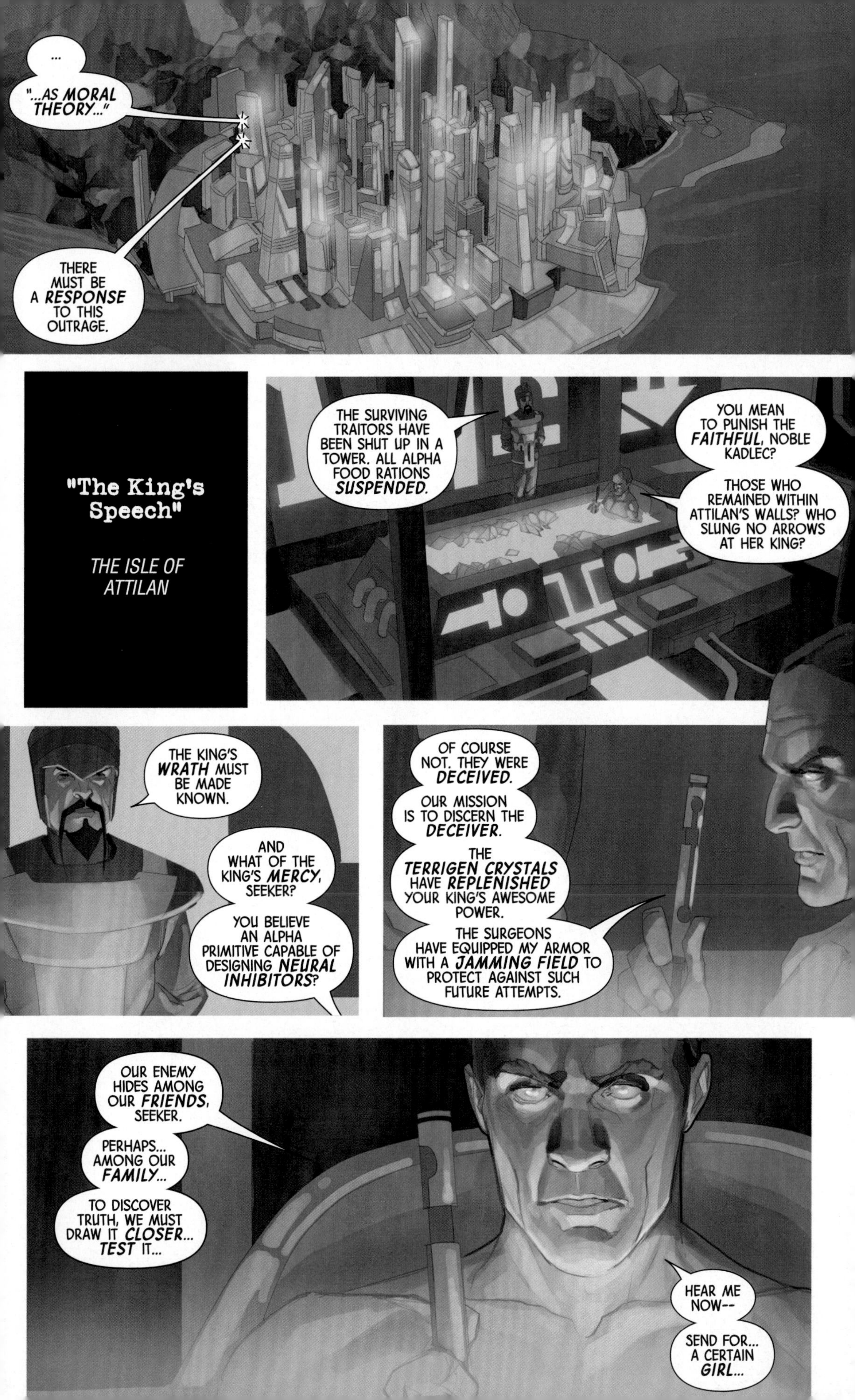
...
"...AS MORAL THEORY..."
THERE MUST BE A RESPONSE TO THIS OUTRAGE.
"The King's Speech"
THE ISLE OF ATTILAN
THE SURVIVING TRAITORS HAVE BEEN SHUT UP IN A TOWER. ALL ALPHA FOOD RATIONS SUSPENDED.
YOU MEAN TO PUNISH THE FAITHFUL, NOBLE KADLEC?
THOSE WHO REMAINED WITHIN ATTILAN'S WALLS? WHO SLUNG NO ARROWS AT HER KING?
THE KING'S WRATH MUST BE MADE KNOWN.
AND WHAT OF THE KING'S MERCY, SEEKER?
YOU BELIEVE AN ALPHA PRIMITIVE CAPABLE OF DESIGNING NEURAL INHIBITORS?
OF COURSE NOT. THEY WERE DECEIVED.
OUR MISSION IS TO DISCERN THE DECEIVER.
THE TERRIGEN CRYSTALS HAVE REPLENISHED YOUR KING'S AWESOME POWER.
THE SURGEONS HAVE EQUIPPED MY ARMOR WITH A JAMMING FIELD TO PROTECT AGAINST SUCH FUTURE ATTEMPTS.
OUR ENEMY HIDES AMONG OUR FRIENDS, SEEKER.
PERHAPS... AMONG OUR FAMILY...
TO DISCOVER TRUTH, WE MUST DRAW IT CLOSER... TEST IT...
HEAR ME NOW--
SEND FOR... A CERTAIN GIRL...

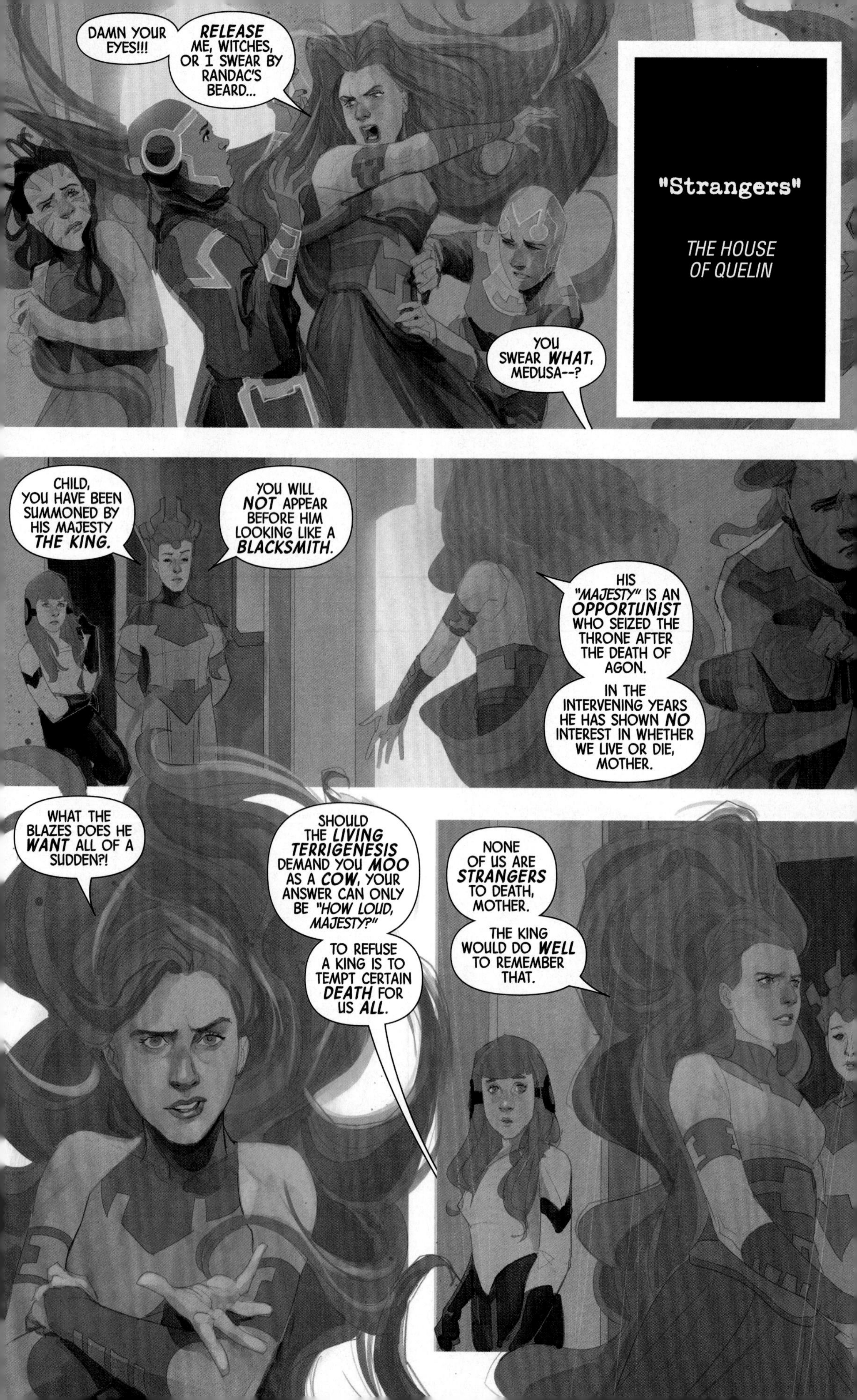
DAMN YOUR EYES!!!
RELEASE ME, WITCHES, OR I SWEAR BY RANDAC'S BEARD...
"Strangers"
THE HOUSE OF QUELIN
YOU SWEAR WHAT, MEDUSA--?
CHILD, YOU HAVE BEEN SUMMONED BY HIS MAJESTY THE KING.
YOU WILL NOT APPEAR BEFORE HIM LOOKING LIKE A BLACKSMITH.
HIS "MAJESTY" IS AN OPPORTUNIST WHO SEIZED THE THRONE AFTER THE DEATH OF AGON.
IN THE INTERVENING YEARS HE HAS SHOWN NO INTEREST IN WHETHER WE LIVE OR DIE, MOTHER.
WHAT THE BLAZES DOES HE WANT ALL OF A SUDDEN?!
SHOULD THE LIVING TERRIGENESIS DEMAND YOU MOO AS A COW, YOUR ANSWER CAN ONLY BE "HOW LOUD, MAJESTY?"
TO REFUSE A KING IS TO TEMPT CERTAIN DEATH FOR US ALL.
NONE OF US ARE STRANGERS TO DEATH, MOTHER.
THE KING WOULD DO WELL TO REMEMBER THAT.

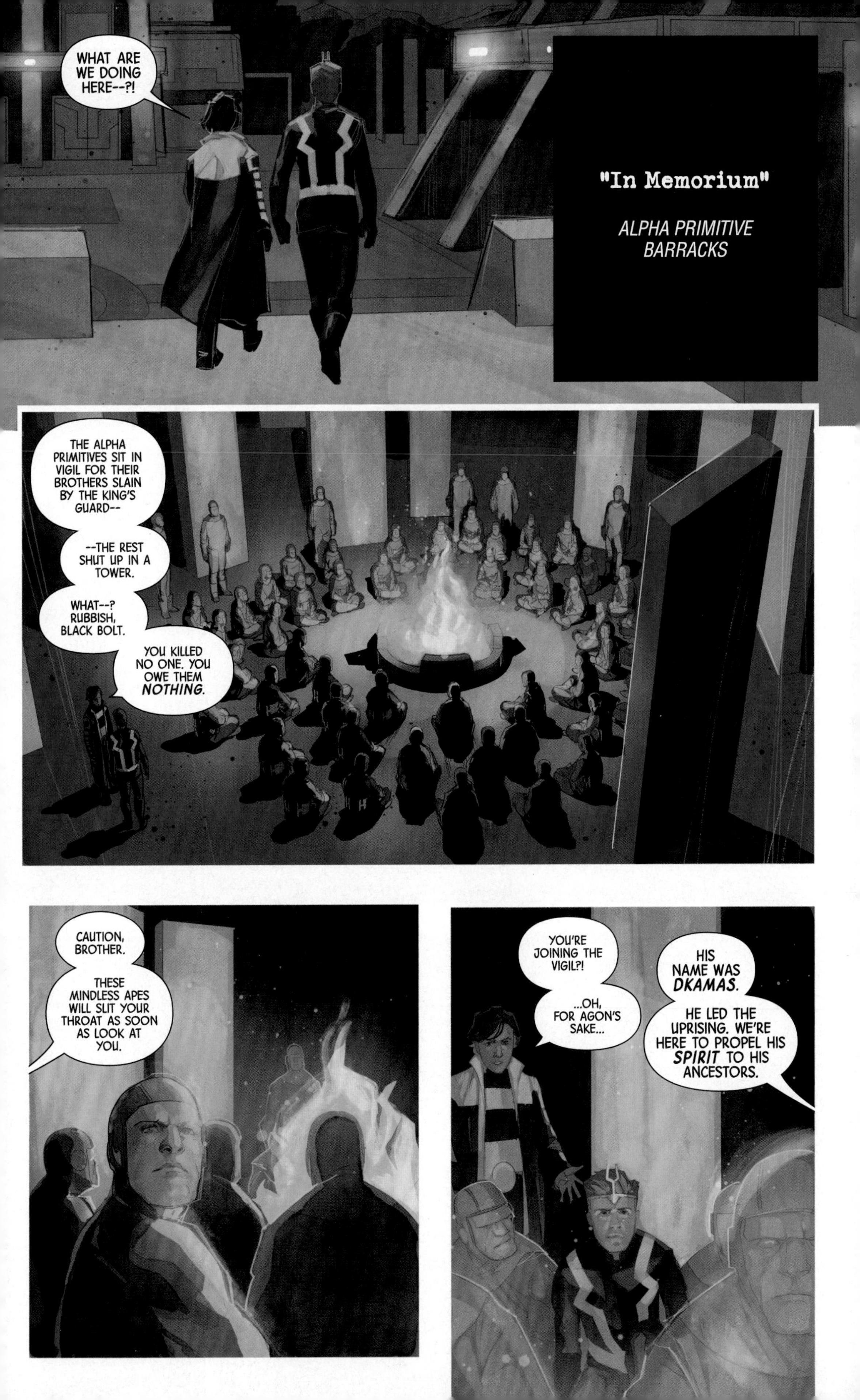
WHAT ARE WE DOING HERE--?!
"In Memorium"
ALPHA PRIMITIVE BARRACKS
THE ALPHA PRIMITIVES SIT IN VIGIL FOR THEIR BROTHERS SLAIN BY THE KING'S GUARD--
--THE REST SHUT UP IN A TOWER.
WHAT--? RUBBISH, BLACK BOLT.
YOU KILLED NO ONE. YOU OWE THEM NOTHING.
CAUTION, BROTHER.
THESE MINDLESS APES WILL SLIT YOUR THROAT AS SOON AS LOOK AT YOU.
YOU'RE JOINING THE VIGIL?!
...OH, FOR AGON'S SAKE...
HIS NAME WAS DKAMAS.
HE LED THE UPRISING. WE'RE HERE TO PROPEL HIS SPIRIT TO HIS ANCESTORS.

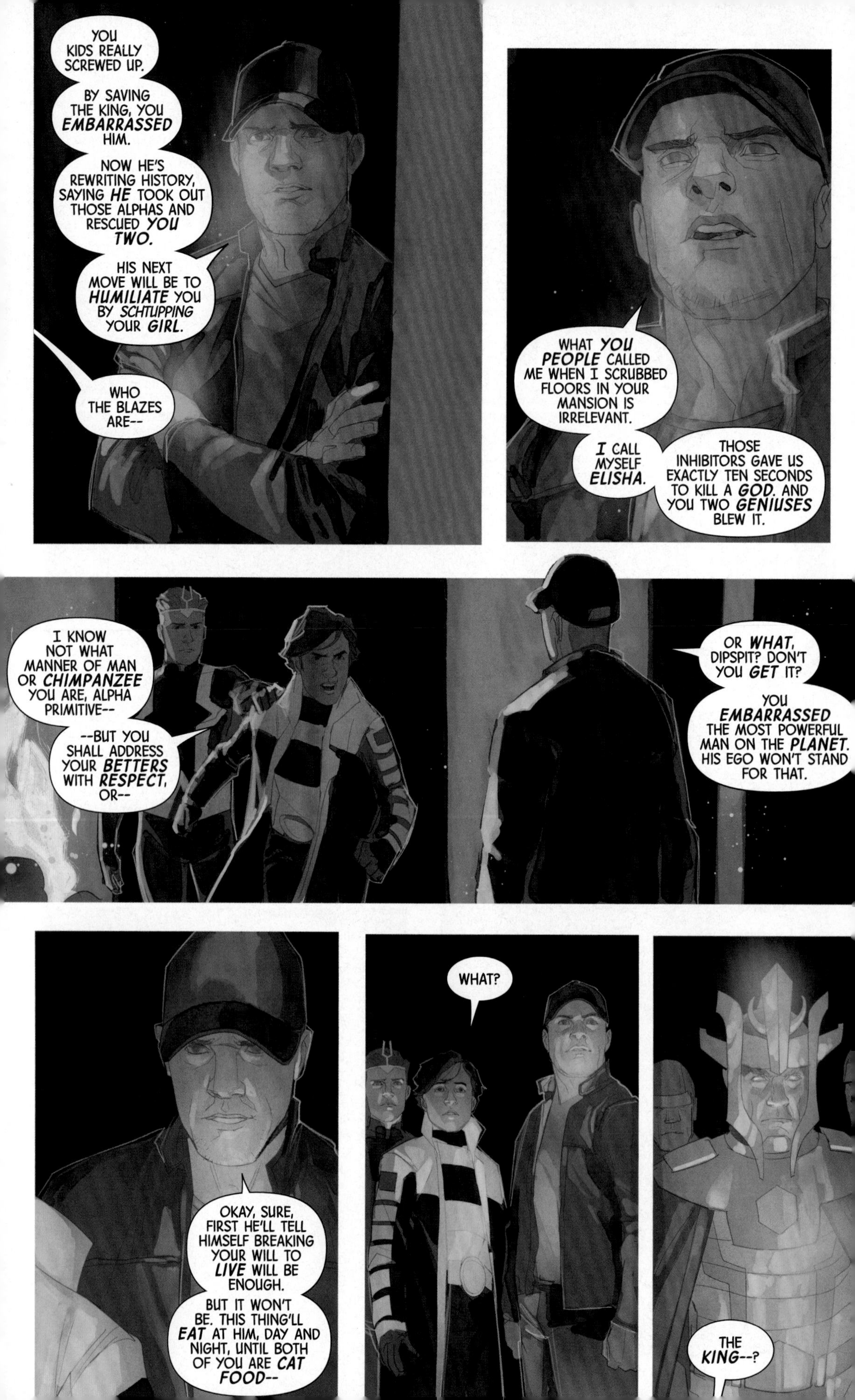
YOU KIDS REALLY SCREWED UP.
BY SAVING THE KING, YOU EMBARRASSED HIM.
NOW HE'S REWRITING HISTORY, SAYING HE TOOK OUT THOSE ALPHAS AND RESCUED YOU TWO.
HIS NEXT MOVE WILL BE TO HUMILIATE YOU BY SCHTUPPING YOUR GIRL.
WHO THE BLAZES ARE--
WHAT YOU PEOPLE CALLED ME WHEN I SCRUBBED FLOORS IN YOUR MANSION IS IRRELEVANT.
I CALL MYSELF ELISHA.
THOSE INHIBITORS GAVE US EXACTLY TEN SECONDS TO KILL A GOD. AND YOU TWO GENIUSES BLEW IT.
I KNOW NOT WHAT MANNER OF MAN OR CHIMPANZEE YOU ARE, ALPHA PRIMITIVE--
--BUT YOU SHALL ADDRESS YOUR BETTERS WITH RESPECT, OR--
OR WHAT, DIPSPIT? DON'T YOU GET IT?
YOU EMBARRASSED THE MOST POWERFUL MAN ON THE PLANET. HIS EGO WON'T STAND FOR THAT.
OKAY, SURE, FIRST HE'LL TELL HIMSELF BREAKING YOUR WILL TO LIVE WILL BE ENOUGH.
BUT IT WON'T BE. THIS THING'LL EAT AT HIM, DAY AND NIGHT, UNTIL BOTH OF YOU ARE CAT FOOD--
WHAT?
THE KING--?

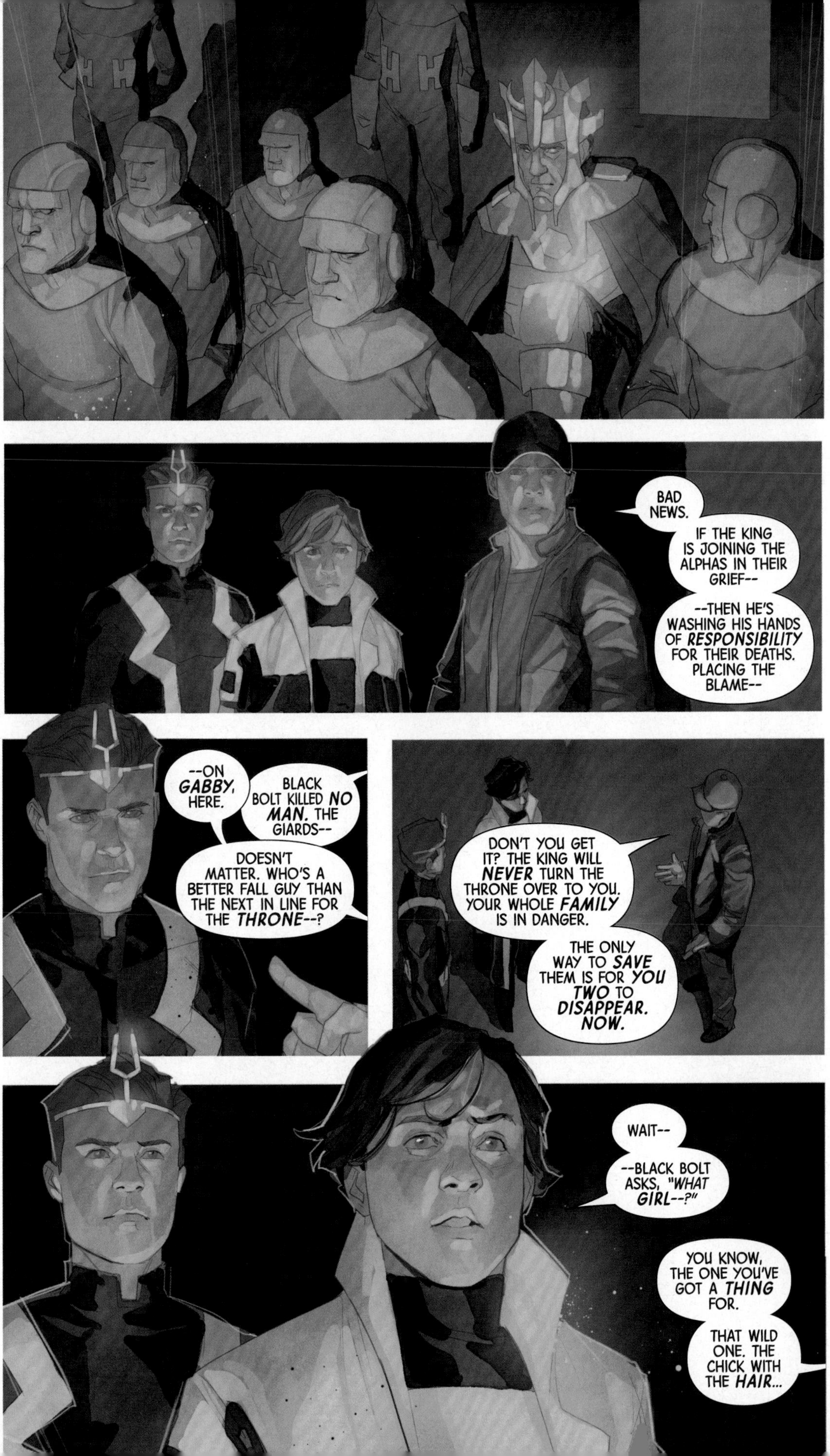
BAD NEWS.
IF THE KING IS JOINING THE ALPHAS IN THEIR GRIEF--
--THEN HE'S WASHING HIS HANDS OF *RESPONSIBILITY* FOR THEIR DEATHS. PLACING THE BLAME--
--ON *GABBY*, HERE.
BLACK BOLT KILLED *NO MAN*. THE GIARDS--
DOESN'T MATTER. WHO'S A BETTER FALL GUY THAN THE NEXT IN LINE FOR THE *THRONE*--?
DON'T YOU GET IT? THE KING WILL *NEVER* TURN THE THRONE OVER TO YOU. YOUR WHOLE *FAMILY* IS IN DANGER.
THE ONLY WAY TO *SAVE* THEM IS FOR *YOU TWO* TO *DISAPPEAR. NOW.*
WAIT--
--BLACK BOLT ASKS, "*WHAT GIRL*--?"
YOU KNOW, THE ONE YOU'VE GOT A *THING* FOR.
THAT WILD ONE. THE CHICK WITH THE *HAIR*...

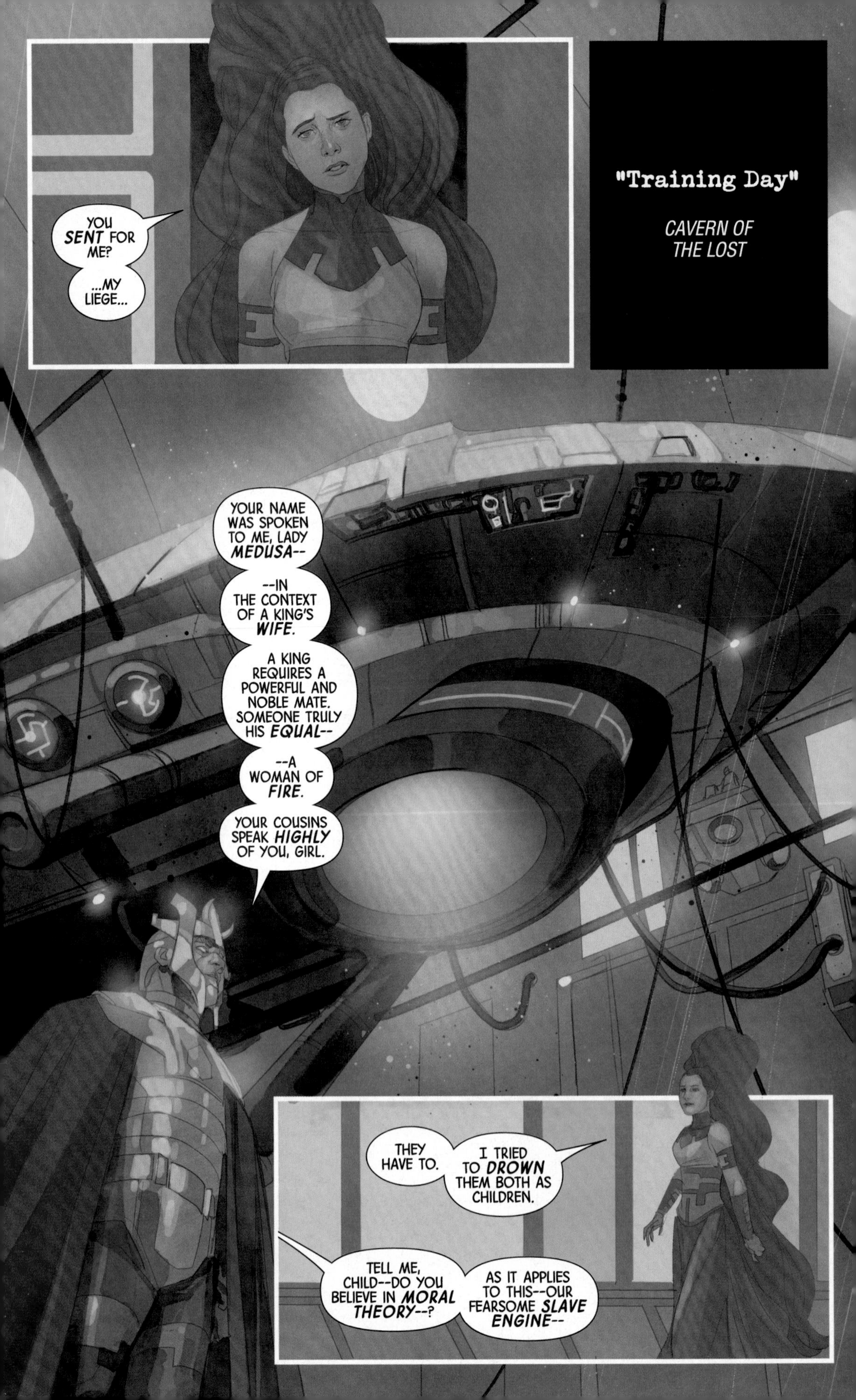
YOU SENT FOR ME?
...MY LIEGE...
"Training Day"
CAVERN OF THE LOST
YOUR NAME WAS SPOKEN TO ME, LADY MEDUSA--
--IN THE CONTEXT OF A KING'S WIFE.
A KING REQUIRES A POWERFUL AND NOBLE MATE. SOMEONE TRULY HIS EQUAL--
--A WOMAN OF FIRE.
YOUR COUSINS SPEAK HIGHLY OF YOU, GIRL.
THEY HAVE TO.
I TRIED TO DROWN THEM BOTH AS CHILDREN.
TELL ME, CHILD--DO YOU BELIEVE IN MORAL THEORY--?
AS IT APPLIES TO THIS--OUR FEARSOME SLAVE ENGINE--

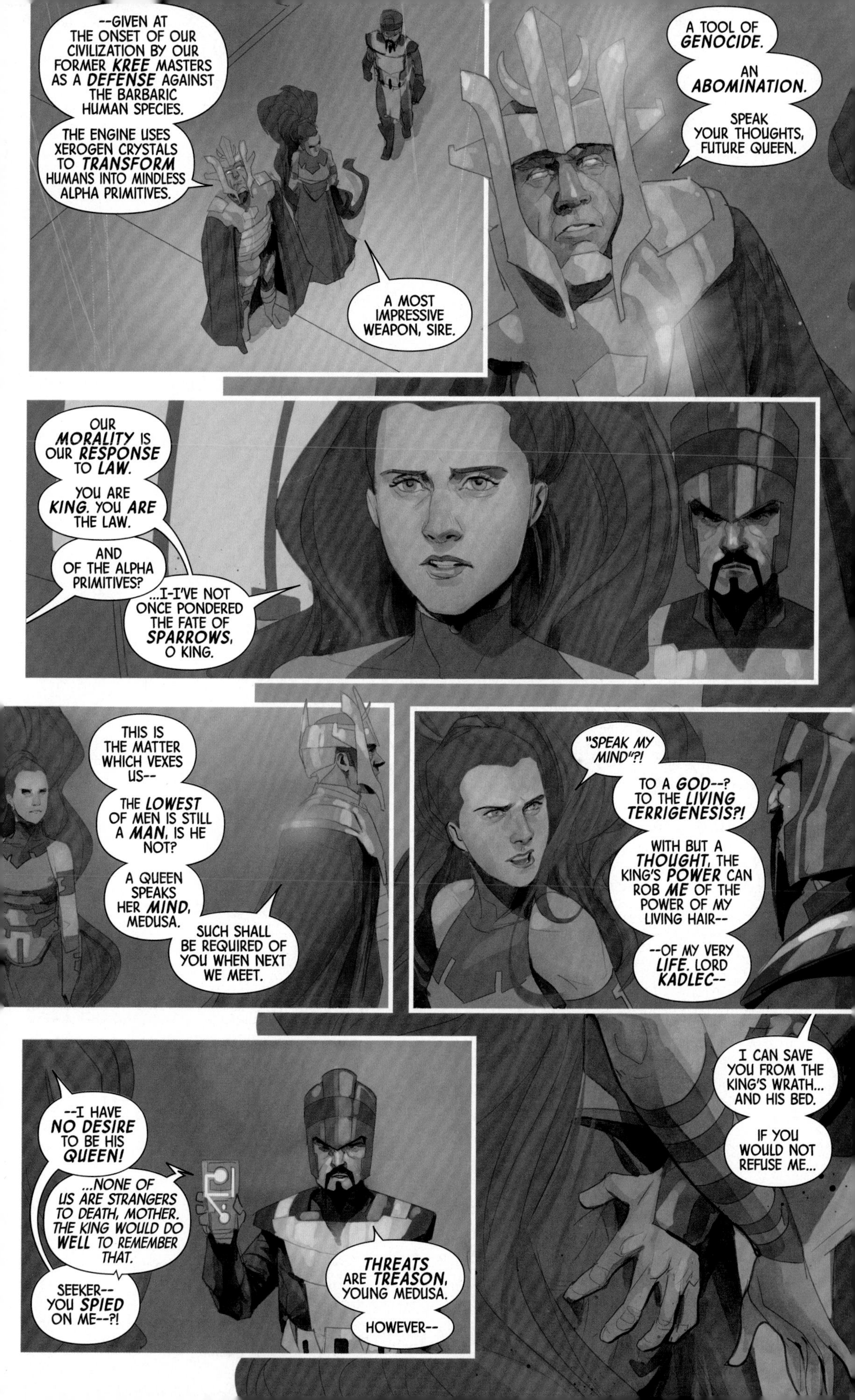
--GIVEN AT THE ONSET OF OUR CIVILIZATION BY OUR FORMER KREE MASTERS AS A DEFENSE AGAINST THE BARBARIC HUMAN SPECIES.
THE ENGINE USES XEROGEN CRYSTALS TO TRANSFORM HUMANS INTO MINDLESS ALPHA PRIMITIVES.
A MOST IMPRESSIVE WEAPON, SIRE.
A TOOL OF GENOCIDE.
AN ABOMINATION.
SPEAK YOUR THOUGHTS, FUTURE QUEEN.
OUR MORALITY IS OUR RESPONSE TO LAW.
YOU ARE KING. YOU ARE THE LAW.
AND OF THE ALPHA PRIMITIVES?
...I-I'VE NOT ONCE PONDERED THE FATE OF SPARROWS, O KING.
THIS IS THE MATTER WHICH VEXES US--
THE LOWEST OF MEN IS STILL A MAN, IS HE NOT?
A QUEEN SPEAKS HER MIND, MEDUSA.
SUCH SHALL BE REQUIRED OF YOU WHEN NEXT WE MEET.
"SPEAK MY MIND"?!
TO A GOD--? TO THE LIVING TERRIGENESIS?!
WITH BUT A THOUGHT, THE KING'S POWER CAN ROB ME OF THE POWER OF MY LIVING HAIR--
--OF MY VERY LIFE. LORD KADLEC--
--I HAVE NO DESIRE TO BE HIS QUEEN!
...NONE OF US ARE STRANGERS TO DEATH, MOTHER. THE KING WOULD DO WELL TO REMEMBER THAT.
SEEKER-- YOU SPIED ON ME--?!
THREATS ARE TREASON, YOUNG MEDUSA.
HOWEVER--
I CAN SAVE YOU FROM THE KING'S WRATH... AND HIS BED.
IF YOU WOULD NOT REFUSE ME...

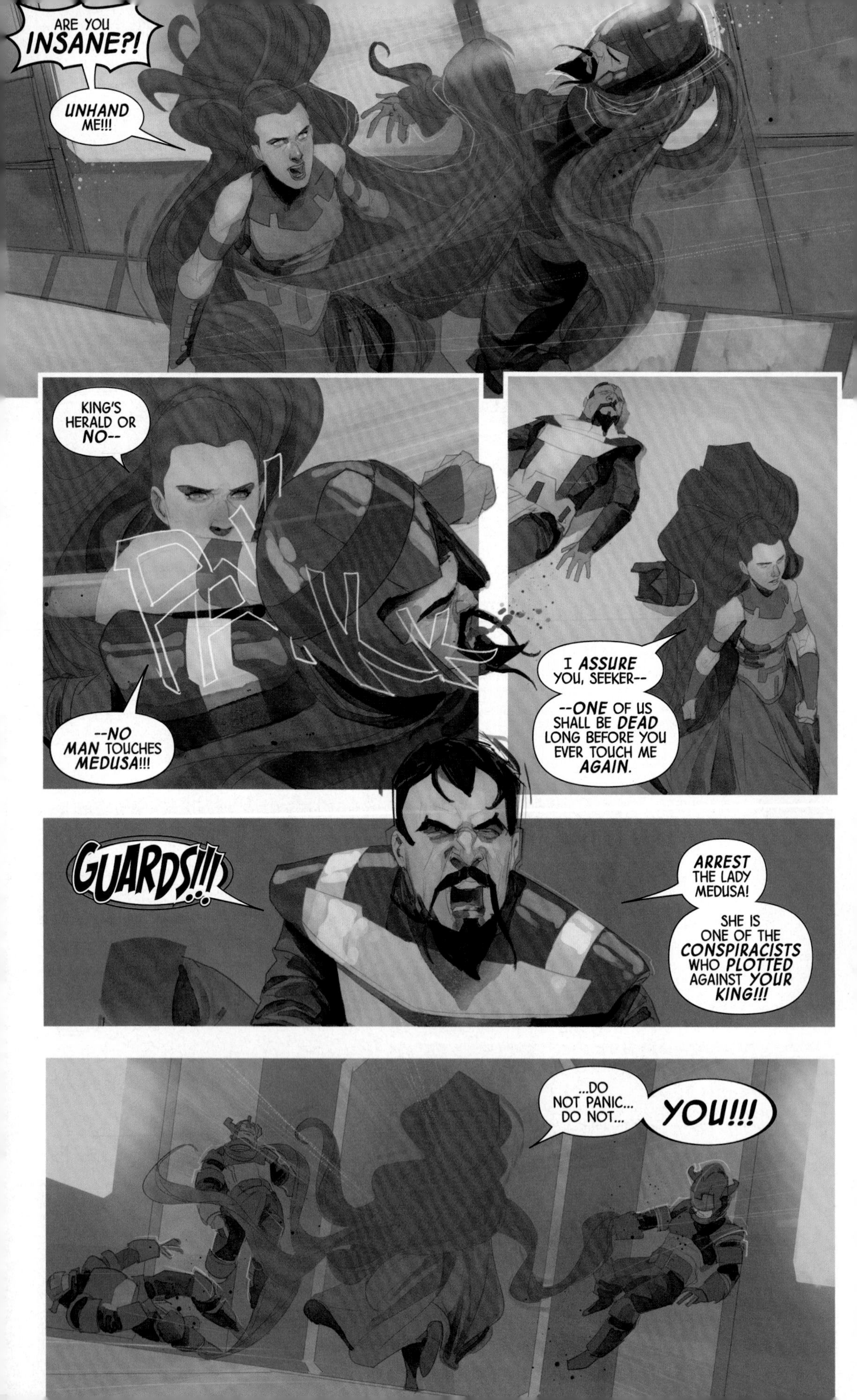
ARE YOU INSANE?!
UNHAND ME!!!
KING'S HERALD OR NO--
--NO MAN TOUCHES MEDUSA!!!
I ASSURE YOU, SEEKER--
--ONE OF US SHALL BE DEAD LONG BEFORE YOU EVER TOUCH ME AGAIN.
GUARDS!!!
ARREST THE LADY MEDUSA!
SHE IS ONE OF THE CONSPIRACISTS WHO PLOTTED AGAINST YOUR KING!!!
...DO NOT PANIC... DO NOT...
YOU!!!

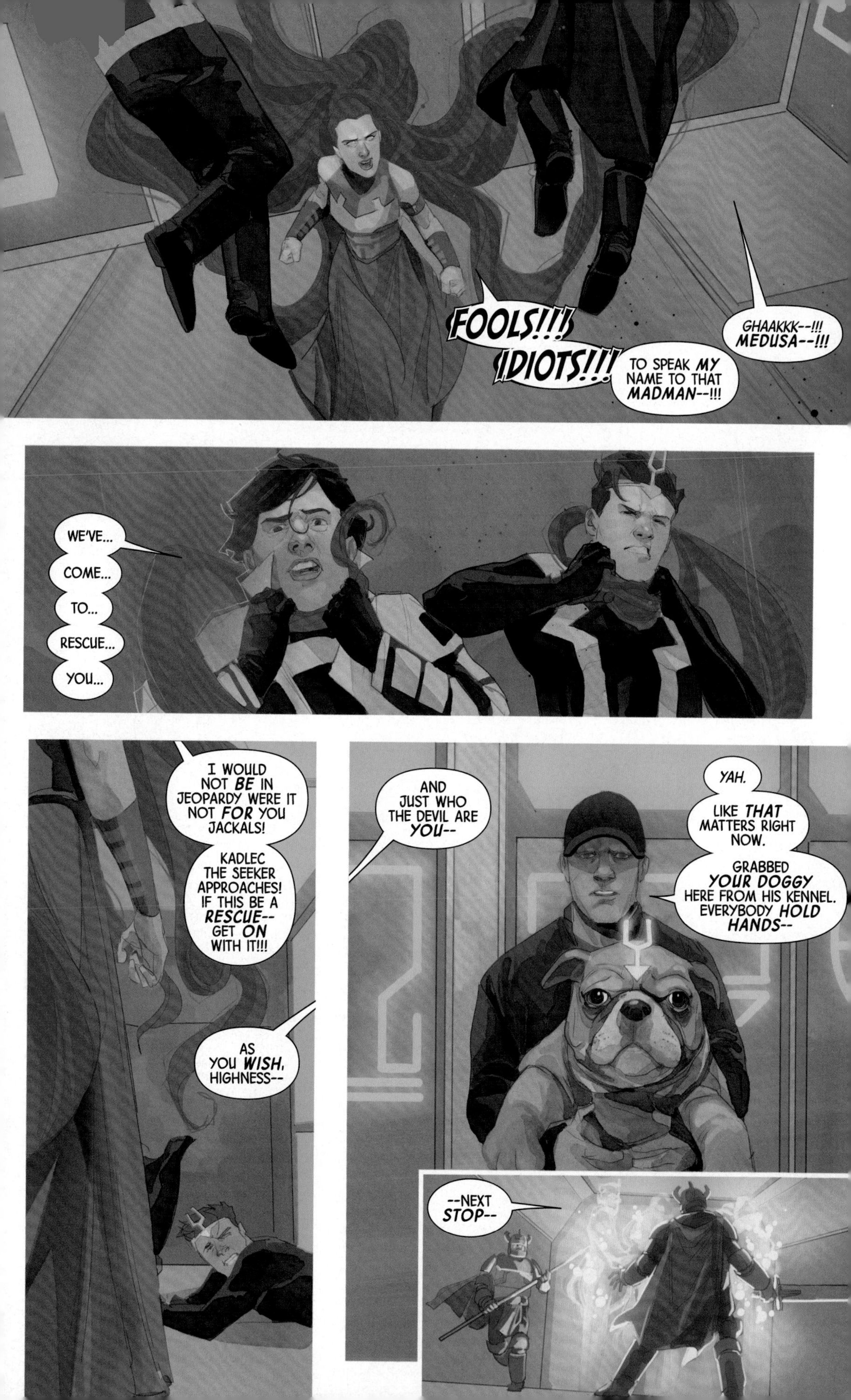
FOOLS!!! IDIOTS!!!
TO SPEAK MY NAME TO THAT MADMAN--!!!
GHAAKKK--!!! MEDUSA--!!!
WE'VE...
COME...
TO...
RESCUE...
YOU...
I WOULD NOT BE IN JEOPARDY WERE IT NOT FOR YOU JACKALS!
KADLEC THE SEEKER APPROACHES! IF THIS BE A RESCUE-- GET ON WITH IT!!!
AS YOU WISH, HIGHNESS--
AND JUST WHO THE DEVIL ARE YOU--
YAH.
LIKE THAT MATTERS RIGHT NOW.
GRABBED YOUR DOGGY HERE FROM HIS KENNEL. EVERYBODY HOLD HANDS--
--NEXT STOP--

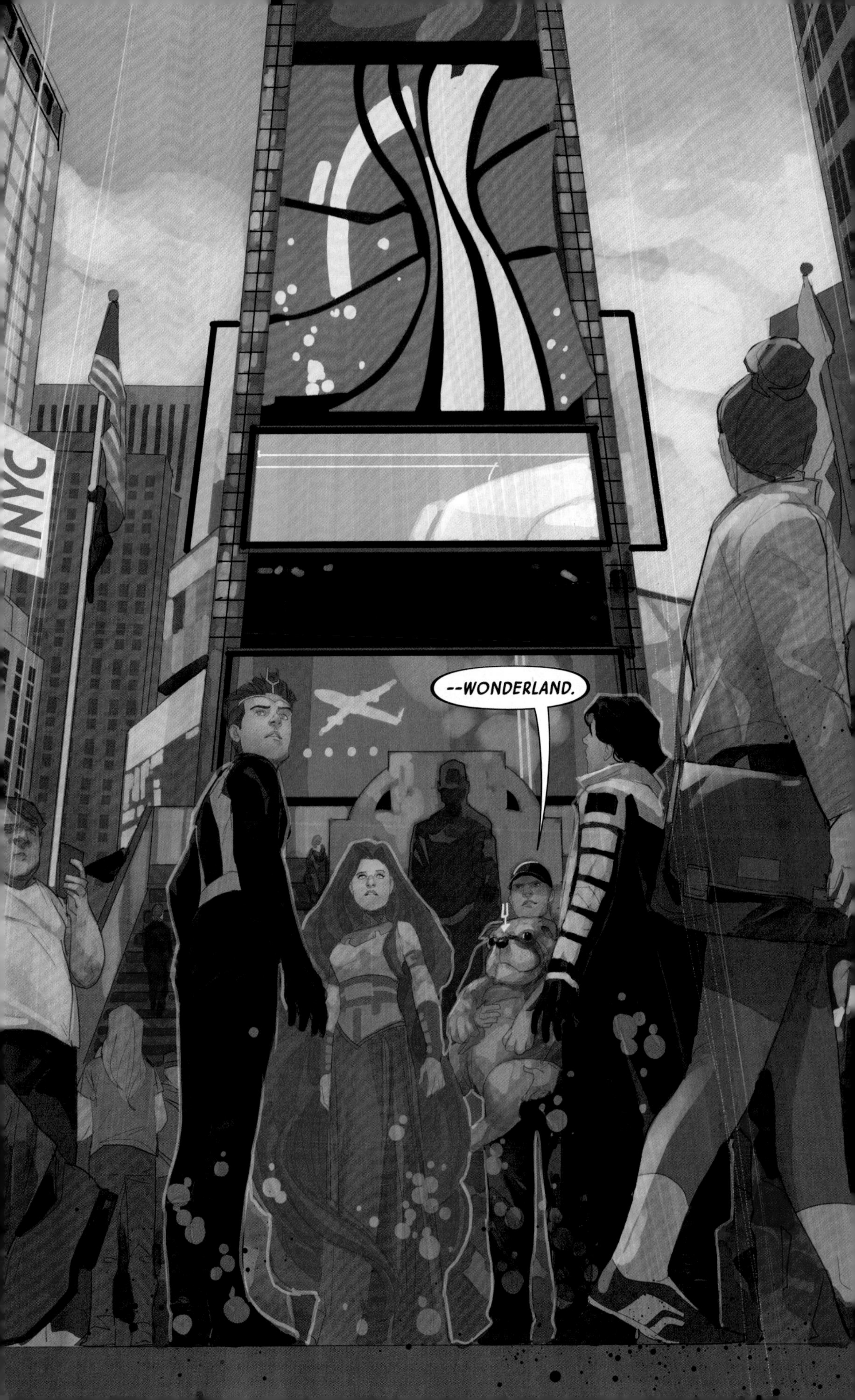
NYC
--WONDERLAND.

TWO

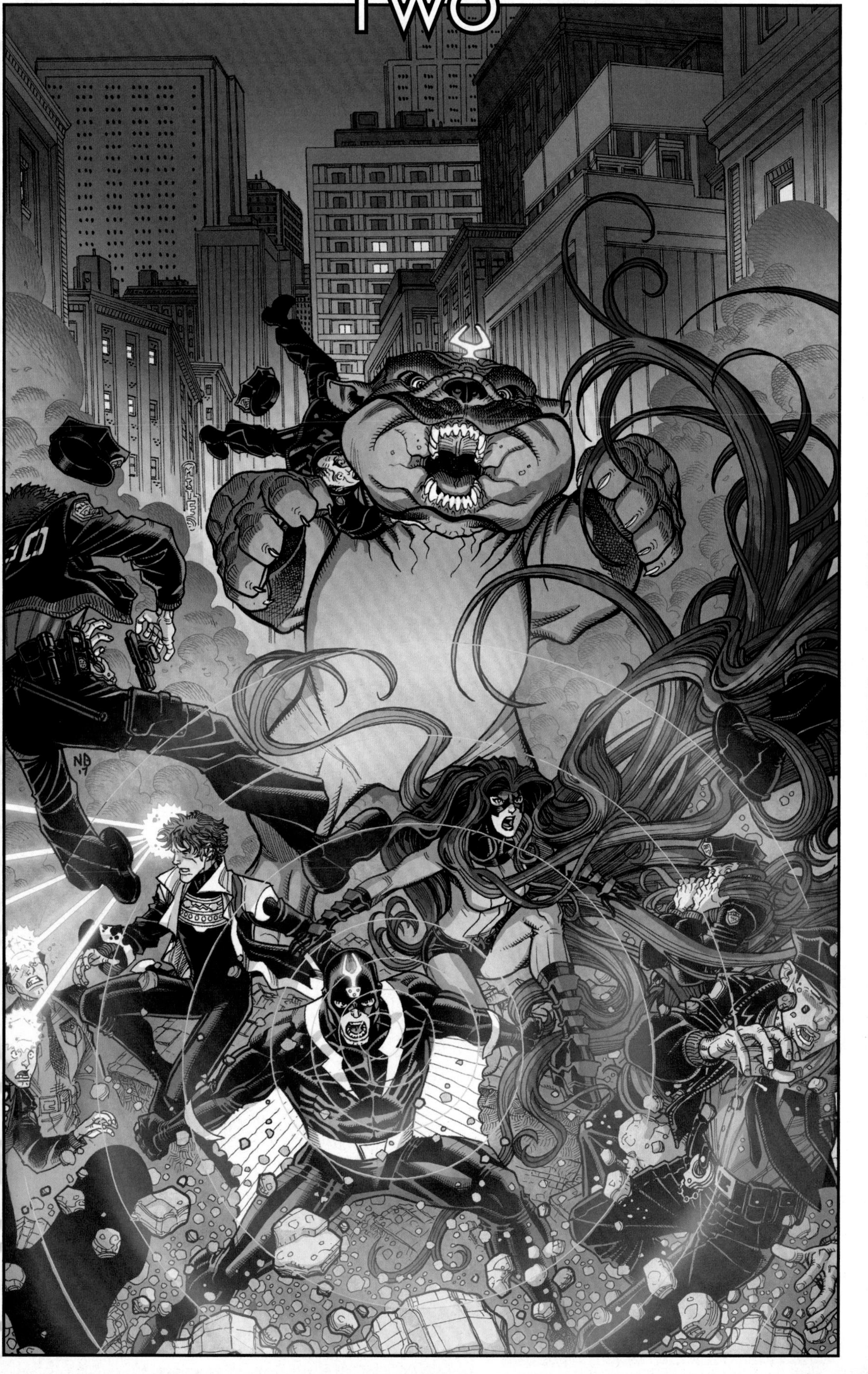

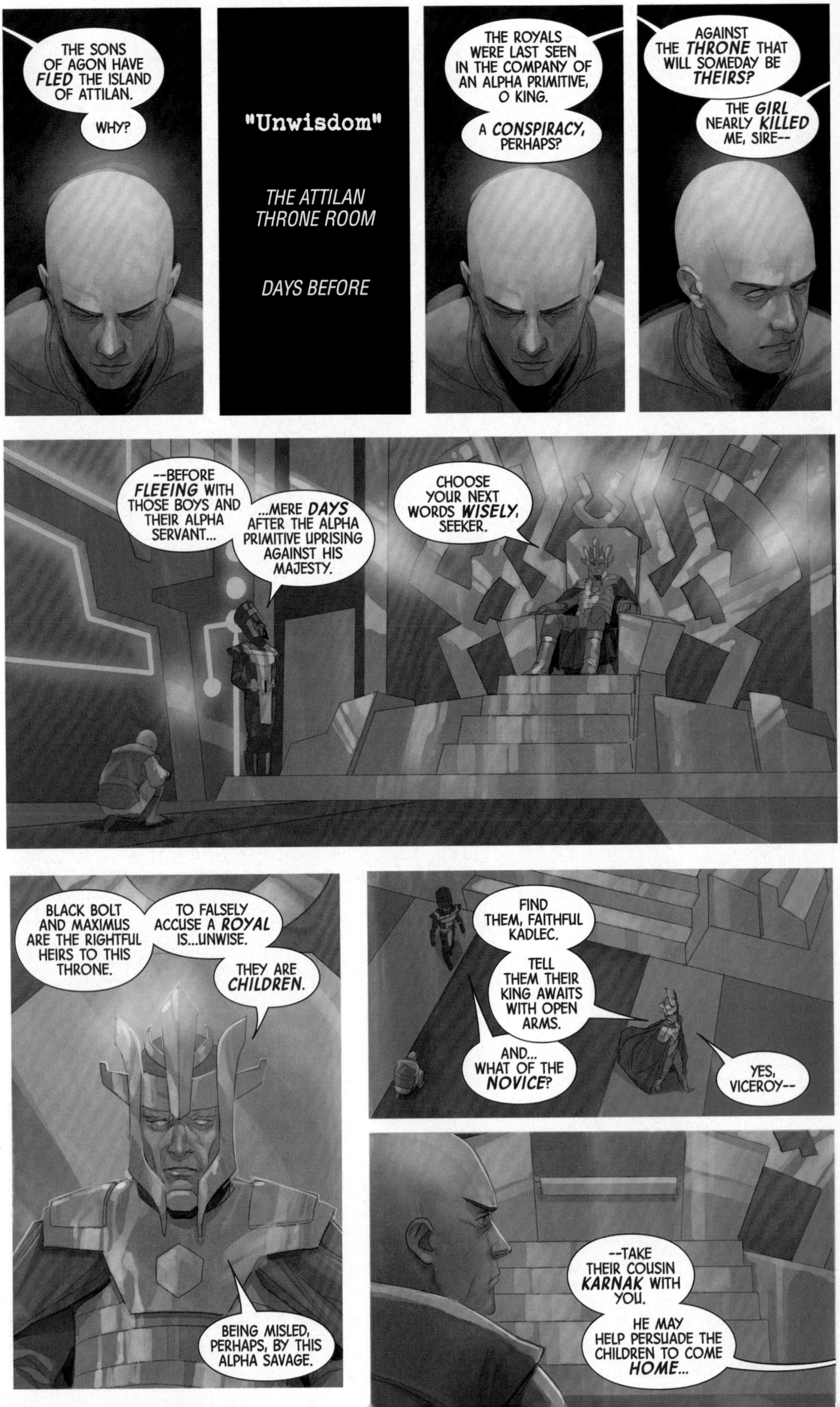

THE SONS OF AGON HAVE FLED THE ISLAND OF ATTILAN.
WHY?
"Unwisdom"
THE ATTILAN THRONE ROOM
DAYS BEFORE
THE ROYALS WERE LAST SEEN IN THE COMPANY OF AN ALPHA PRIMITIVE, O KING.
A CONSPIRACY, PERHAPS?
AGAINST THE THRONE THAT WILL SOMEDAY BE THEIRS?
THE GIRL NEARLY KILLED ME, SIRE--
--BEFORE FLEEING WITH THOSE BOYS AND THEIR ALPHA SERVANT...
...MERE DAYS AFTER THE ALPHA PRIMITIVE UPRISING AGAINST HIS MAJESTY.
CHOOSE YOUR NEXT WORDS WISELY, SEEKER.
BLACK BOLT AND MAXIMUS ARE THE RIGHTFUL HEIRS TO THIS THRONE.
TO FALSELY ACCUSE A ROYAL IS...UNWISE.
THEY ARE CHILDREN.
BEING MISLED, PERHAPS, BY THIS ALPHA SAVAGE.
FIND THEM, FAITHFUL KADLEC.
TELL THEM THEIR KING AWAITS WITH OPEN ARMS.
AND... WHAT OF THE NOVICE?
YES, VICEROY--
--TAKE THEIR COUSIN KARNAK WITH YOU.
HE MAY HELP PERSUADE THE CHILDREN TO COME HOME...

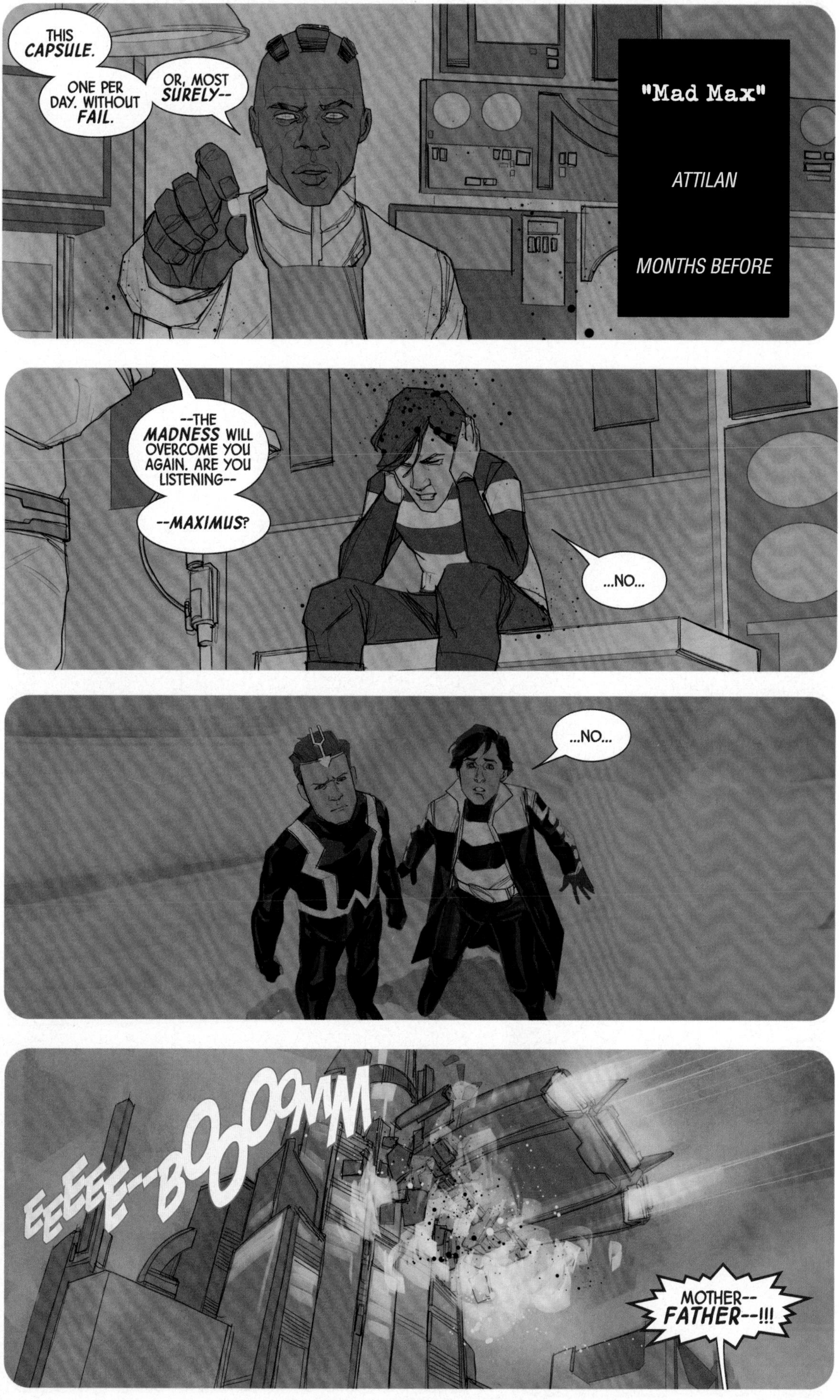
"Mad Max"
ATTILAN
MONTHS BEFORE
THIS CAPSULE.
ONE PER DAY. WITHOUT FAIL.
OR, MOST SURELY--
--THE MADNESS WILL OVERCOME YOU AGAIN. ARE YOU LISTENING--
--MAXIMUS?
...NO...
...NO...
EEEEE--BOOOOMM
MOTHER-- FATHER--!!!

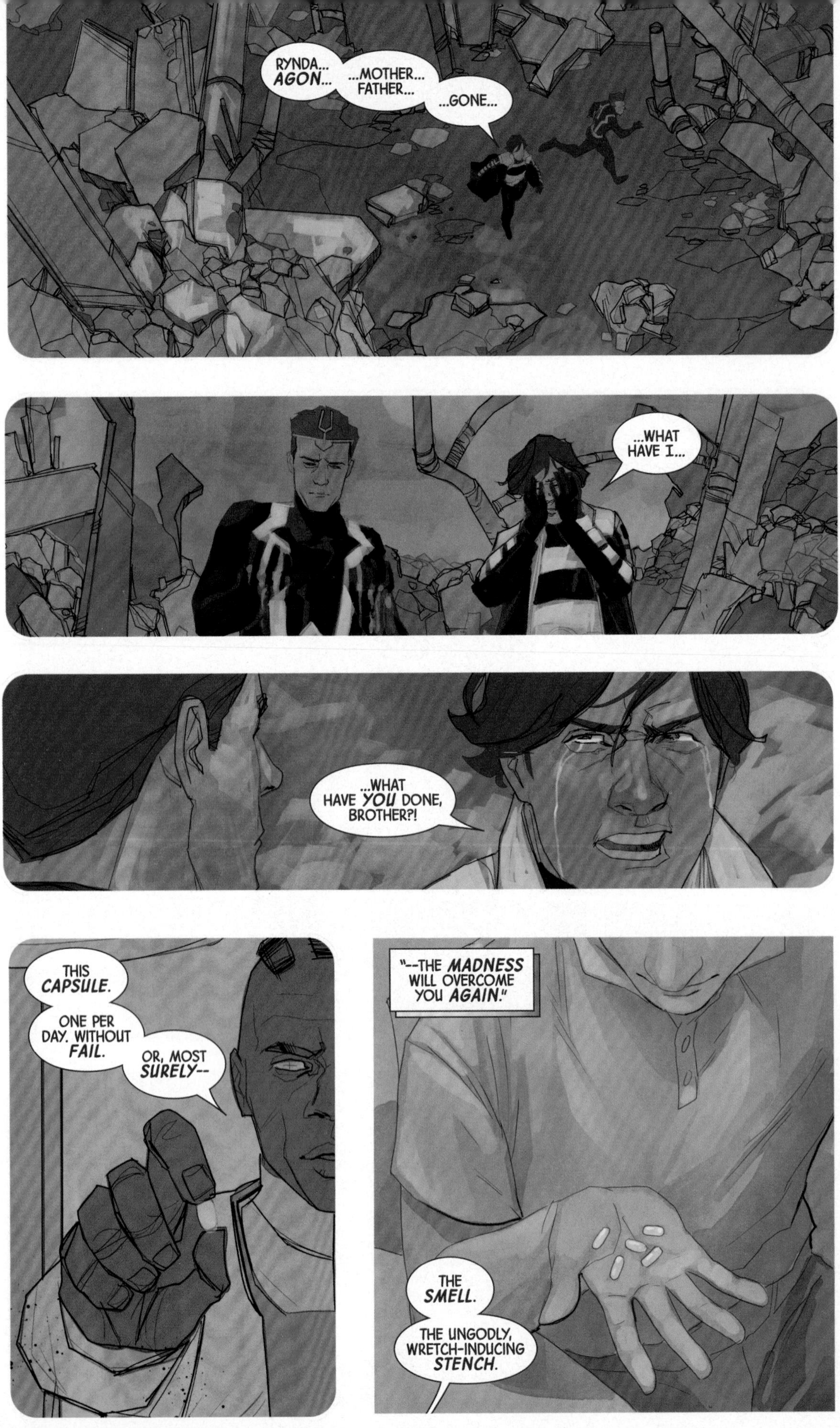
RYNDA... AGON...
...MOTHER... FATHER...
...GONE...
...WHAT HAVE I...
...WHAT HAVE YOU DONE, BROTHER?!
THIS CAPSULE.
ONE PER DAY. WITHOUT FAIL.
OR, MOST SURELY--
"--THE MADNESS WILL OVERCOME YOU AGAIN."
THE SMELL.
THE UNGODLY, WRETCH-INDUCING STENCH.

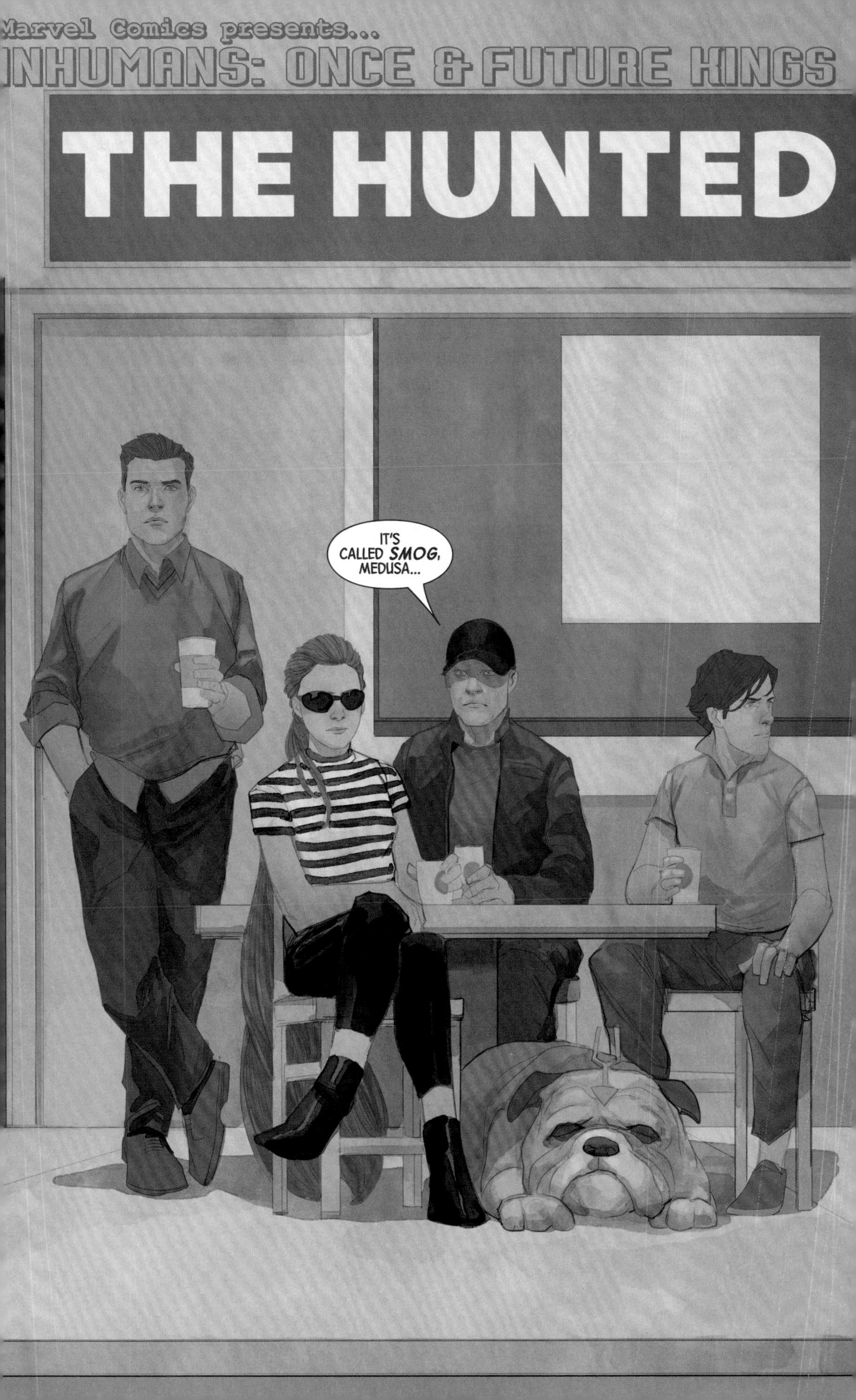
Marvel Comics presents...
INHUMANS: ONCE & FUTURE KINGS
THE HUNTED
IT'S CALLED SMOG, MEDUSA...

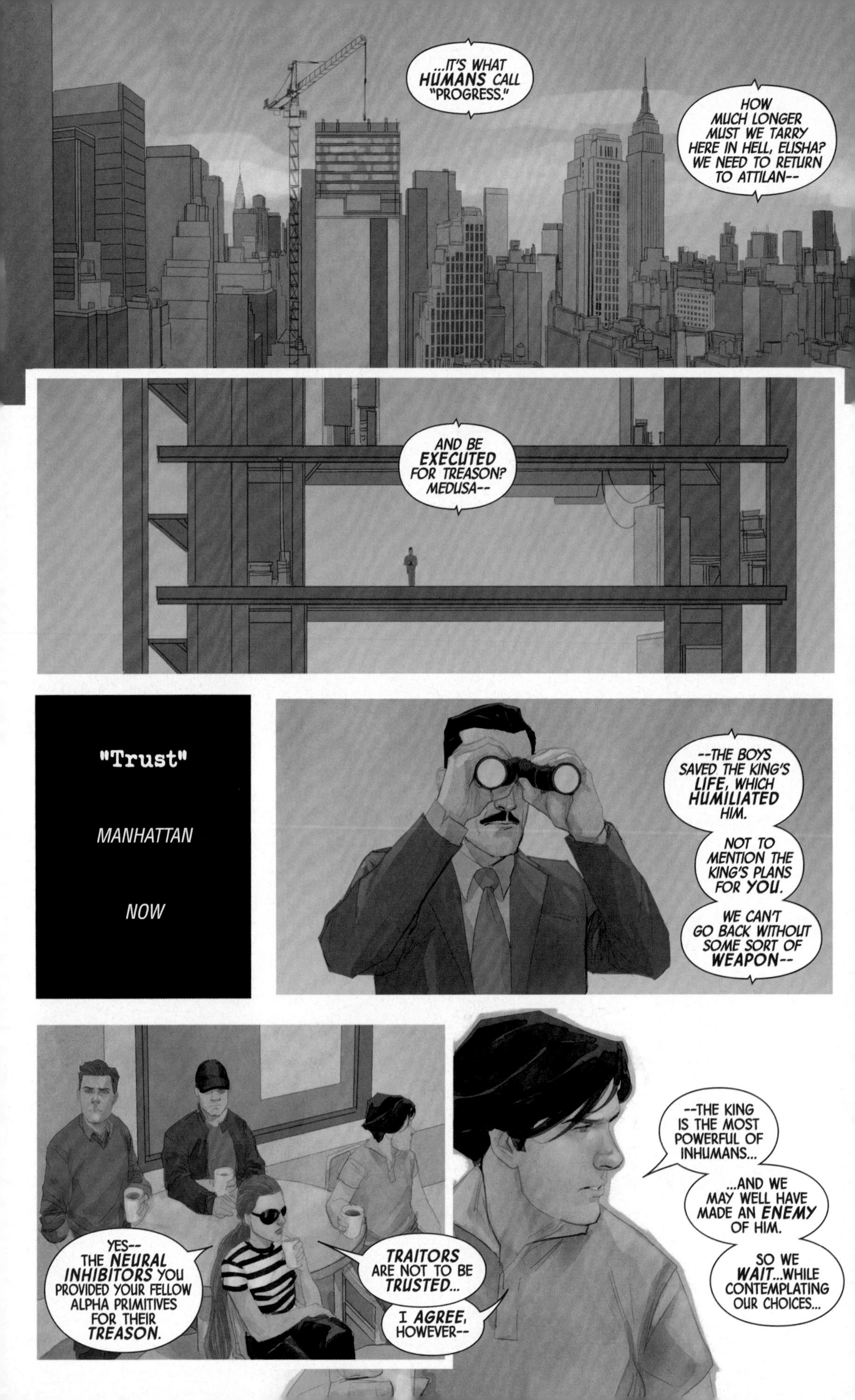
...IT'S WHAT HUMANS CALL "PROGRESS."
HOW MUCH LONGER MUST WE TARRY HERE IN HELL, ELISHA? WE NEED TO RETURN TO ATTILAN--
AND BE EXECUTED FOR TREASON? MEDUSA--
"Trust"
MANHATTAN
NOW
--THE BOYS SAVED THE KING'S LIFE, WHICH HUMILIATED HIM.
NOT TO MENTION THE KING'S PLANS FOR YOU.
WE CAN'T GO BACK WITHOUT SOME SORT OF WEAPON--
YES-- THE NEURAL INHIBITORS YOU PROVIDED YOUR FELLOW ALPHA PRIMITIVES FOR THEIR TREASON.
TRAITORS ARE NOT TO BE TRUSTED...
I AGREE, HOWEVER--
--THE KING IS THE MOST POWERFUL OF INHUMANS...
...AND WE MAY WELL HAVE MADE AN ENEMY OF HIM.
SO WE WAIT...WHILE CONTEMPLATING OUR CHOICES...

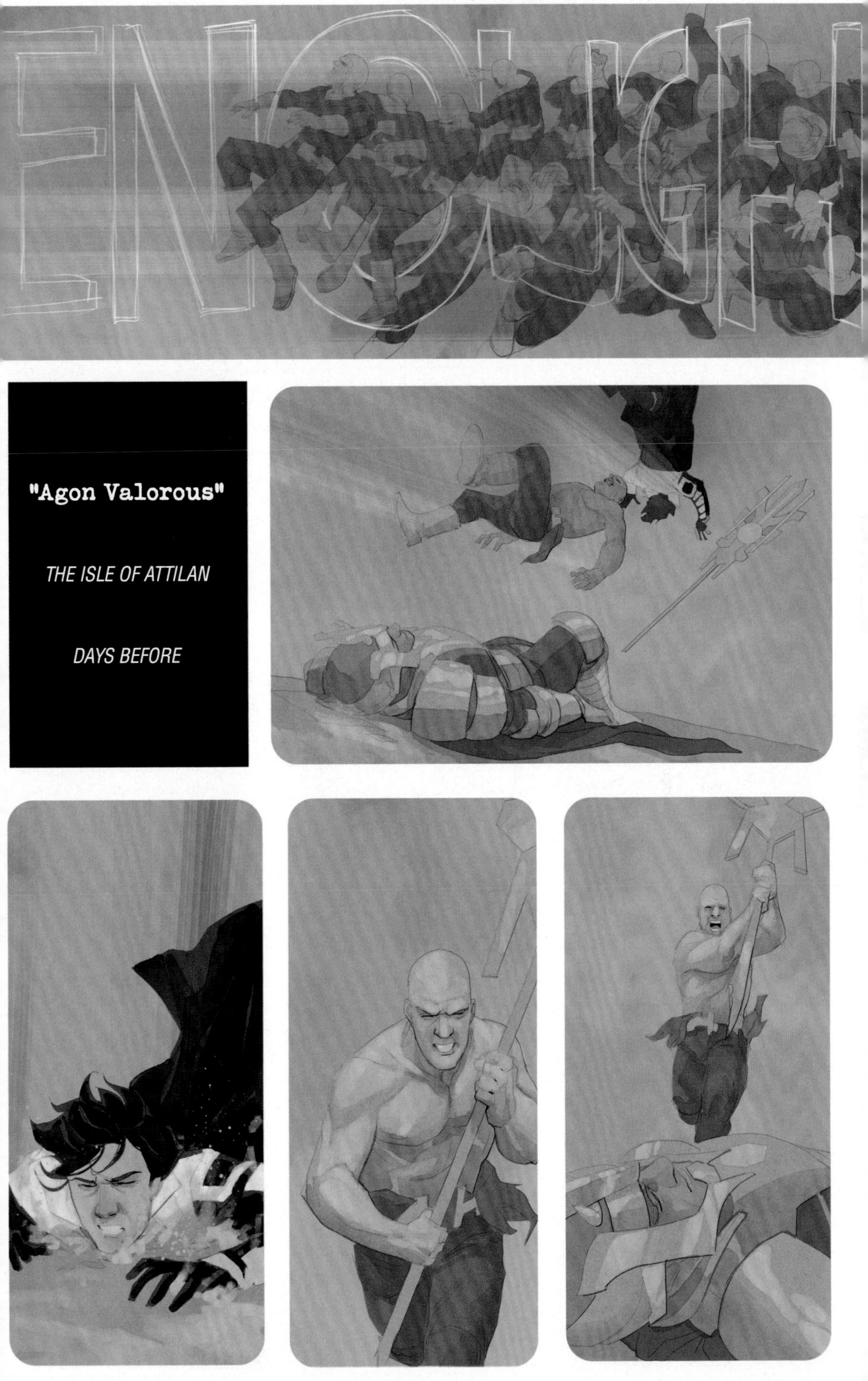
ENOUGH
"Agon Valorous"
THE ISLE OF ATTILAN
DAYS BEFORE

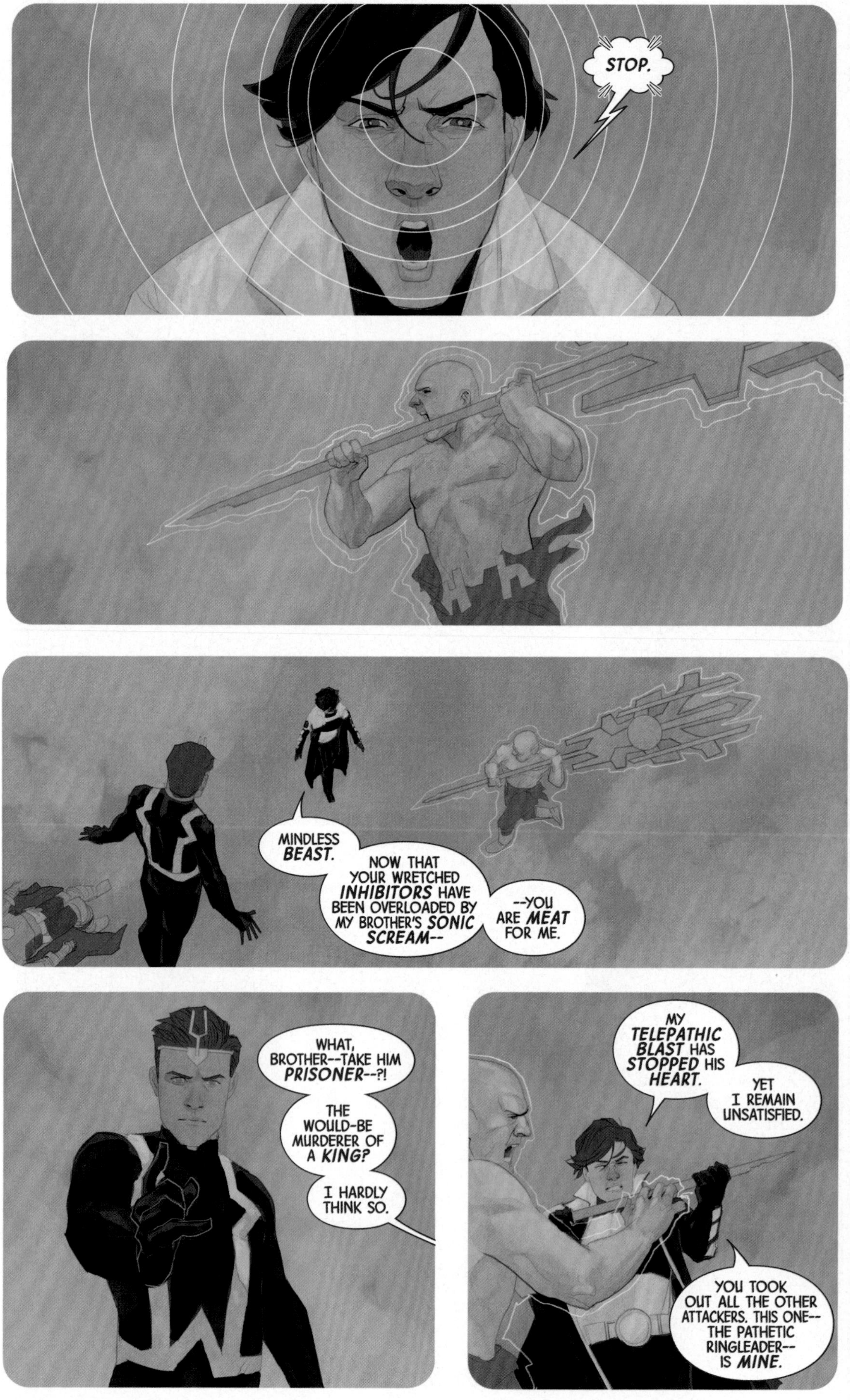
STOP.
MINDLESS BEAST.
NOW THAT YOUR WRETCHED INHIBITORS HAVE BEEN OVERLOADED BY MY BROTHER'S SONIC SCREAM--
--YOU ARE MEAT FOR ME.
WHAT, BROTHER--TAKE HIM PRISONER--?!
THE WOULD-BE MURDERER OF A KING?
I HARDLY THINK SO.
MY TELEPATHIC BLAST HAS STOPPED HIS HEART.
YET I REMAIN UNSATISFIED.
YOU TOOK OUT ALL THE OTHER ATTACKERS. THIS ONE--THE PATHETIC RINGLEADER--IS MINE.

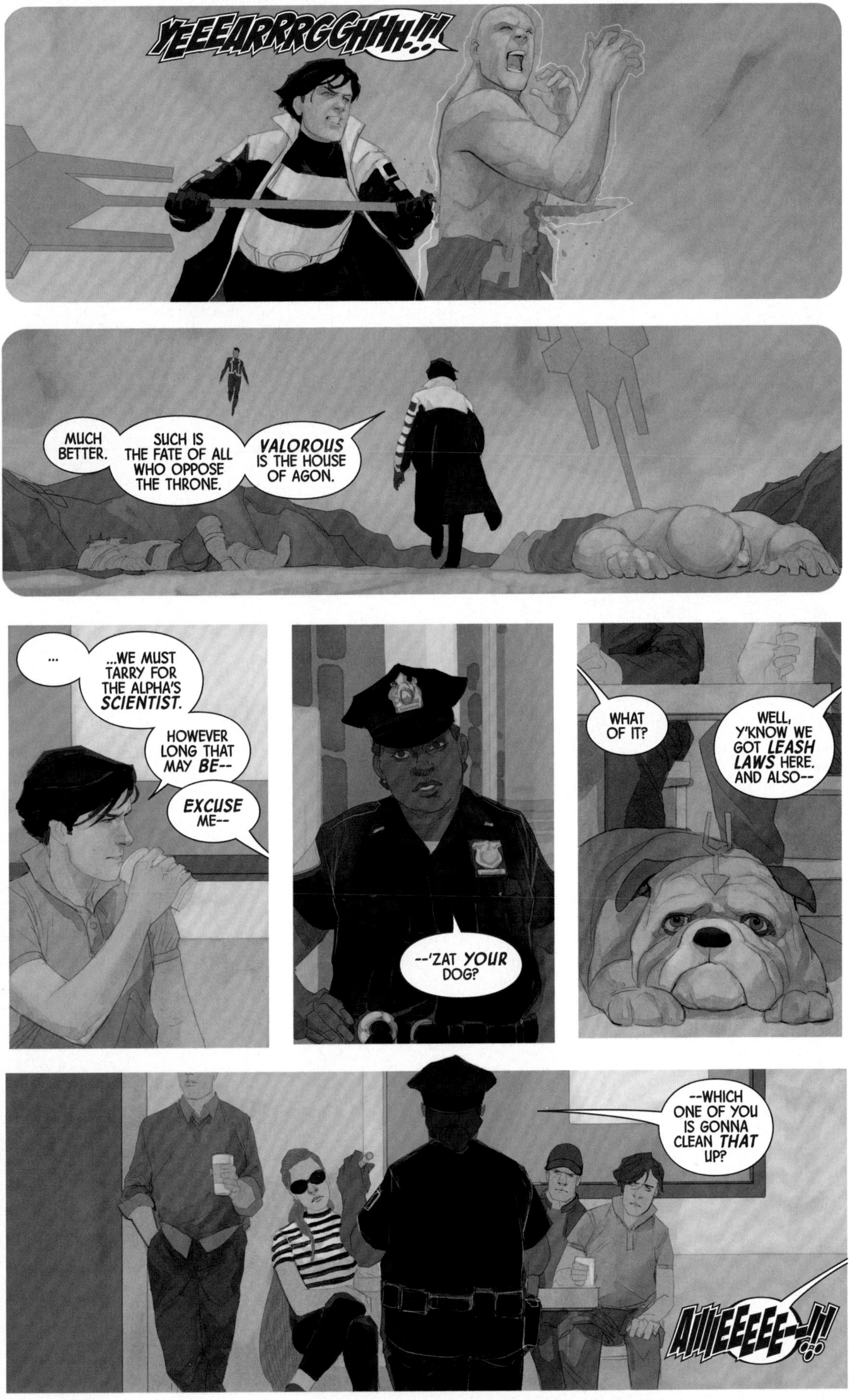

YEEEARRRGGHHH!!!
MUCH BETTER.
SUCH IS THE FATE OF ALL WHO OPPOSE THE THRONE.
VALOROUS IS THE HOUSE OF AGON.
...
...WE MUST TARRY FOR THE ALPHA'S SCIENTIST.
HOWEVER LONG THAT MAY BE--
EXCUSE ME--
--'ZAT YOUR DOG?
WHAT OF IT?
WELL, Y'KNOW WE GOT LEASH LAWS HERE. AND ALSO--
--WHICH ONE OF YOU IS GONNA CLEAN THAT UP?
AIIIEEEEE--!!!

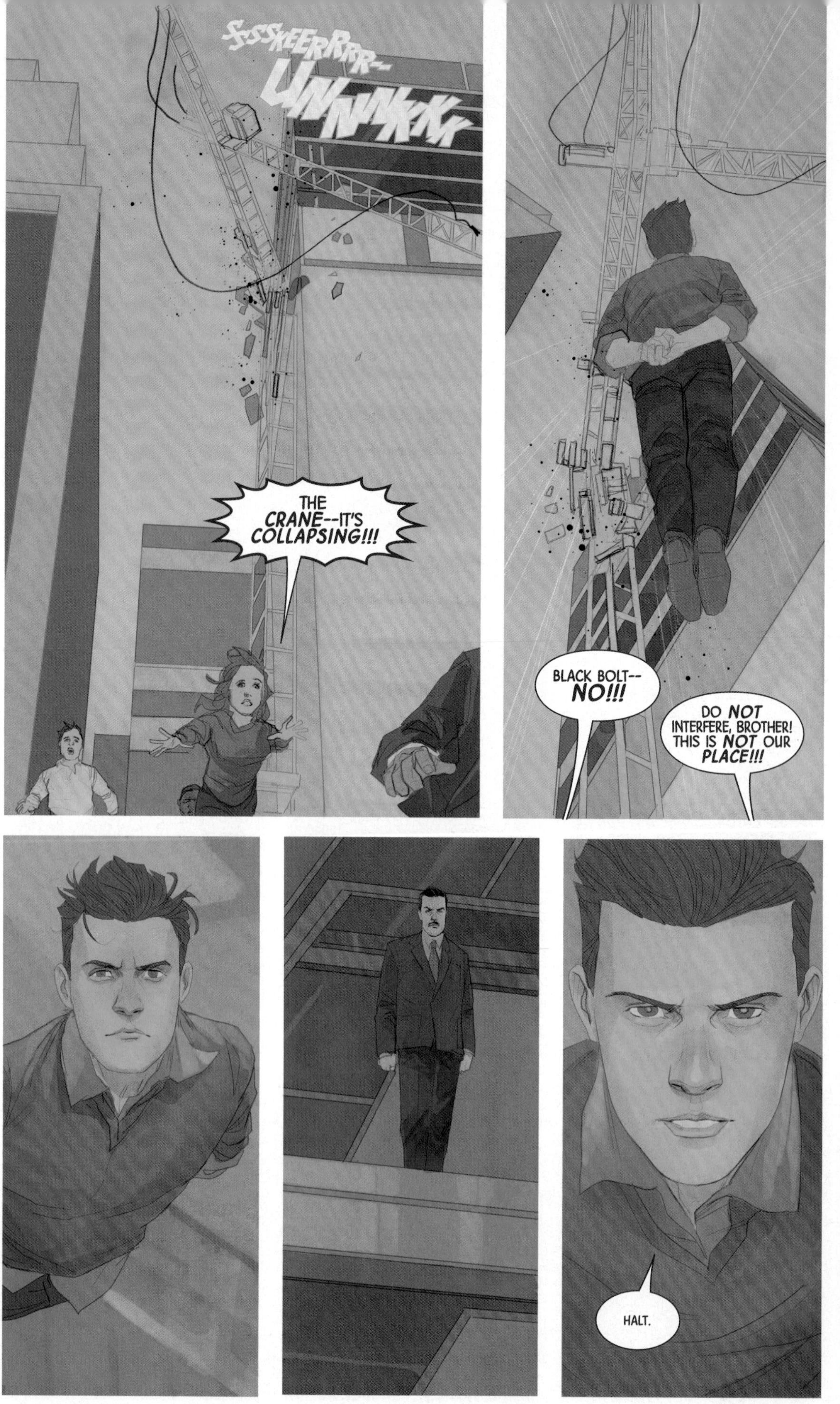
SSSSKEERRRR--UNNNKKK
THE CRANE--IT'S COLLAPSING!!!
BLACK BOLT-- NO!!!
DO NOT INTERFERE, BROTHER! THIS IS NOT OUR PLACE!!!
HALT.

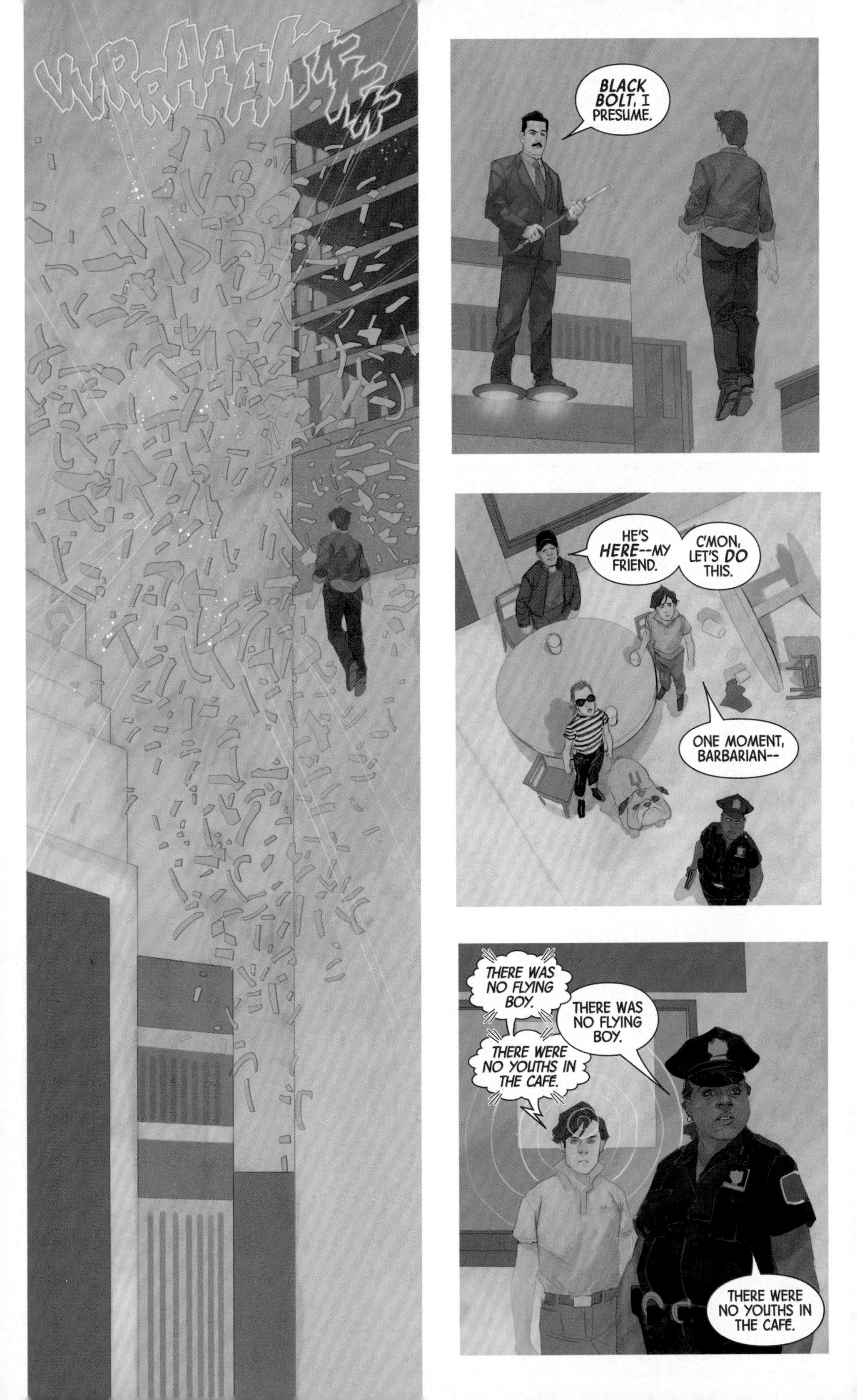
VVRAAAMK
BLACK BOLT, I PRESUME.
HE'S HERE--MY FRIEND.
C'MON, LET'S DO THIS.
ONE MOMENT, BARBARIAN--
THERE WAS NO FLYING BOY.
THERE WAS NO FLYING BOY.
THERE WERE NO YOUTHS IN THE CAFÉ.
THERE WERE NO YOUTHS IN THE CAFÉ.

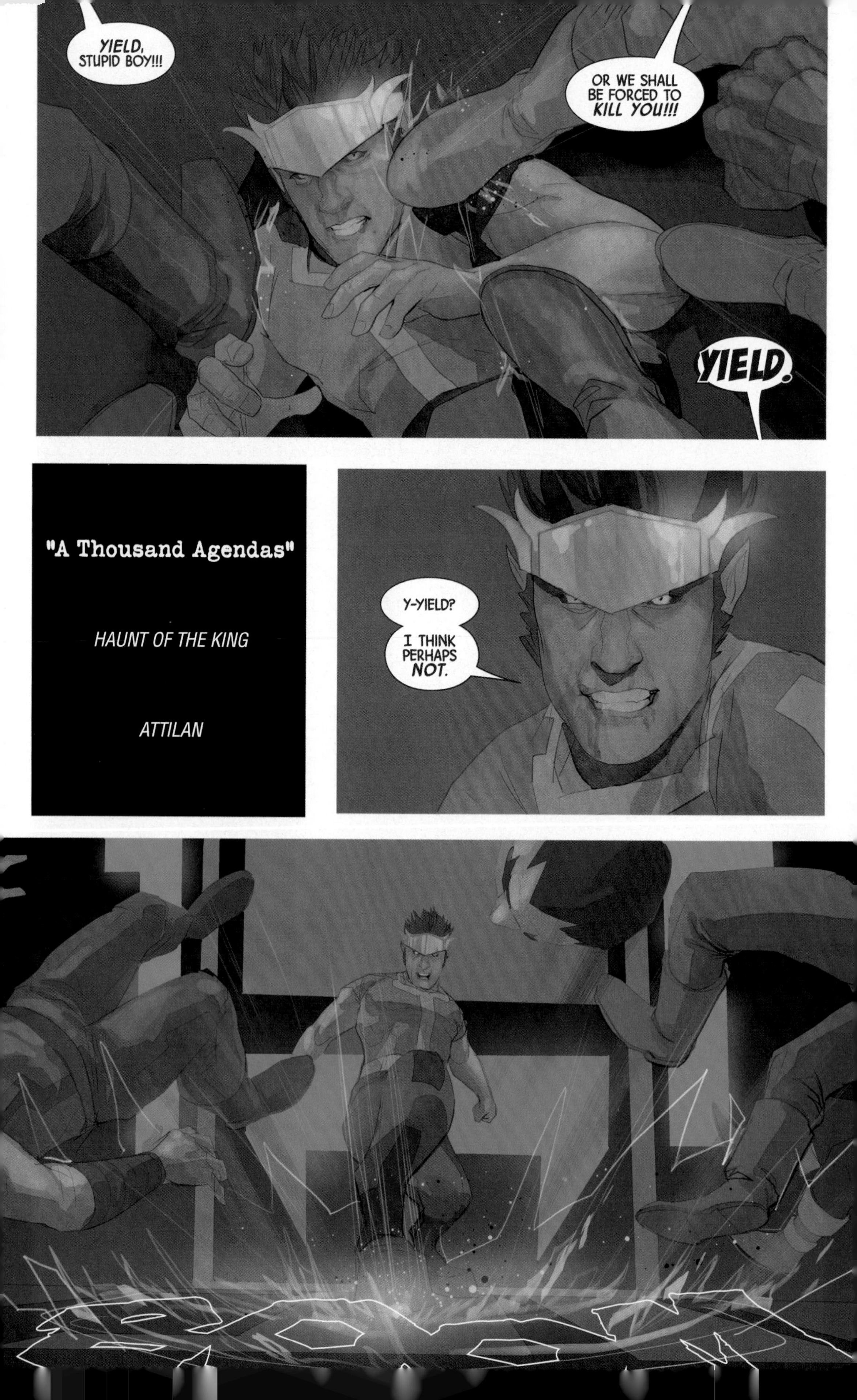
YIELD, STUPID BOY!!!
OR WE SHALL BE FORCED TO KILL YOU!!!
YIELD.
"A Thousand Agendas"
HAUNT OF THE KING
ATTILAN
Y-YIELD?
I THINK PERHAPS NOT.

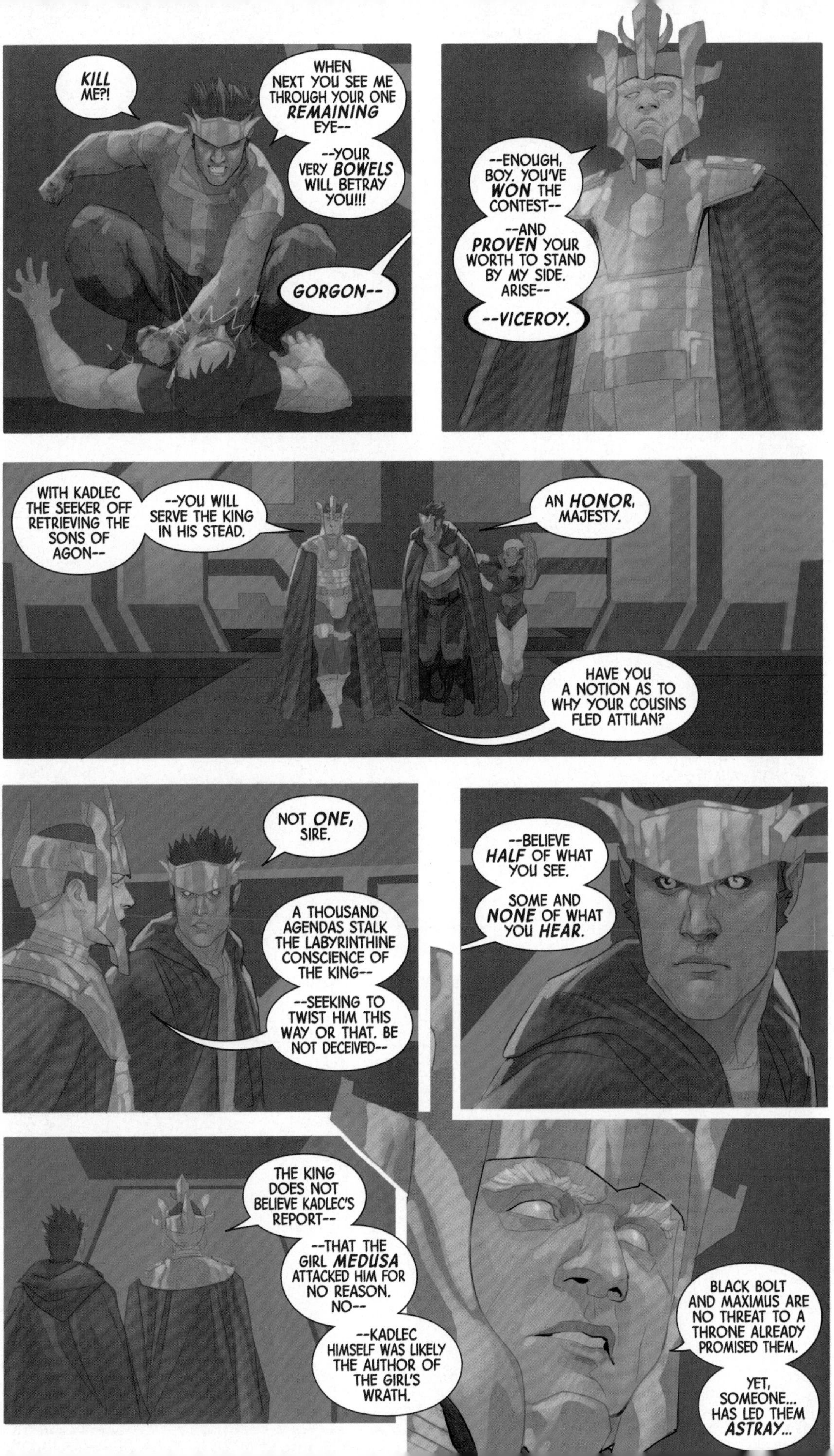
KILL ME?!
WHEN NEXT YOU SEE ME THROUGH YOUR ONE REMAINING EYE--
--YOUR VERY BOWELS WILL BETRAY YOU!!!
GORGON--
--ENOUGH, BOY. YOU'VE WON THE CONTEST--
--AND PROVEN YOUR WORTH TO STAND BY MY SIDE. ARISE--
--VICEROY.
WITH KADLEC THE SEEKER OFF RETRIEVING THE SONS OF AGON--
--YOU WILL SERVE THE KING IN HIS STEAD.
AN HONOR, MAJESTY.
HAVE YOU A NOTION AS TO WHY YOUR COUSINS FLED ATTILAN?
NOT ONE, SIRE.
A THOUSAND AGENDAS STALK THE LABYRINTHINE CONSCIENCE OF THE KING--
--SEEKING TO TWIST HIM THIS WAY OR THAT. BE NOT DECEIVED--
--BELIEVE HALF OF WHAT YOU SEE.
SOME AND NONE OF WHAT YOU HEAR.
THE KING DOES NOT BELIEVE KADLEC'S REPORT--
--THAT THE GIRL MEDUSA ATTACKED HIM FOR NO REASON. NO--
--KADLEC HIMSELF WAS LIKELY THE AUTHOR OF THE GIRL'S WRATH.
BLACK BOLT AND MAXIMUS ARE NO THREAT TO A THRONE ALREADY PROMISED THEM.
YET, SOMEONE... HAS LED THEM ASTRAY...

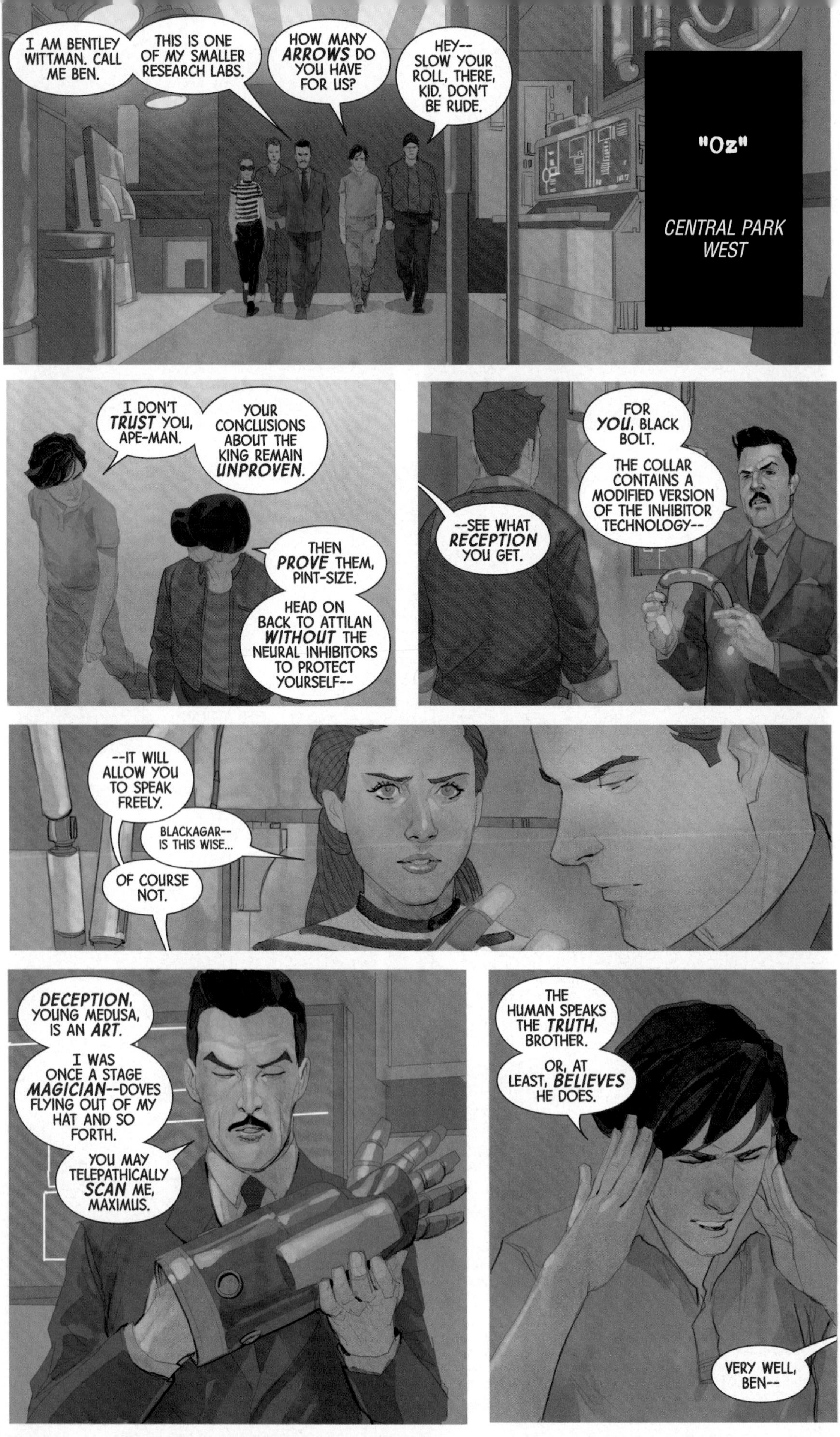
"Oz"
CENTRAL PARK WEST
I AM BENTLEY WITTMAN. CALL ME BEN.
THIS IS ONE OF MY SMALLER RESEARCH LABS.
HOW MANY ARROWS DO YOU HAVE FOR US?
HEY-- SLOW YOUR ROLL, THERE, KID. DON'T BE RUDE.
I DON'T TRUST YOU, APE-MAN.
YOUR CONCLUSIONS ABOUT THE KING REMAIN UNPROVEN.
THEN PROVE THEM, PINT-SIZE.
HEAD ON BACK TO ATTILAN WITHOUT THE NEURAL INHIBITORS TO PROTECT YOURSELF--
--SEE WHAT RECEPTION YOU GET.
FOR YOU, BLACK BOLT.
THE COLLAR CONTAINS A MODIFIED VERSION OF THE INHIBITOR TECHNOLOGY--
--IT WILL ALLOW YOU TO SPEAK FREELY.
BLACKAGAR-- IS THIS WISE...
OF COURSE NOT.
DECEPTION, YOUNG MEDUSA, IS AN ART.
I WAS ONCE A STAGE MAGICIAN--DOVES FLYING OUT OF MY HAT AND SO FORTH.
YOU MAY TELEPATHICALLY SCAN ME, MAXIMUS.
THE HUMAN SPEAKS THE TRUTH, BROTHER.
OR, AT LEAST, BELIEVES HE DOES.
VERY WELL, BEN--

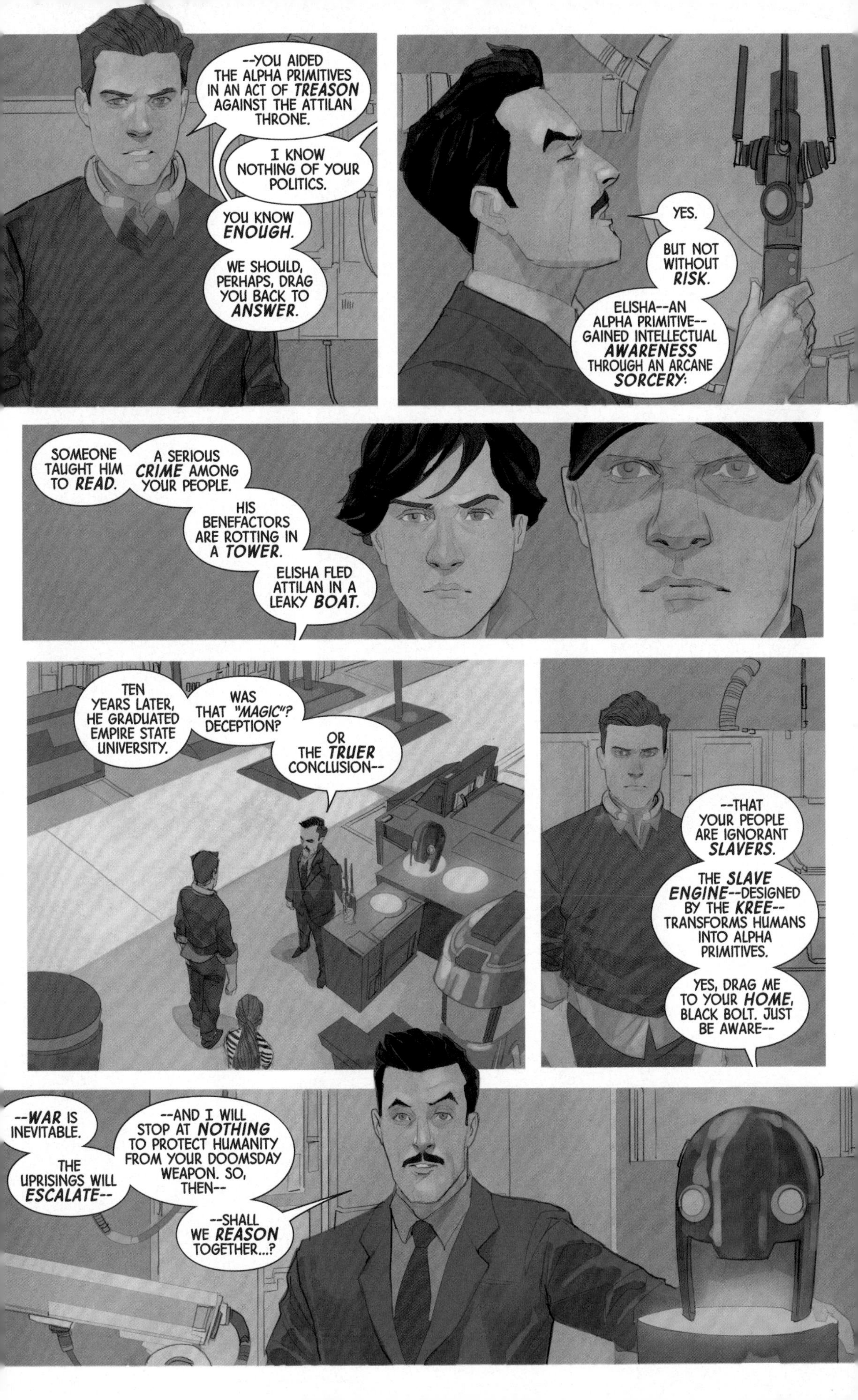
--YOU AIDED THE ALPHA PRIMITIVES IN AN ACT OF TREASON AGAINST THE ATTILAN THRONE.
I KNOW NOTHING OF YOUR POLITICS.
YOU KNOW ENOUGH.
WE SHOULD, PERHAPS, DRAG YOU BACK TO ANSWER.
YES.
BUT NOT WITHOUT RISK.
ELISHA--AN ALPHA PRIMITIVE--GAINED INTELLECTUAL AWARENESS THROUGH AN ARCANE SORCERY:
SOMEONE TAUGHT HIM TO READ.
A SERIOUS CRIME AMONG YOUR PEOPLE.
HIS BENEFACTORS ARE ROTTING IN A TOWER.
ELISHA FLED ATTILAN IN A LEAKY BOAT.
TEN YEARS LATER, HE GRADUATED EMPIRE STATE UNIVERSITY.
WAS THAT "MAGIC"? DECEPTION?
OR THE TRUER CONCLUSION--
--THAT YOUR PEOPLE ARE IGNORANT SLAVERS.
THE SLAVE ENGINE--DESIGNED BY THE KREE--TRANSFORMS HUMANS INTO ALPHA PRIMITIVES.
YES, DRAG ME TO YOUR HOME, BLACK BOLT. JUST BE AWARE--
--WAR IS INEVITABLE.
THE UPRISINGS WILL ESCALATE--
--AND I WILL STOP AT NOTHING TO PROTECT HUMANITY FROM YOUR DOOMSDAY WEAPON. SO, THEN--
--SHALL WE REASON TOGETHER...?

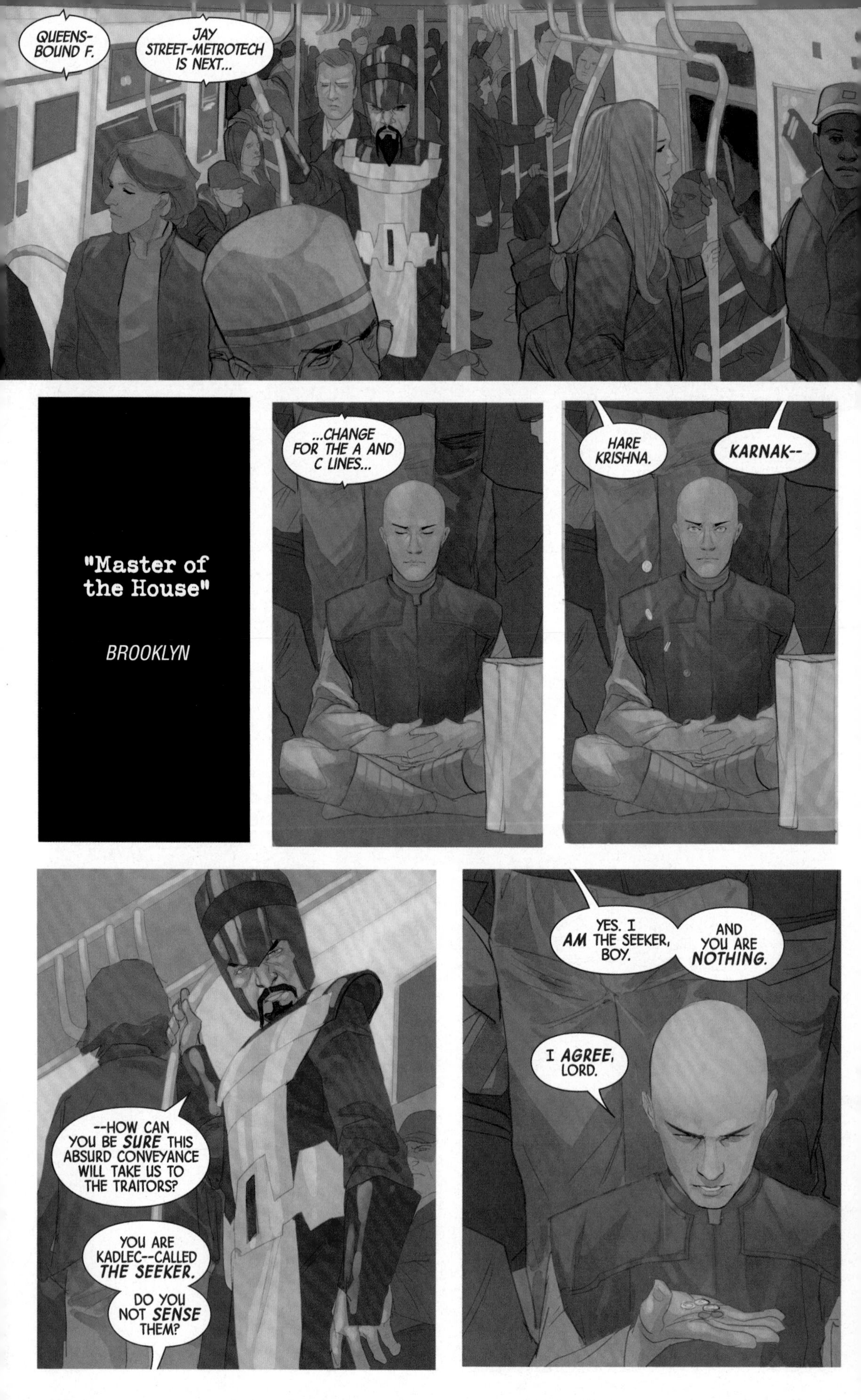
QUEENS-BOUND F.
JAY STREET-METROTECH IS NEXT...
"Master of the House"
BROOKLYN
...CHANGE FOR THE A AND C LINES...
HARE KRISHNA.
KARNAK--
--HOW CAN YOU BE SURE THIS ABSURD CONVEYANCE WILL TAKE US TO THE TRAITORS?
YOU ARE KADLEC--CALLED THE SEEKER.
DO YOU NOT SENSE THEM?
YES. I AM THE SEEKER, BOY.
AND YOU ARE NOTHING.
I AGREE, LORD.

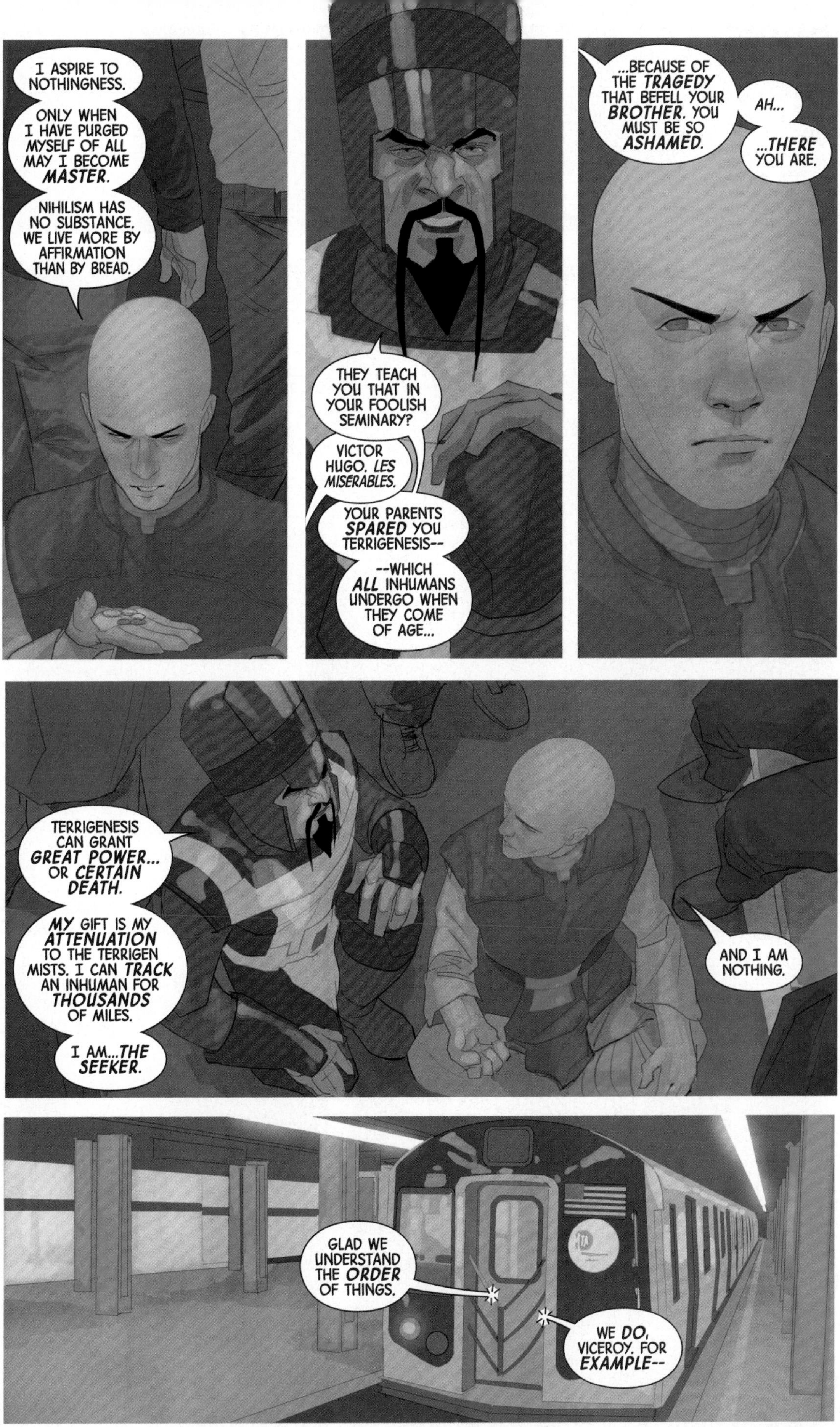

I ASPIRE TO NOTHINGNESS.
ONLY WHEN I HAVE PURGED MYSELF OF ALL MAY I BECOME MASTER.
NIHILISM HAS NO SUBSTANCE. WE LIVE MORE BY AFFIRMATION THAN BY BREAD.
THEY TEACH YOU THAT IN YOUR FOOLISH SEMINARY?
VICTOR HUGO. LES MISÉRABLES.
YOUR PARENTS SPARED YOU TERRIGENESIS--
--WHICH ALL INHUMANS UNDERGO WHEN THEY COME OF AGE...
...BECAUSE OF THE TRAGEDY THAT BEFELL YOUR BROTHER. YOU MUST BE SO ASHAMED.
AH...
...THERE YOU ARE.
TERRIGENESIS CAN GRANT GREAT POWER... OR CERTAIN DEATH.
MY GIFT IS MY ATTENUATION TO THE TERRIGEN MISTS. I CAN TRACK AN INHUMAN FOR THOUSANDS OF MILES.
I AM...THE SEEKER.
AND I AM NOTHING.
GLAD WE UNDERSTAND THE ORDER OF THINGS.
WE DO, VICEROY. FOR EXAMPLE--

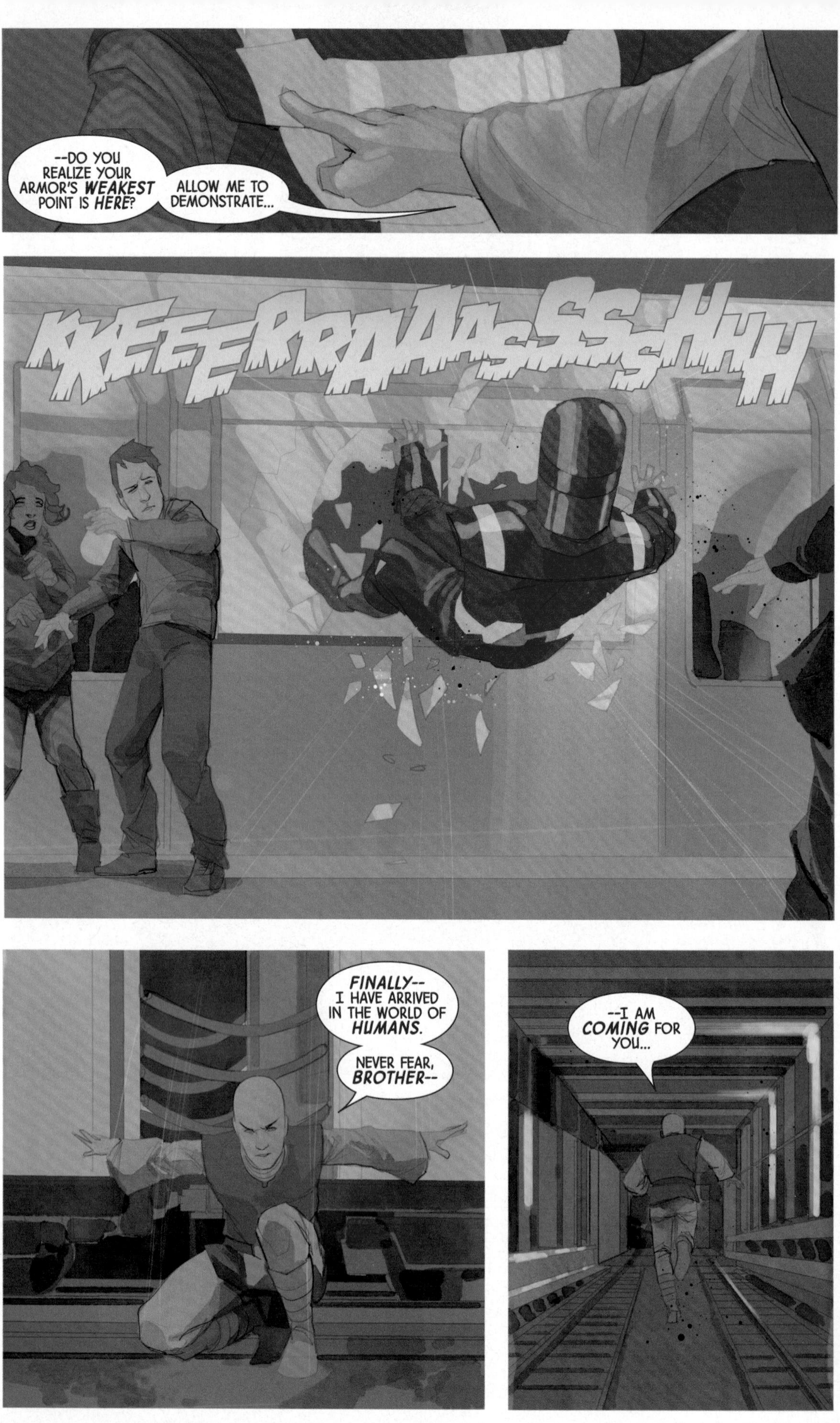
--DO YOU REALIZE YOUR ARMOR'S WEAKEST POINT IS HERE?
ALLOW ME TO DEMONSTRATE...
KKEEERRAAASSSHHH
FINALLY-- I HAVE ARRIVED IN THE WORLD OF HUMANS.
NEVER FEAR, BROTHER--
--I AM COMING FOR YOU...

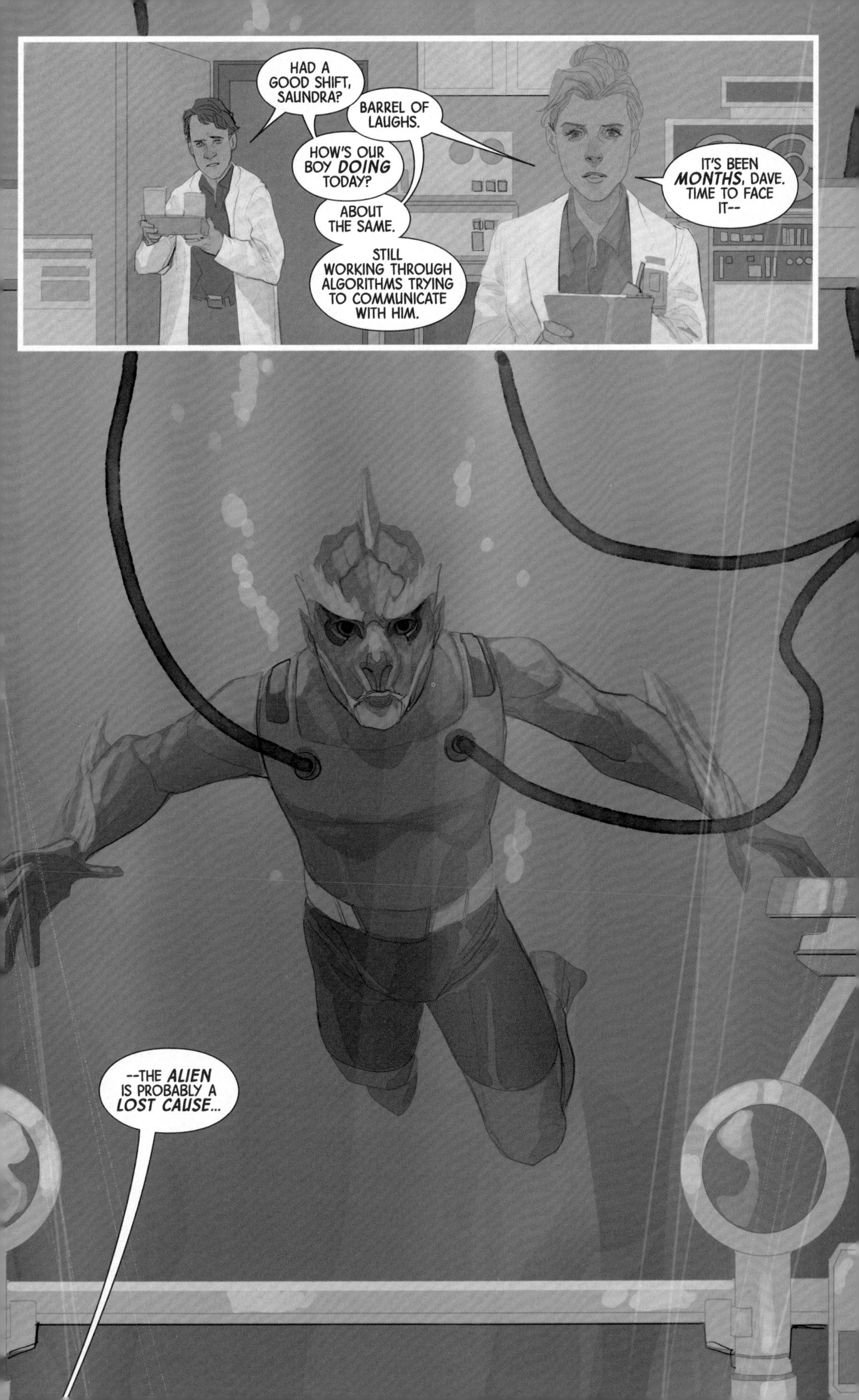

HAD A GOOD SHIFT, SAUNDRA?
BARREL OF LAUGHS.
HOW'S OUR BOY DOING TODAY?
ABOUT THE SAME.
STILL WORKING THROUGH ALGORITHMS TRYING TO COMMUNICATE WITH HIM.
IT'S BEEN MONTHS, DAVE. TIME TO FACE IT--
--THE ALIEN IS PROBABLY A LOST CAUSE...

THREE

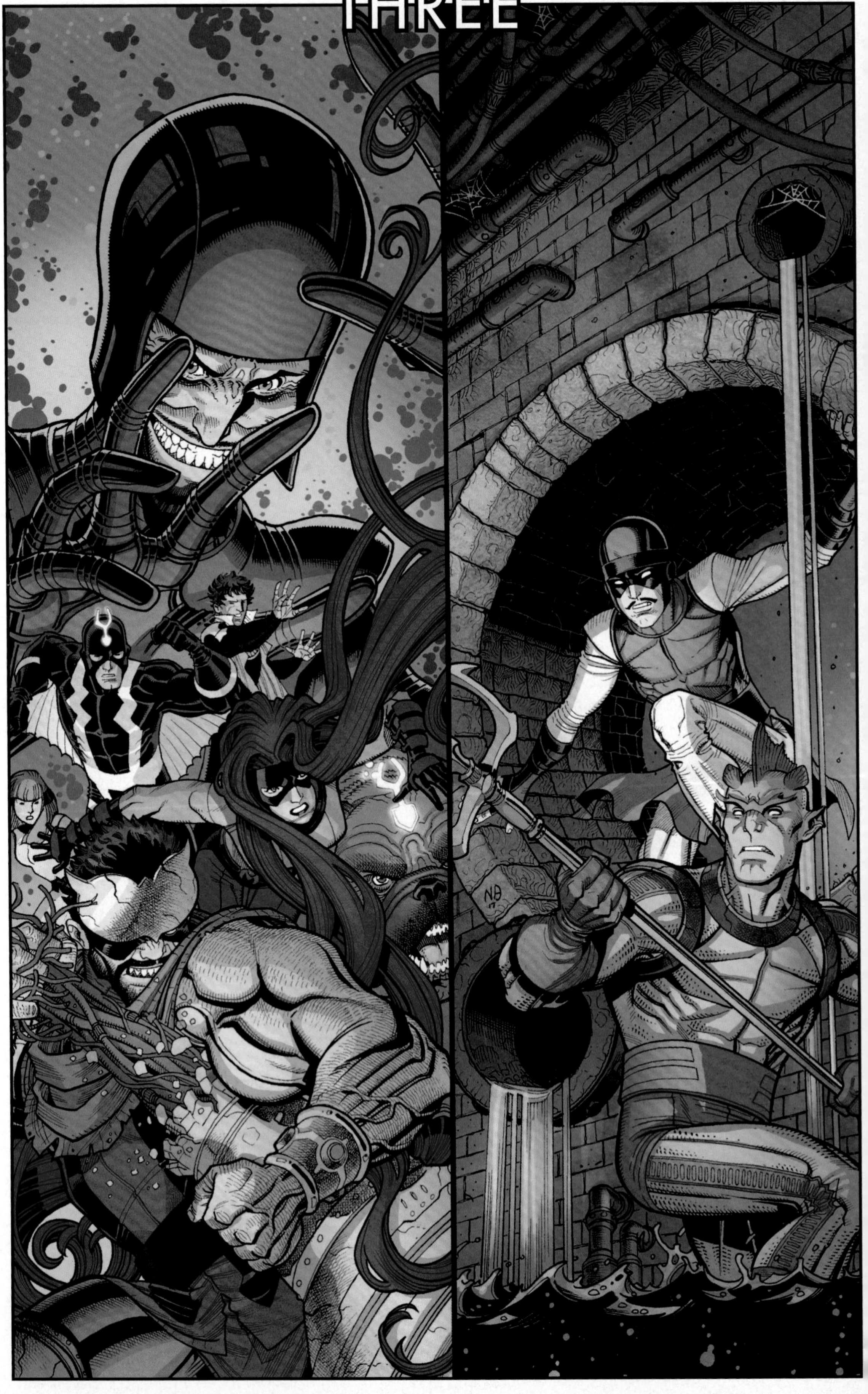

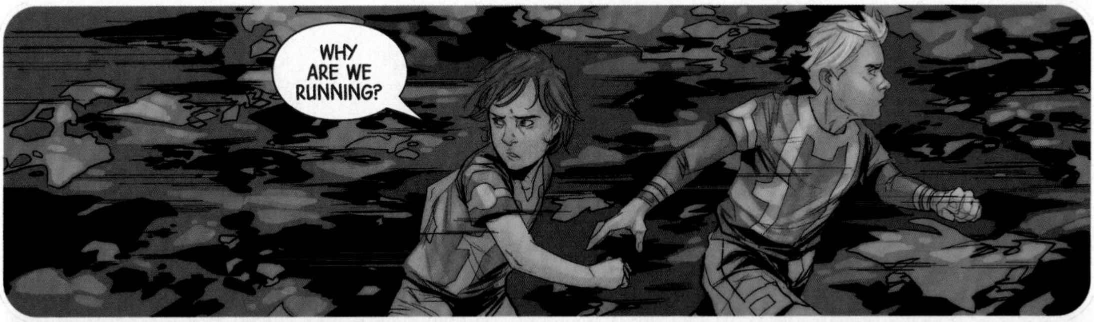
WHY ARE WE RUNNING?

"Home"

THE BEREN WOOD, BEFORE THE DEATH OF AGON

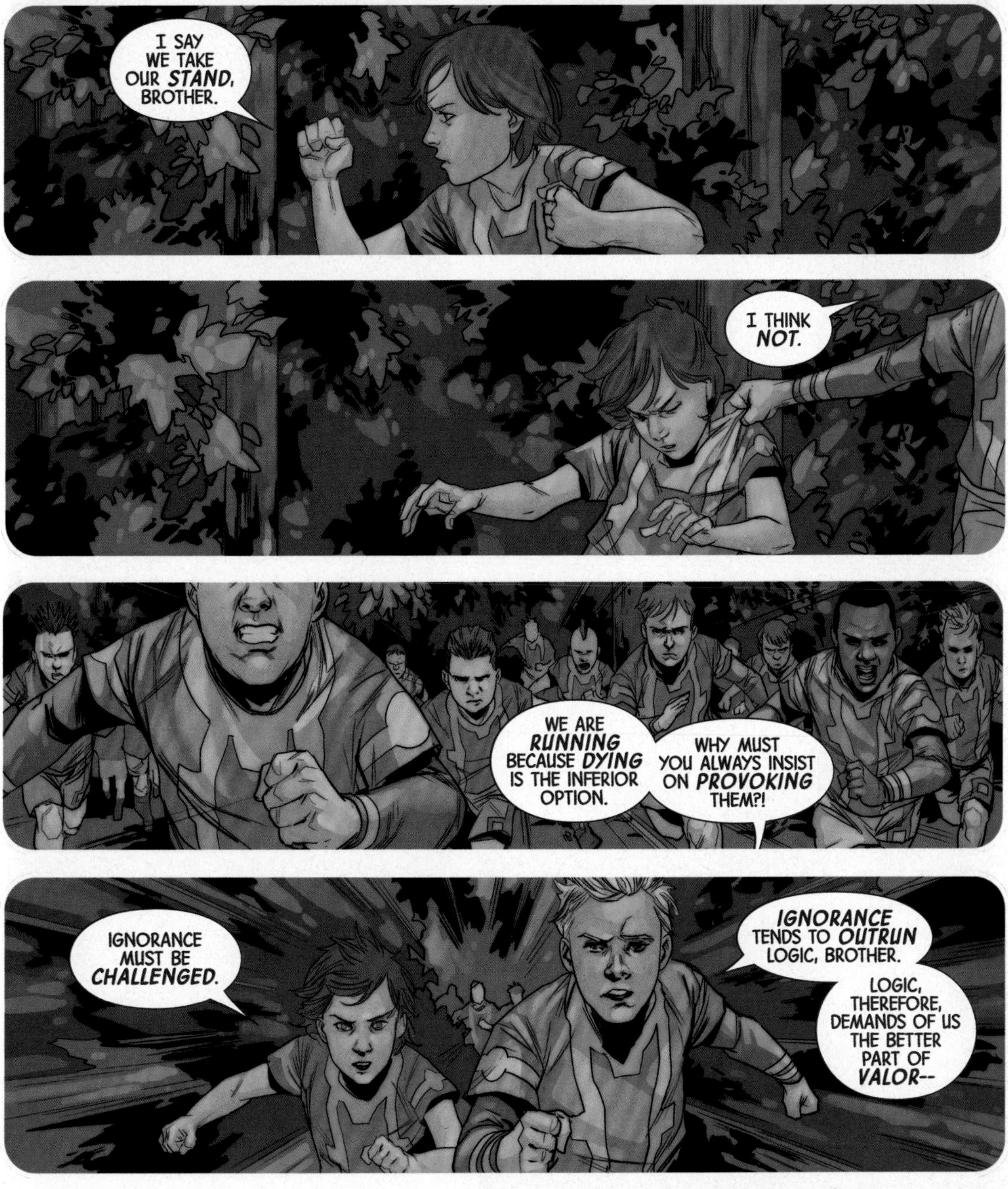
I SAY WE TAKE OUR STAND, BROTHER.
I THINK NOT.
WE ARE RUNNING BECAUSE DYING IS THE INFERIOR OPTION.
WHY MUST YOU ALWAYS INSIST ON PROVOKING THEM?!
IGNORANCE MUST BE CHALLENGED.
IGNORANCE TENDS TO OUTRUN LOGIC, BROTHER.
LOGIC, THEREFORE, DEMANDS OF US THE BETTER PART OF VALOR--

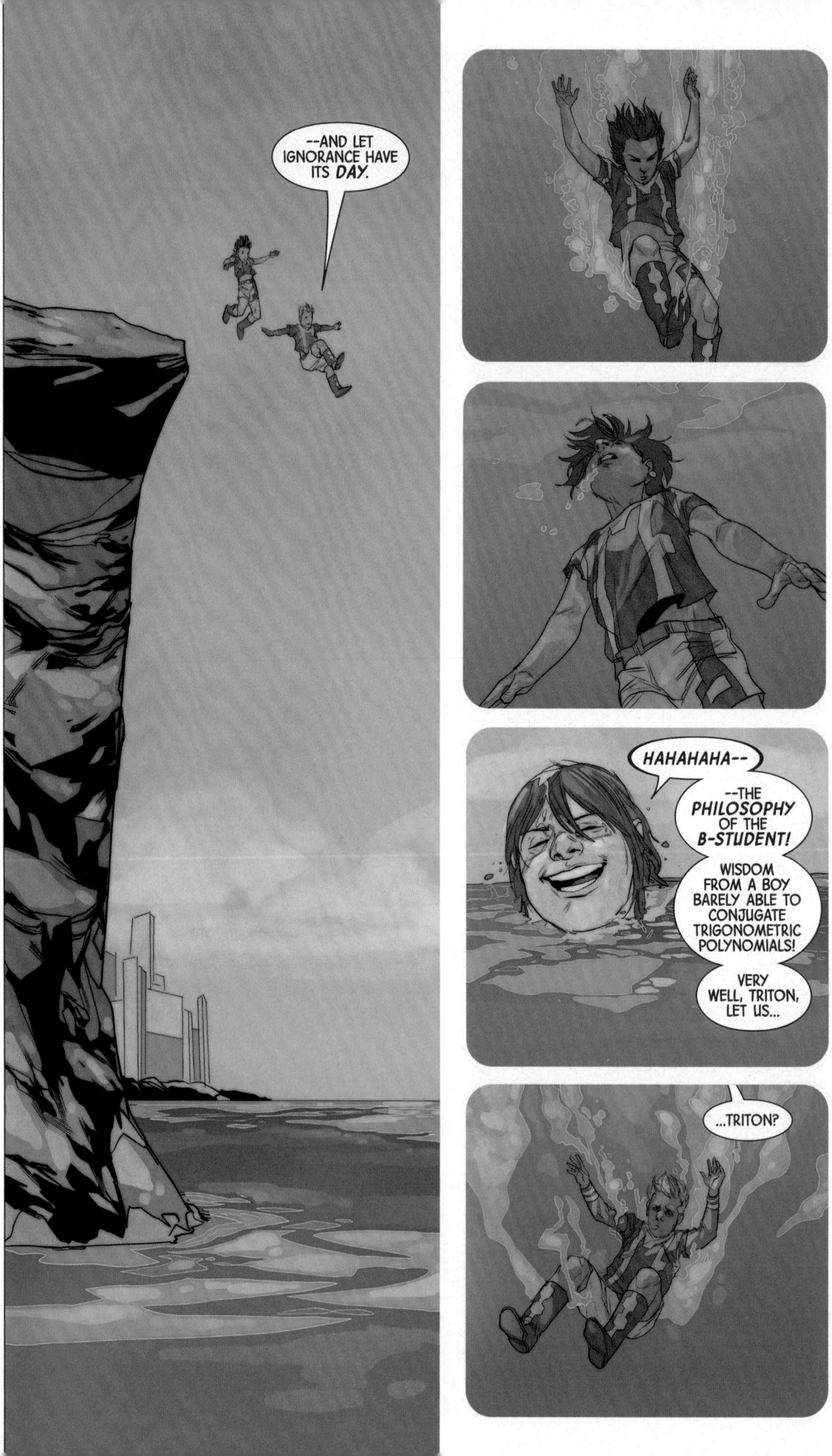
--AND LET IGNORANCE HAVE ITS DAY.
HAHAHAHA--
--THE PHILOSOPHY OF THE B-STUDENT!
WISDOM FROM A BOY BARELY ABLE TO CONJUGATE TRIGONOMETRIC POLYNOMIALS!
VERY WELL, TRITON, LET US...
...TRITON?

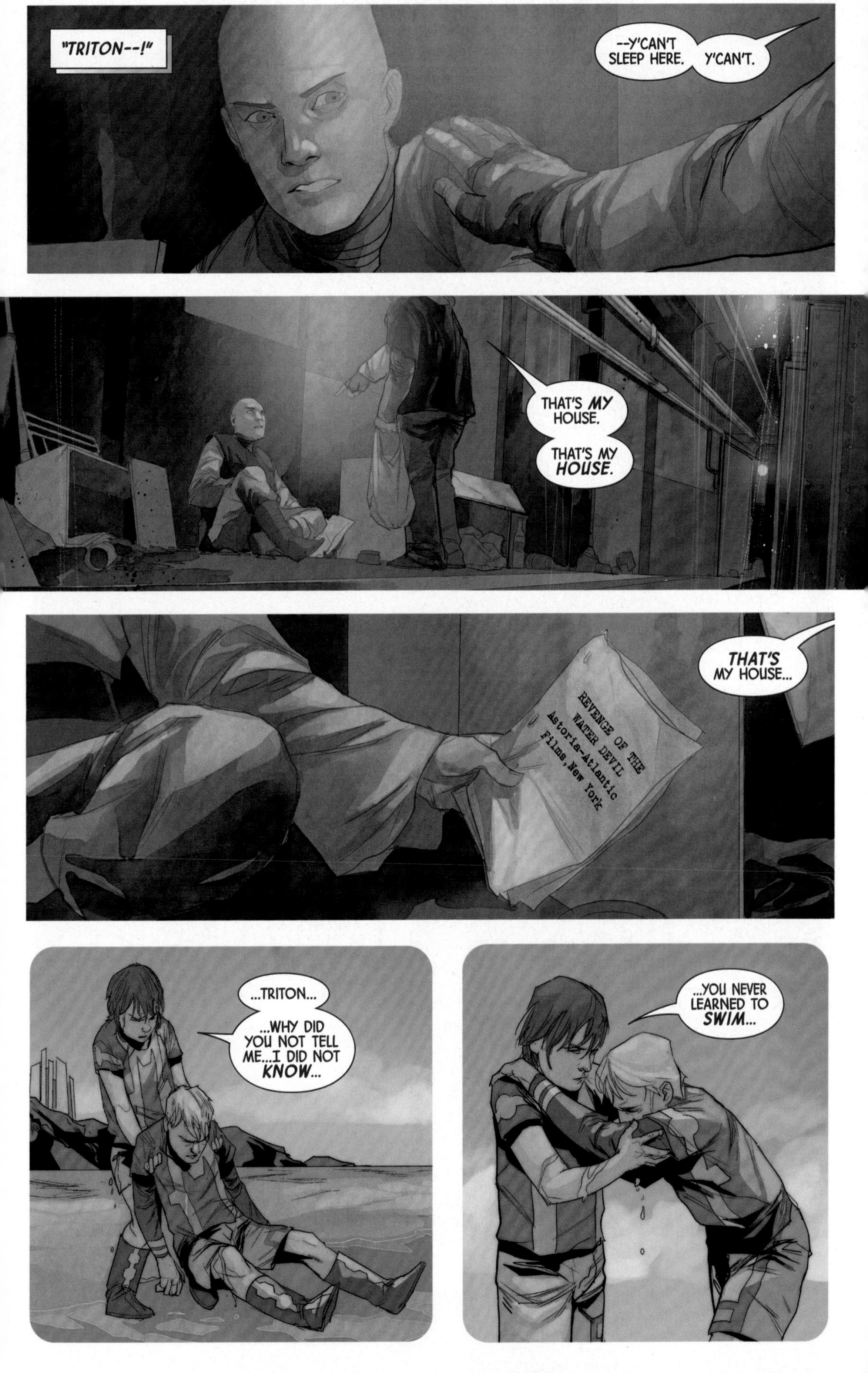
"TRITON--!"
--Y'CAN'T SLEEP HERE.
Y'CAN'T.
THAT'S MY HOUSE.
THAT'S MY HOUSE.
REVENGE OF THE WATER DEVIL Astoria-Atlantic Films,New York
THAT'S MY HOUSE...
...TRITON...
...WHY DID YOU NOT TELL ME...I DID NOT KNOW...
...YOU NEVER LEARNED TO SWIM...

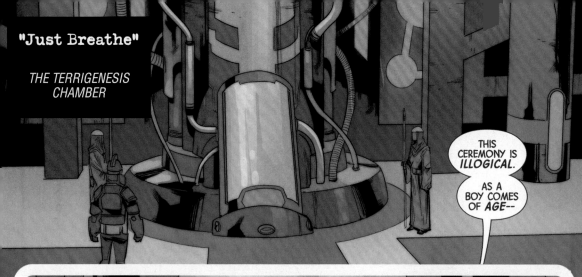

"Just Breathe"

THE TERRIGENESIS CHAMBER

THIS CEREMONY IS *ILLOGICAL.*

AS A BOY COMES OF *AGE*--

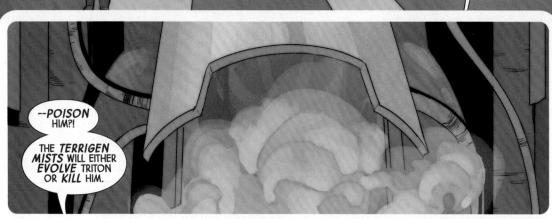

--*POISON* HIM?!

THE *TERRIGEN MISTS* WILL EITHER *EVOLVE* TRITON OR *KILL* HIM.

IT IS OUR *WAY,* KARNAK.

IT IS *IGNORANCE,* MOTHER. INHUMANS ARE BORNE OF *SCIENCE*--

--YET WE CLING TO *RITUAL.*

WHY NOT SLING A DOZEN *ARROWS* INTO MY BROTHER'S CHEST IN ORDER TO COUNT THE *HEARTBEATS?*

JUST AS *LOGICAL...*

...

...AND SO NOW BEHOLD...

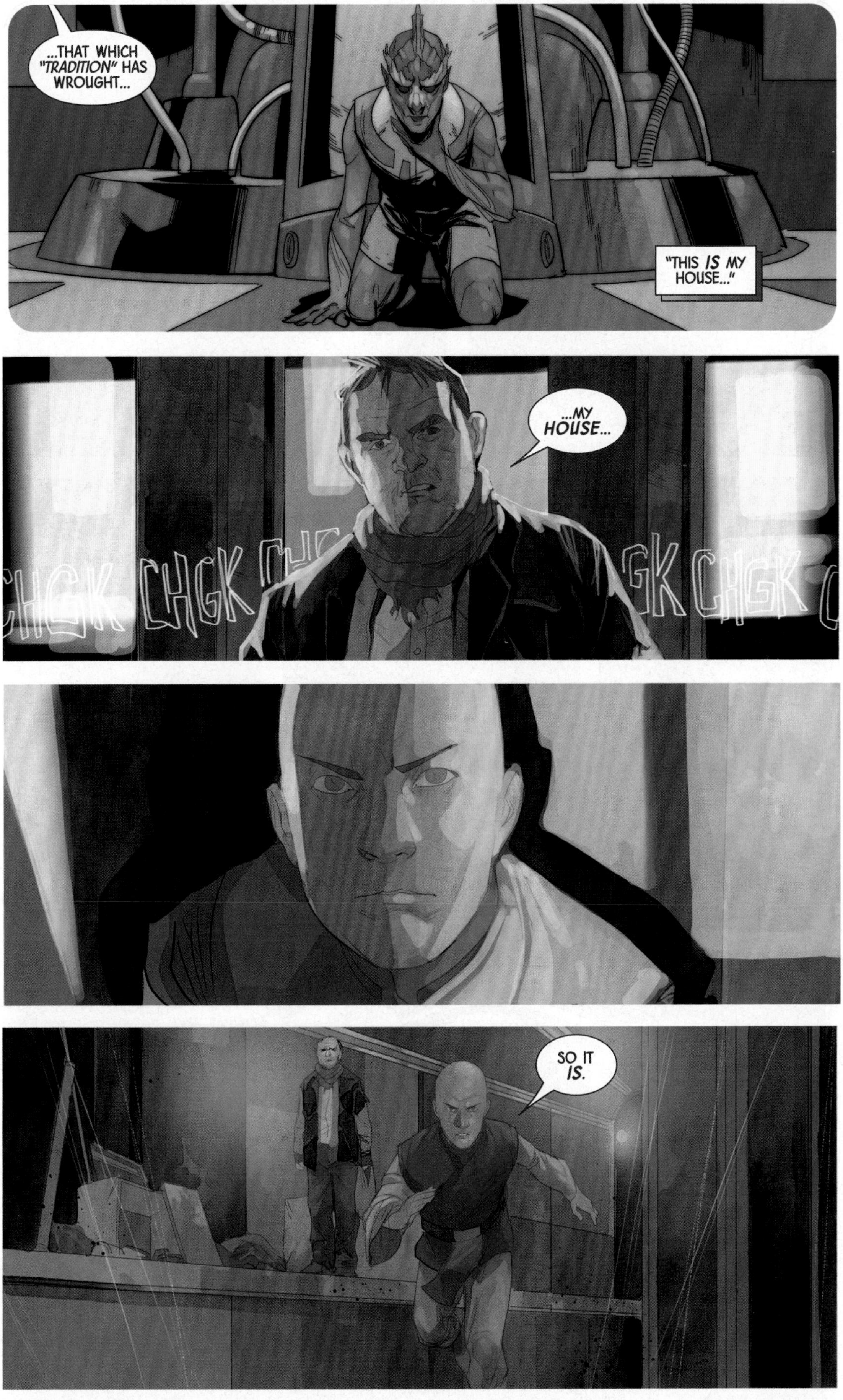
...THAT WHICH "TRADITION" HAS WROUGHT...
"THIS IS MY HOUSE..."
...MY HOUSE...
CHGK CHGK CHGK CHGK
SO IT IS.

THE ATTENUATOR REMAINS IN YOUR PALM.

SEE--

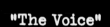

"The Voice"

KENNEDY AIRPORT, NOW

ACTIVE--

--DEFEAT.

THE MODIFIED *NEURAL INHIBITOR* IN YOUR COLLAR RING IS ALWAYS *ACTIVE*--

--ALLOWING YOU TO *SPEAK* WITHOUT TRIGGERING YOUR SONIC POWER-- UNTIL YOU DEFEAT IT.

THE DAMNABLE AIRPORT *NOISE*--

--WILL *PERFECTLY* MASK OUR *DRILL*, YOUNG MAXIMUS.

NOW, AT *MY* COMMAND--

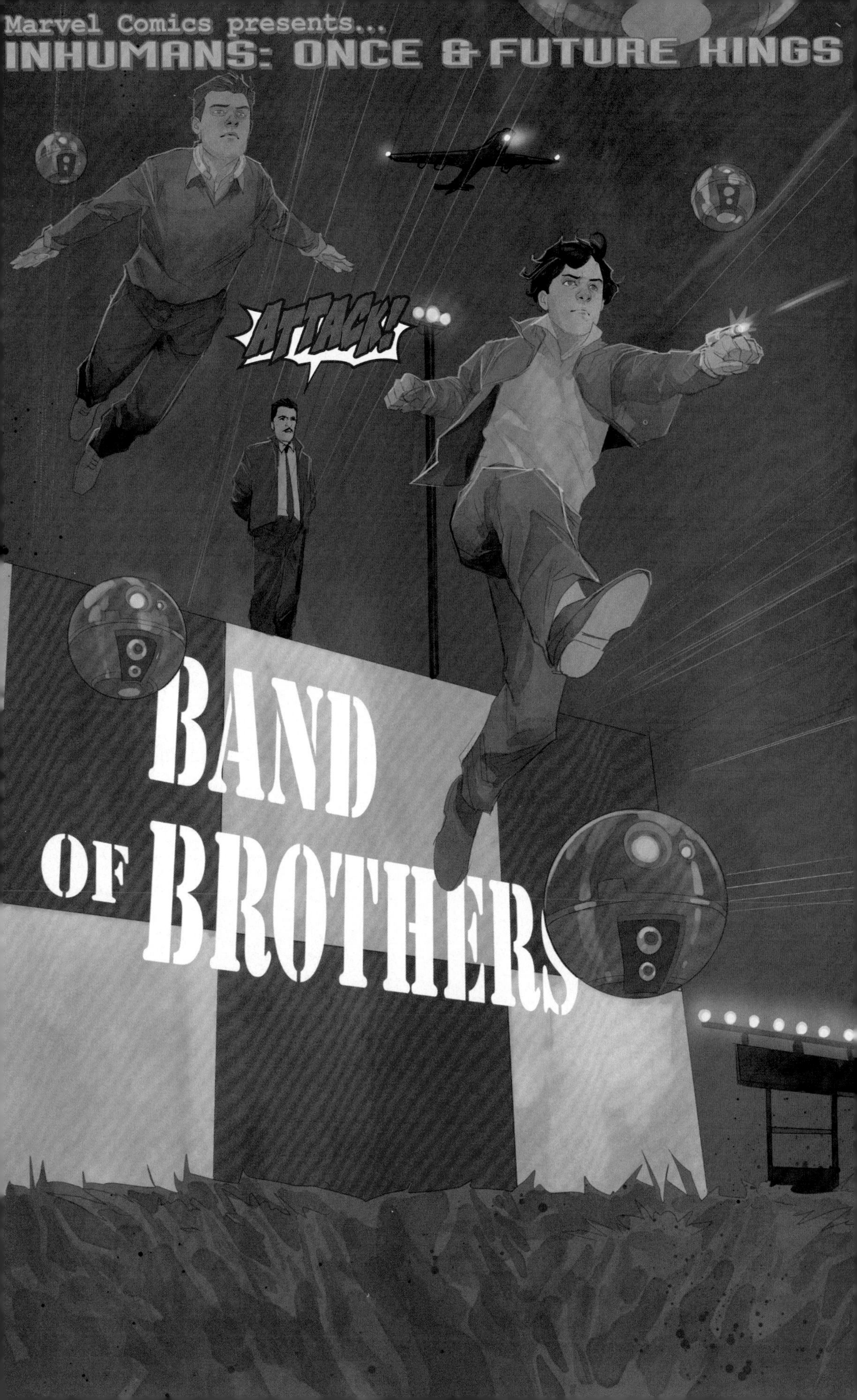
Marvel Comics presents...
INHUMANS: ONCE & FUTURE KINGS
ATTACK!
BAND OF BROTHERS

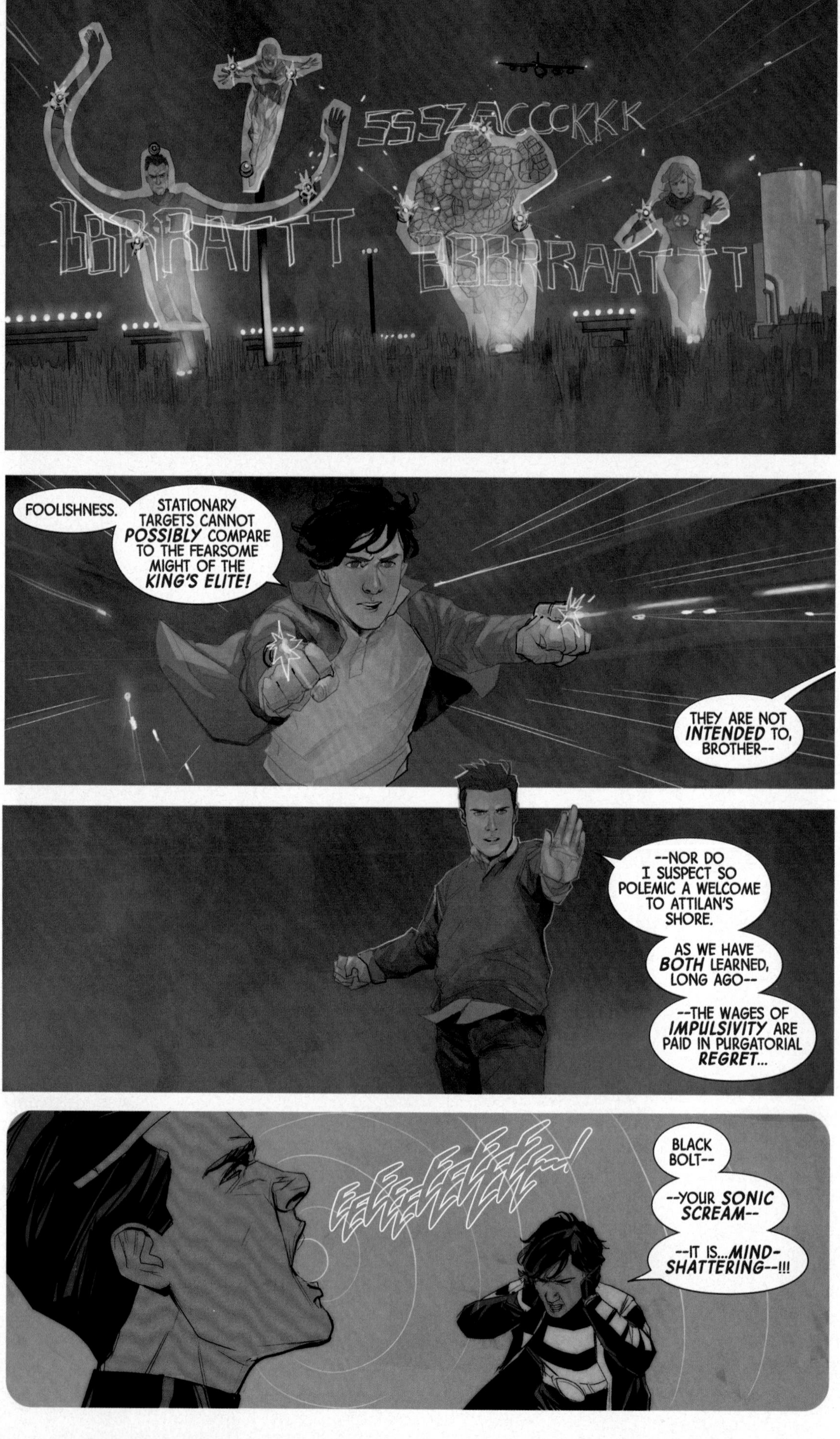
SSSZACCCKKK
BBRRATTT
BBBRRAATTTT
FOOLISHNESS.
STATIONARY TARGETS CANNOT POSSIBLY COMPARE TO THE FEARSOME MIGHT OF THE KING'S ELITE!
THEY ARE NOT INTENDED TO, BROTHER--
--NOR DO I SUSPECT SO POLEMIC A WELCOME TO ATTILAN'S SHORE.
AS WE HAVE BOTH LEARNED, LONG AGO--
--THE WAGES OF IMPULSIVITY ARE PAID IN PURGATORIAL REGRET...
BLACK BOLT--
--YOUR SONIC SCREAM--
--IT IS...MIND-SHATTERING--!!!

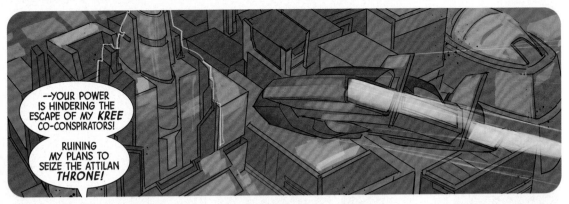

--YOUR POWER IS HINDERING THE ESCAPE OF MY *KREE* CO-CONSPIRATORS!

RUINING MY PLANS TO SEIZE THE ATTILAN *THRONE!*

NO!!! THE ROYAL PALACE--!!!

MOTHER-- *FATHER--!!!*

EEEEE--BOOOOMM

THIS *CAPSULE,* YOUNG MAXIMUS.

ONE PER DAY. WITHOUT *FAIL.*

OR, MOST *SURELY,* THE MADNESS WILL OVERCOME YOU *AGAIN.*

NOW, BLACK BOLT...

...LOOSEN YOUR CLENCHED FIST JUST A *BIT...*

...*FOCUS* YOUR POWER. TARGET THE GLASS ATOP THE METAL STAND-UP. WITH PRECISION AND CONTROL...

...IT SHOULD REQUIRE THE MEREST *WHISPER...*

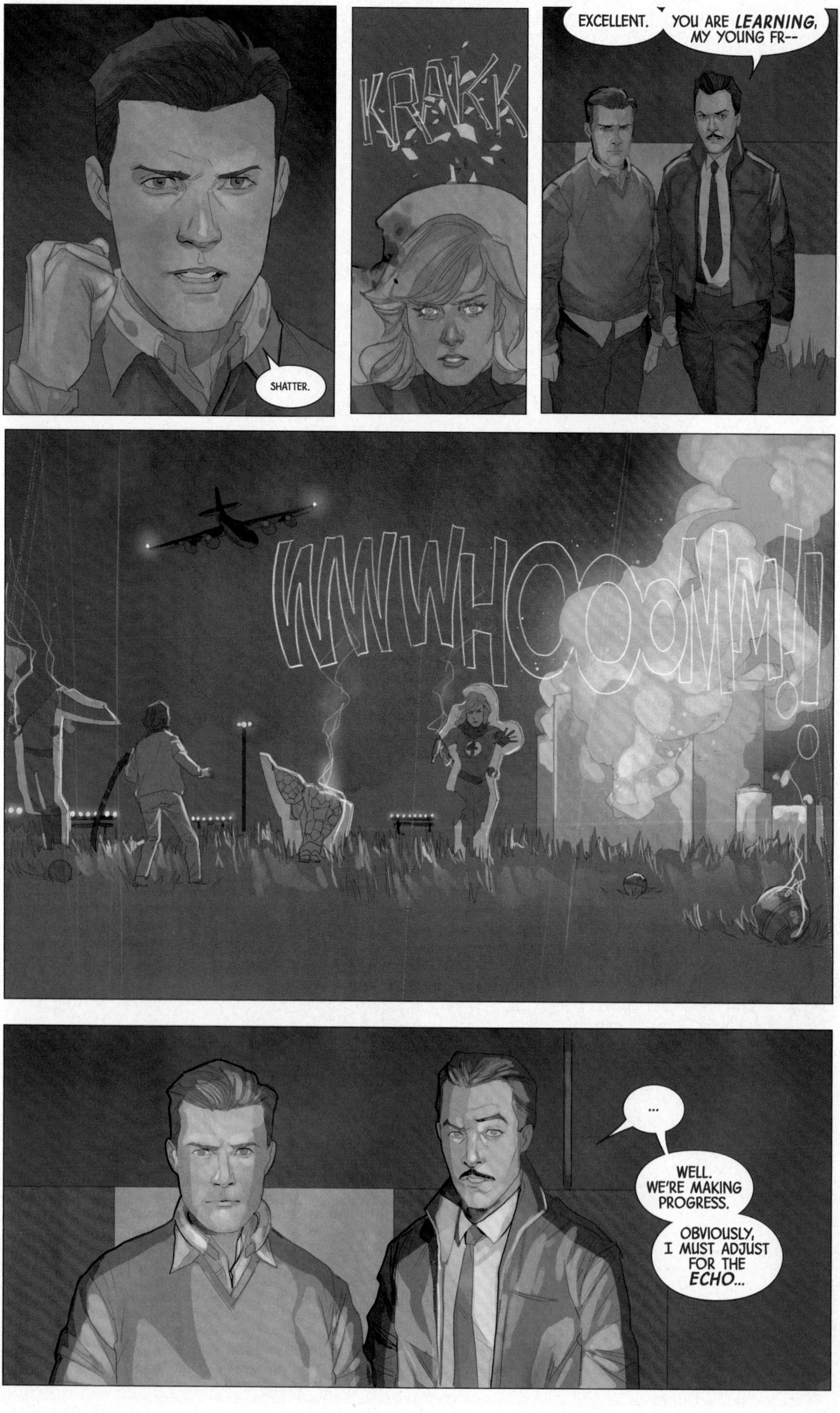
SHATTER.
KRAKK
EXCELLENT.
YOU ARE LEARNING, MY YOUNG FR--
WWWHOOOMM!!
...
WELL. WE'RE MAKING PROGRESS.
OBVIOUSLY, I MUST ADJUST FOR THE ECHO...

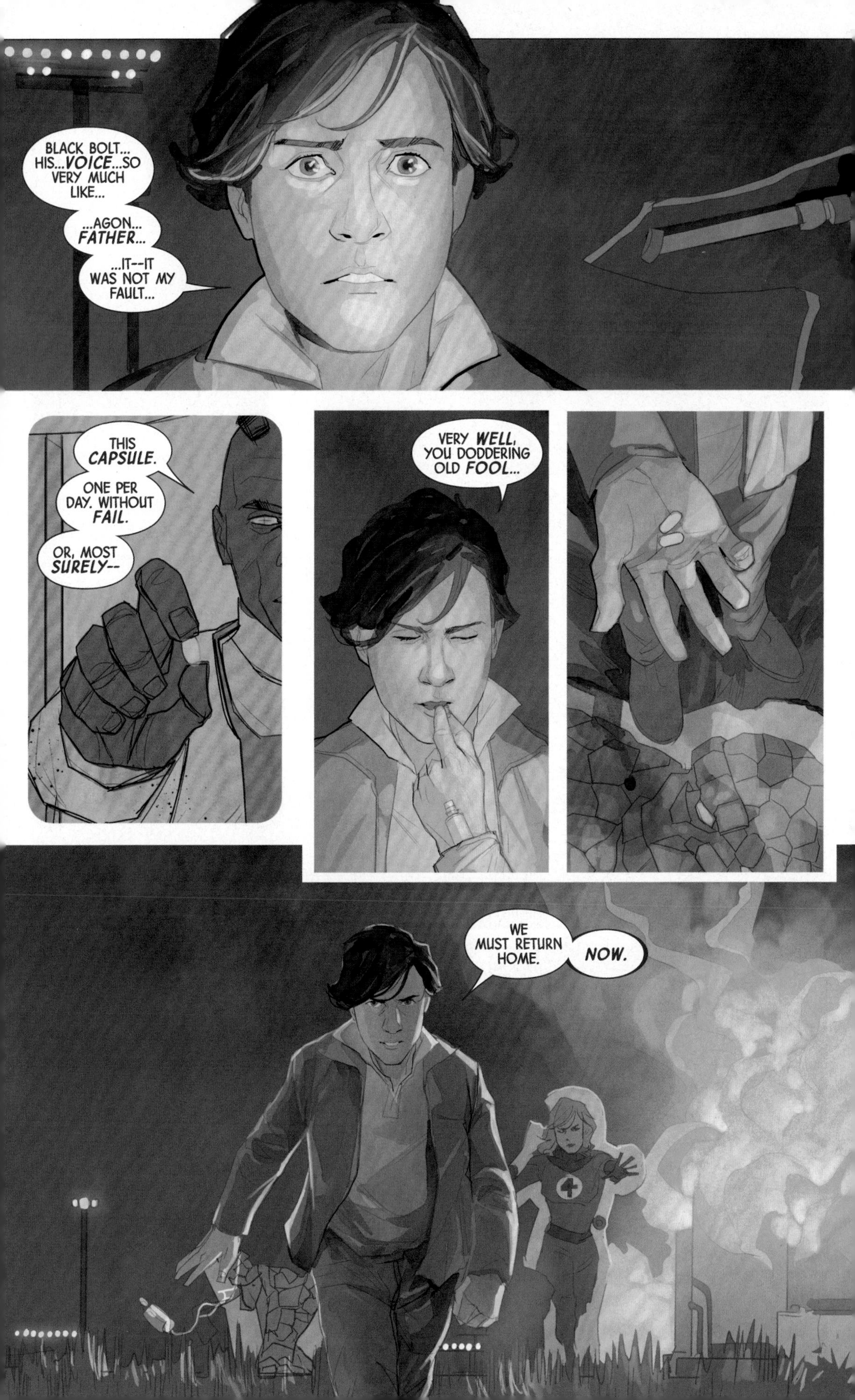

BLACK BOLT... HIS...VOICE...SO VERY MUCH LIKE...
...AGON... FATHER...
...IT--IT WAS NOT MY FAULT...
THIS CAPSULE.
ONE PER DAY. WITHOUT FAIL.
OR, MOST SURELY--
VERY WELL, YOU DODDERING OLD FOOL...
WE MUST RETURN HOME.
NOW.

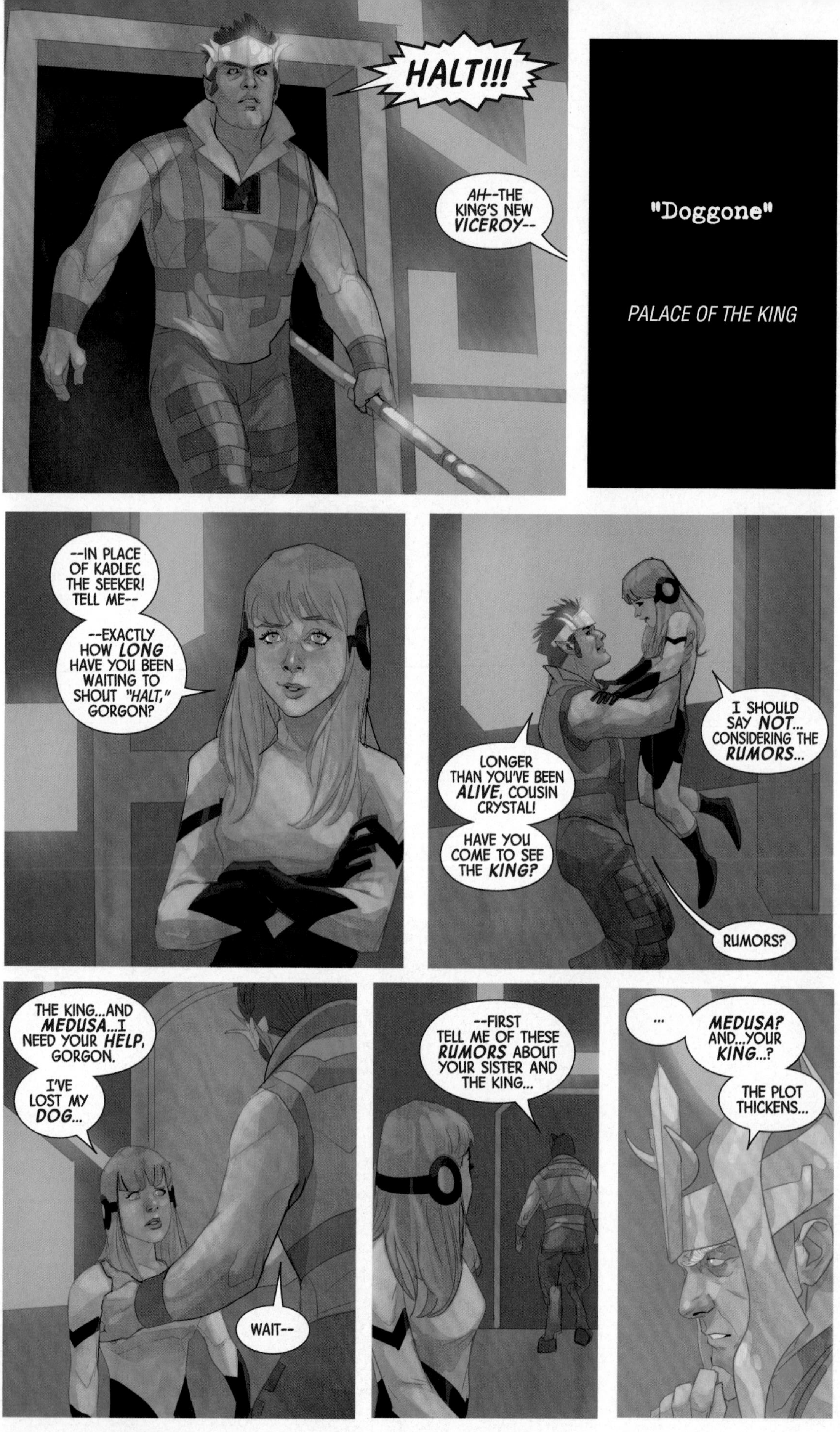
HALT!!!
AH--THE KING'S NEW VICEROY--
"Doggone"
PALACE OF THE KING
--IN PLACE OF KADLEC THE SEEKER! TELL ME--
--EXACTLY HOW LONG HAVE YOU BEEN WAITING TO SHOUT "HALT," GORGON?
LONGER THAN YOU'VE BEEN ALIVE, COUSIN CRYSTAL!
HAVE YOU COME TO SEE THE KING?
I SHOULD SAY NOT... CONSIDERING THE RUMORS...
RUMORS?
THE KING...AND MEDUSA...I NEED YOUR HELP, GORGON.
I'VE LOST MY DOG...
WAIT--
--FIRST TELL ME OF THESE RUMORS ABOUT YOUR SISTER AND THE KING...
...
MEDUSA? AND...YOUR KING...?
THE PLOT THICKENS...

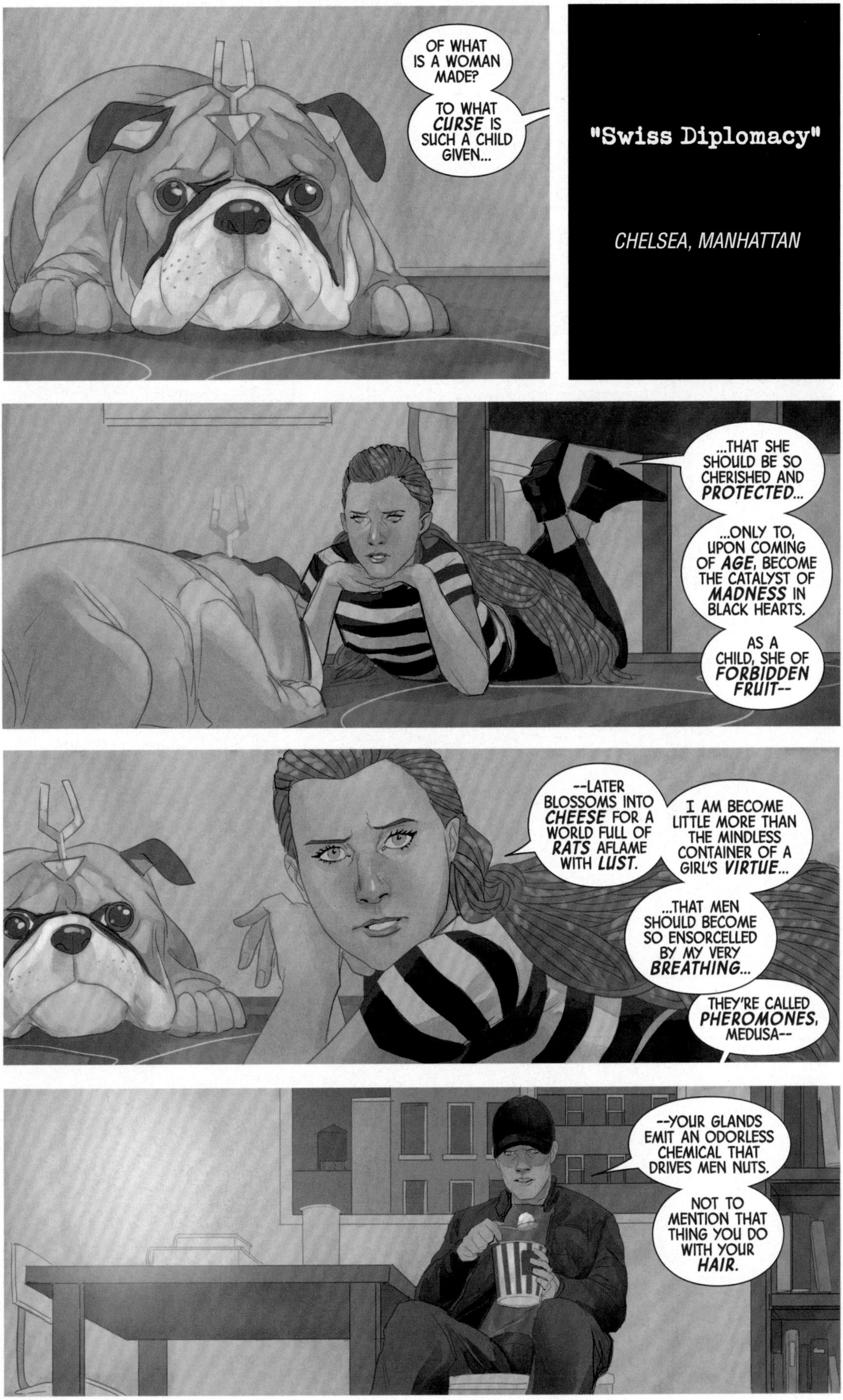

OF WHAT IS A WOMAN MADE?
TO WHAT CURSE IS SUCH A CHILD GIVEN...
"Swiss Diplomacy"
CHELSEA, MANHATTAN
...THAT SHE SHOULD BE SO CHERISHED AND PROTECTED...
...ONLY TO, UPON COMING OF AGE, BECOME THE CATALYST OF MADNESS IN BLACK HEARTS.
AS A CHILD, SHE OF FORBIDDEN FRUIT--
--LATER BLOSSOMS INTO CHEESE FOR A WORLD FULL OF RATS AFLAME WITH LUST.
I AM BECOME LITTLE MORE THAN THE MINDLESS CONTAINER OF A GIRL'S VIRTUE...
...THAT MEN SHOULD BECOME SO ENSORCELLED BY MY VERY BREATHING...
THEY'RE CALLED PHEROMONES, MEDUSA--
--YOUR GLANDS EMIT AN ODORLESS CHEMICAL THAT DRIVES MEN NUTS.
NOT TO MENTION THAT THING YOU DO WITH YOUR HAIR.

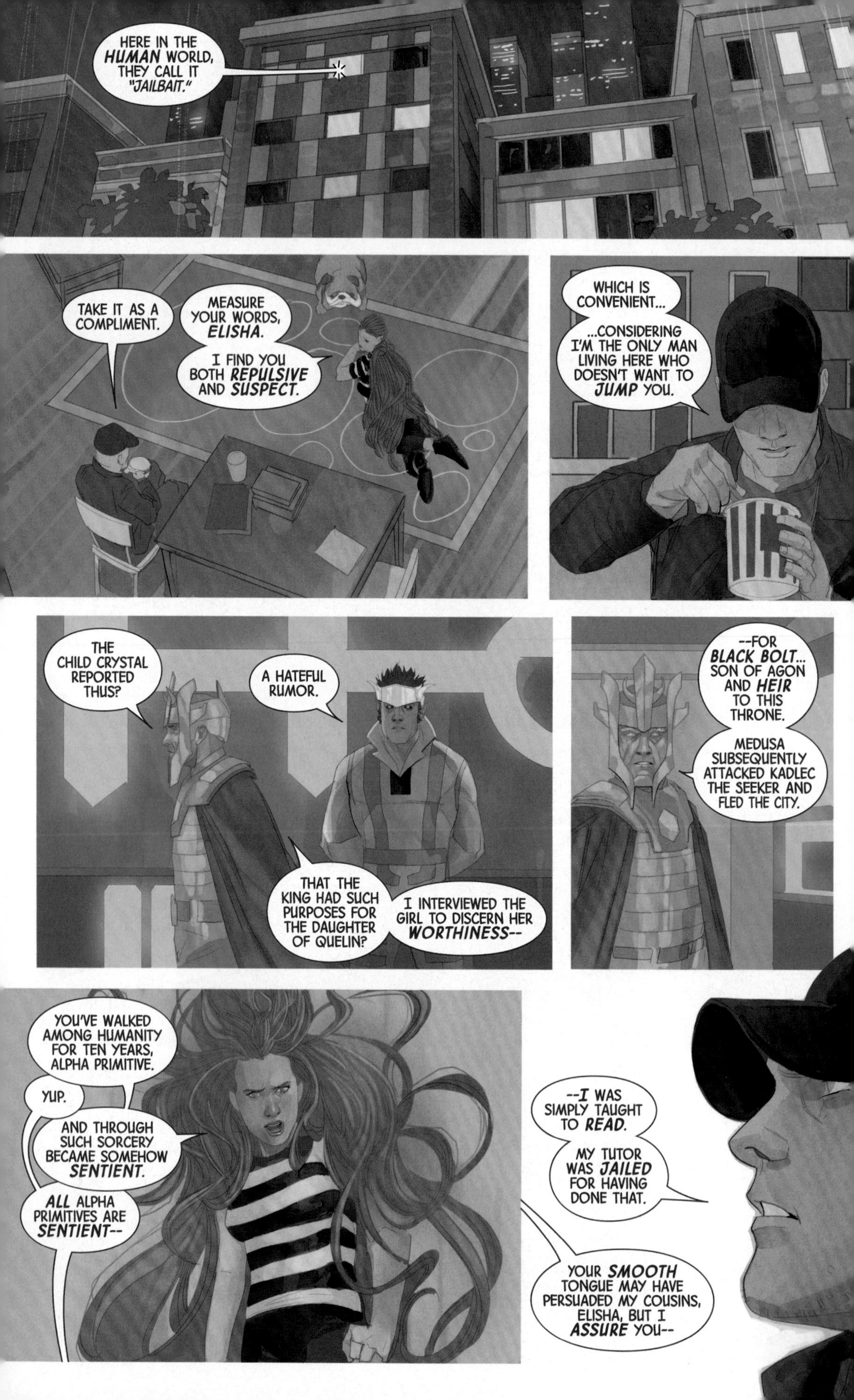
HERE IN THE HUMAN WORLD, THEY CALL IT "JAILBAIT."
TAKE IT AS A COMPLIMENT.
MEASURE YOUR WORDS, ELISHA.
I FIND YOU BOTH REPULSIVE AND SUSPECT.
WHICH IS CONVENIENT...
...CONSIDERING I'M THE ONLY MAN LIVING HERE WHO DOESN'T WANT TO JUMP YOU.
THE CHILD CRYSTAL REPORTED THUS?
A HATEFUL RUMOR.
THAT THE KING HAD SUCH PURPOSES FOR THE DAUGHTER OF QUELIN?
I INTERVIEWED THE GIRL TO DISCERN HER WORTHINESS--
--FOR BLACK BOLT... SON OF AGON AND HEIR TO THIS THRONE.
MEDUSA SUBSEQUENTLY ATTACKED KADLEC THE SEEKER AND FLED THE CITY.
YOU'VE WALKED AMONG HUMANITY FOR TEN YEARS, ALPHA PRIMITIVE.
YUP.
AND THROUGH SUCH SORCERY BECAME SOMEHOW SENTIENT.
ALL ALPHA PRIMITIVES ARE SENTIENT--
--I WAS SIMPLY TAUGHT TO READ.
MY TUTOR WAS JAILED FOR HAVING DONE THAT.
YOUR SMOOTH TONGUE MAY HAVE PERSUADED MY COUSINS, ELISHA, BUT I ASSURE YOU--

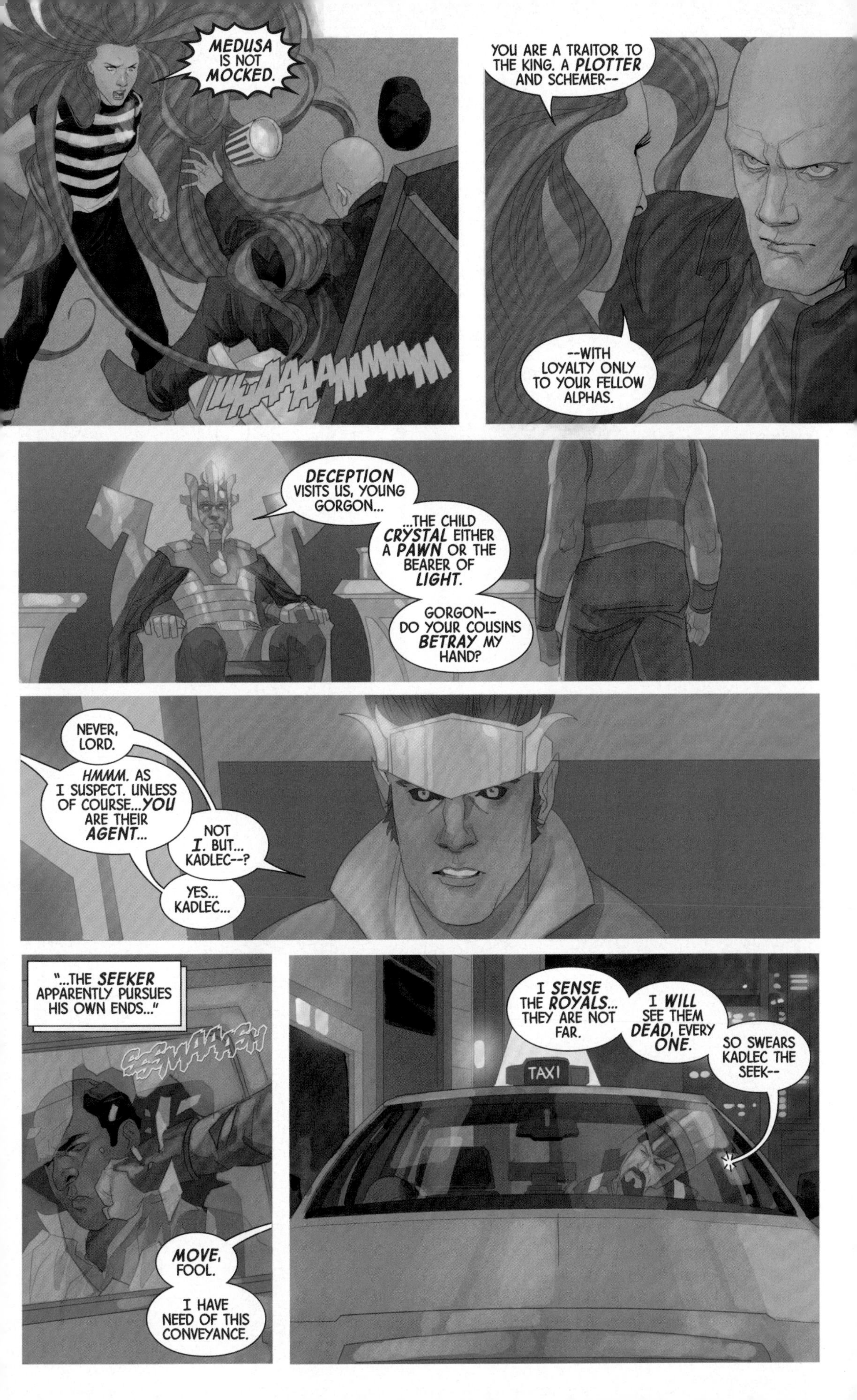
MEDUSA IS NOT MOCKED.
WHAAAAMMMMM
YOU ARE A TRAITOR TO THE KING. A PLOTTER AND SCHEMER--
--WITH LOYALTY ONLY TO YOUR FELLOW ALPHAS.
DECEPTION VISITS US, YOUNG GORGON...
...THE CHILD CRYSTAL EITHER A PAWN OR THE BEARER OF LIGHT.
GORGON-- DO YOUR COUSINS BETRAY MY HAND?
NEVER, LORD.
HMMM. AS I SUSPECT. UNLESS OF COURSE...YOU ARE THEIR AGENT...
NOT I. BUT... KADLEC--?
YES... KADLEC...
"...THE SEEKER APPARENTLY PURSUES HIS OWN ENDS..."
SSSMAAASH
MOVE, FOOL.
I HAVE NEED OF THIS CONVEYANCE.
TAXI
I SENSE THE ROYALS... THEY ARE NOT FAR.
I WILL SEE THEM DEAD, EVERY ONE.
SO SWEARS KADLEC THE SEEK--

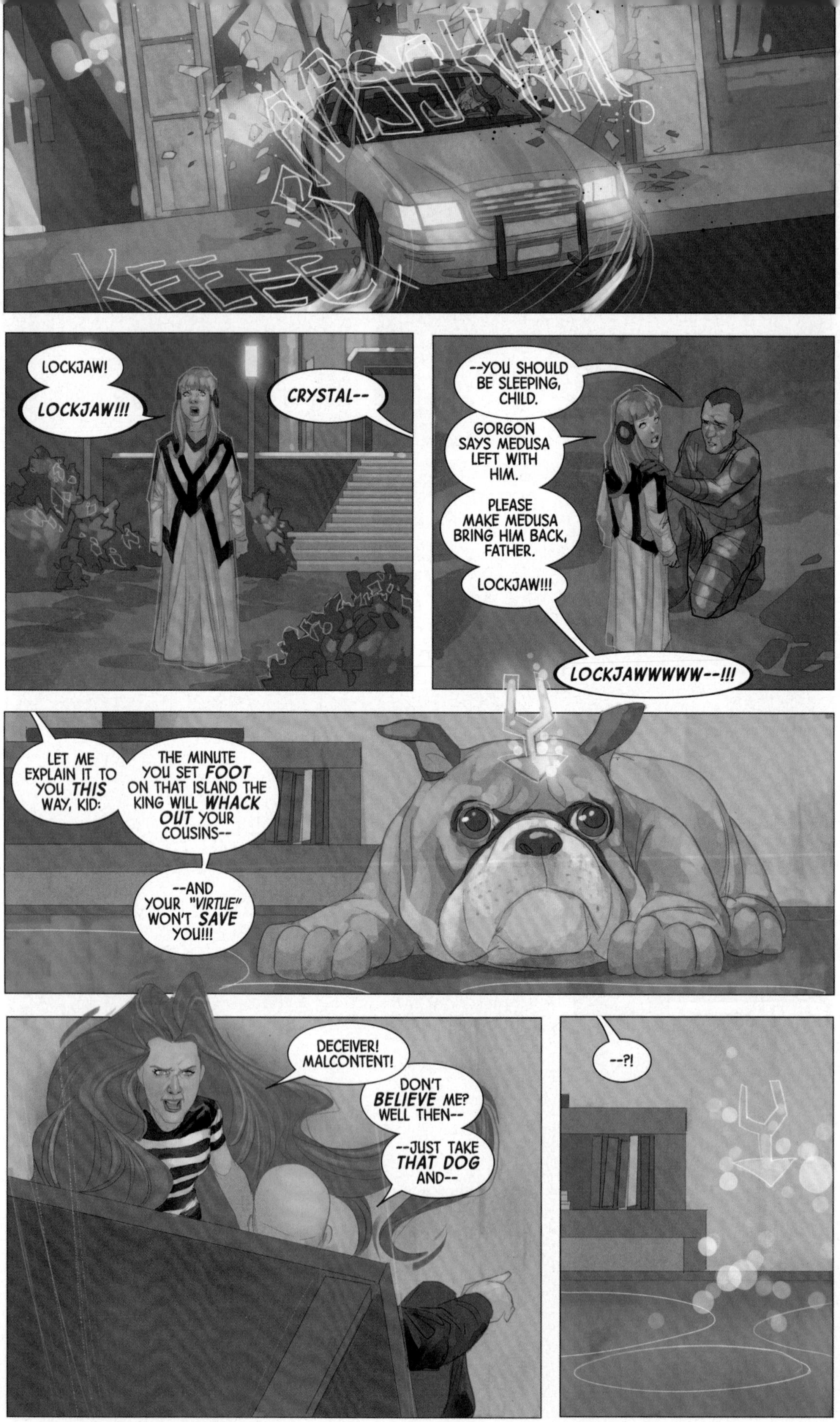
KRRSSHH!
KEEEE
LOCKJAW!
LOCKJAW!!!
CRYSTAL--
--YOU SHOULD BE SLEEPING, CHILD.
GORGON SAYS MEDUSA LEFT WITH HIM.
PLEASE MAKE MEDUSA BRING HIM BACK, FATHER.
LOCKJAW!!!
LOCKJAWWWWW--!!!
LET ME EXPLAIN IT TO YOU THIS WAY, KID:
THE MINUTE YOU SET FOOT ON THAT ISLAND THE KING WILL WHACK OUT YOUR COUSINS--
--AND YOUR "VIRTUE" WON'T SAVE YOU!!!
DECEIVER! MALCONTENT!
DON'T BELIEVE ME? WELL THEN--
--JUST TAKE THAT DOG AND--
--?!

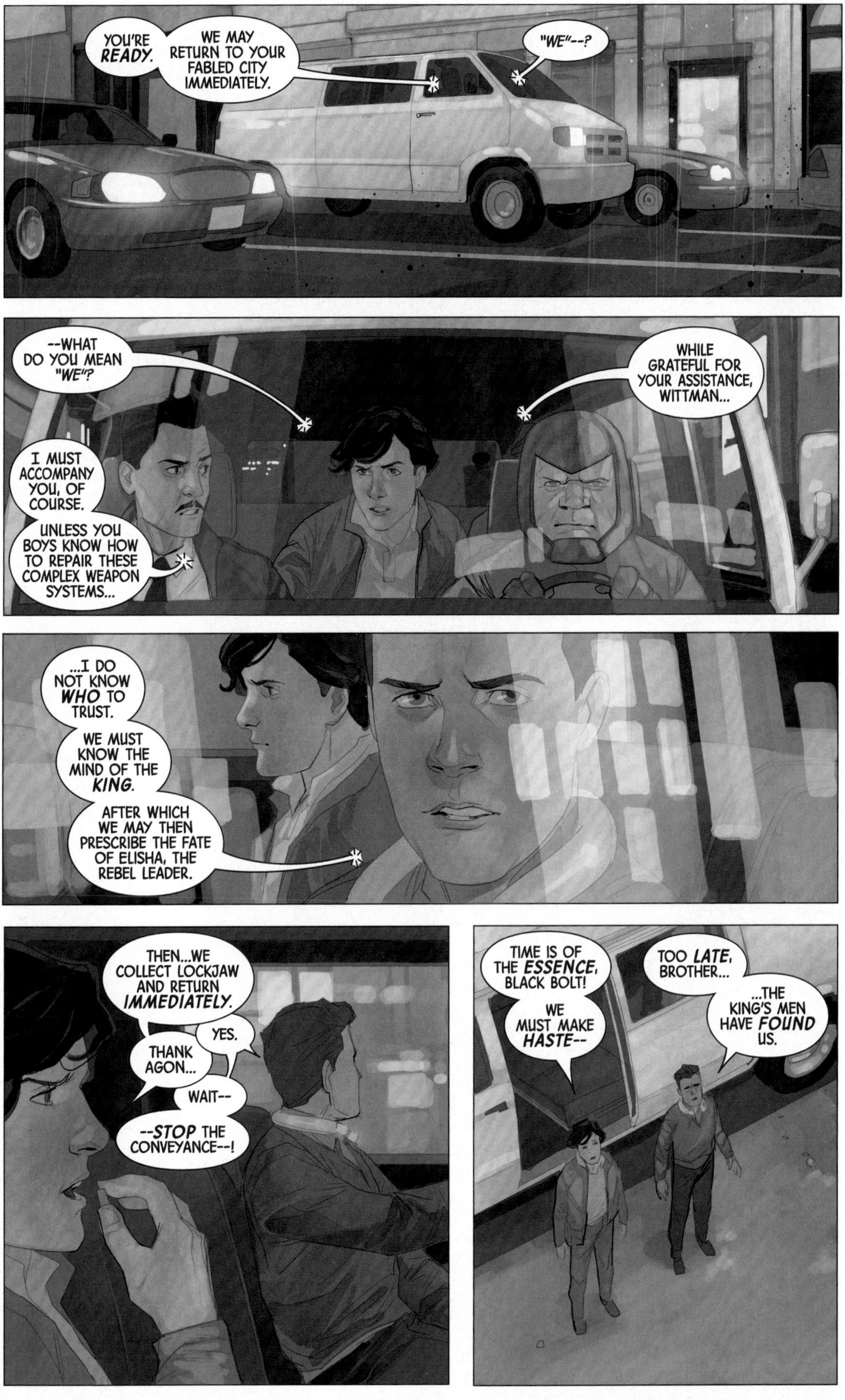
YOU'RE READY.
WE MAY RETURN TO YOUR FABLED CITY IMMEDIATELY.
"WE"--?
--WHAT DO YOU MEAN "WE"?
WHILE GRATEFUL FOR YOUR ASSISTANCE, WITTMAN...
I MUST ACCOMPANY YOU, OF COURSE.
UNLESS YOU BOYS KNOW HOW TO REPAIR THESE COMPLEX WEAPON SYSTEMS...
...I DO NOT KNOW WHO TO TRUST.
WE MUST KNOW THE MIND OF THE KING.
AFTER WHICH WE MAY THEN PRESCRIBE THE FATE OF ELISHA, THE REBEL LEADER.
THEN...WE COLLECT LOCKJAW AND RETURN IMMEDIATELY.
YES.
THANK AGON...
WAIT--
--STOP THE CONVEYANCE--!
TIME IS OF THE ESSENCE, BLACK BOLT!
WE MUST MAKE HASTE--
TOO LATE, BROTHER...
...THE KING'S MEN HAVE FOUND US.

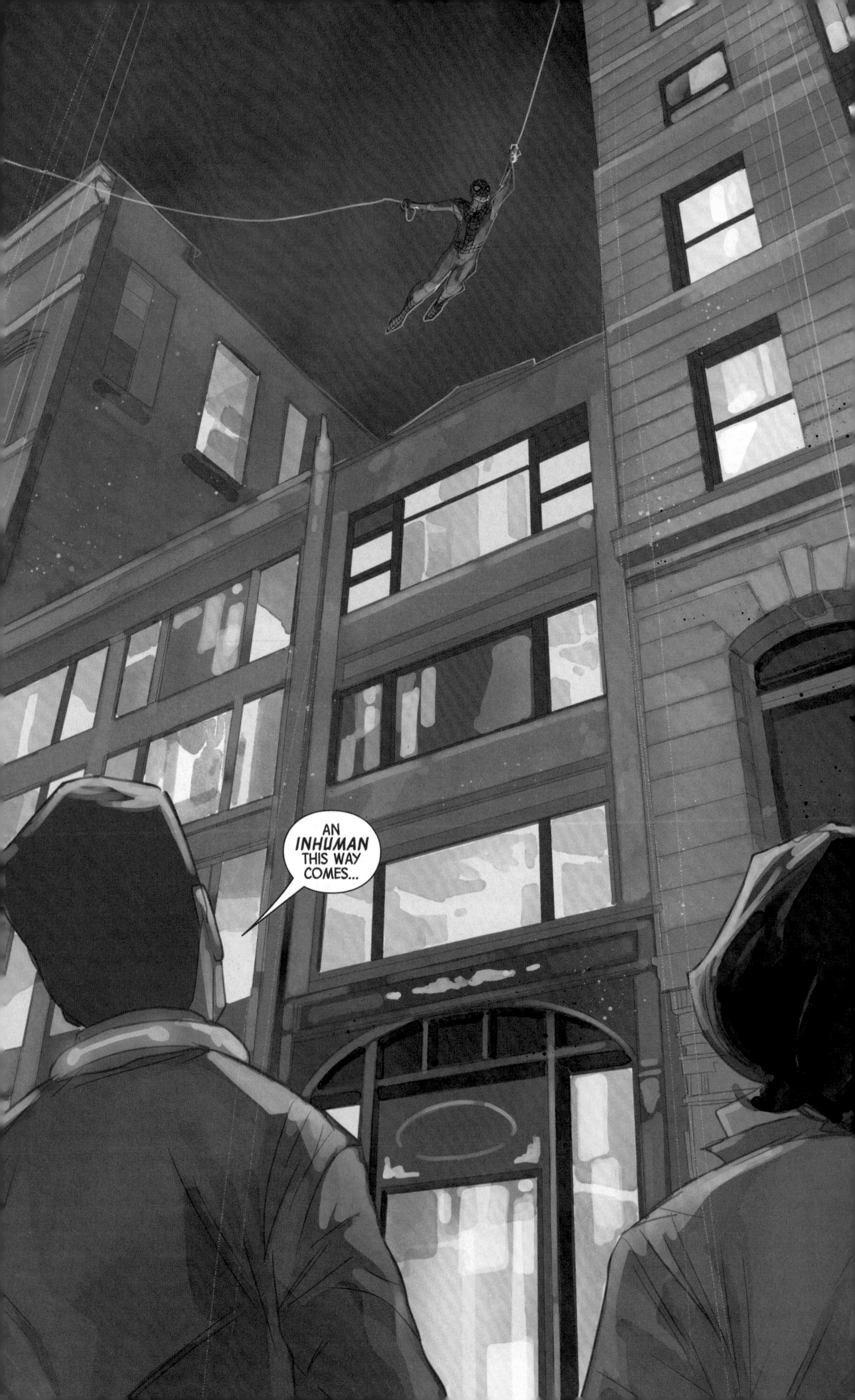
AN INHUMAN THIS WAY COMES...

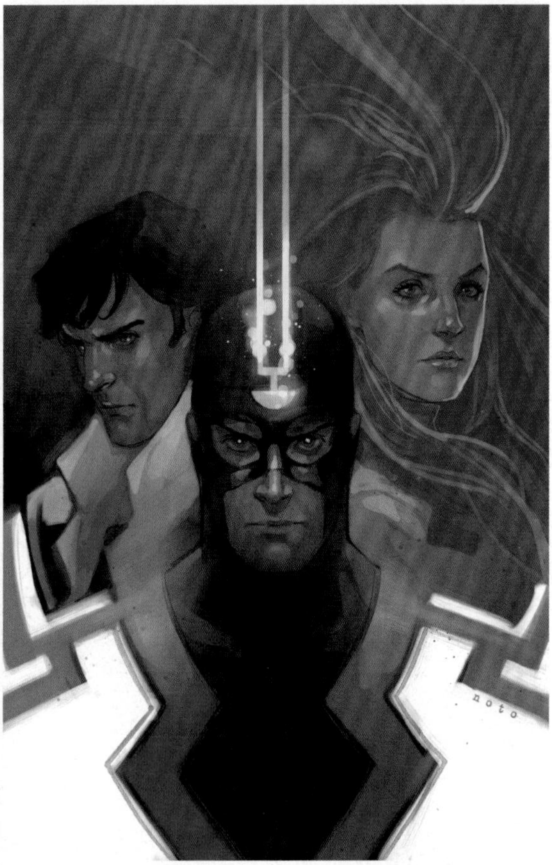

ONE VARIANT BY **PHIL NOTO**

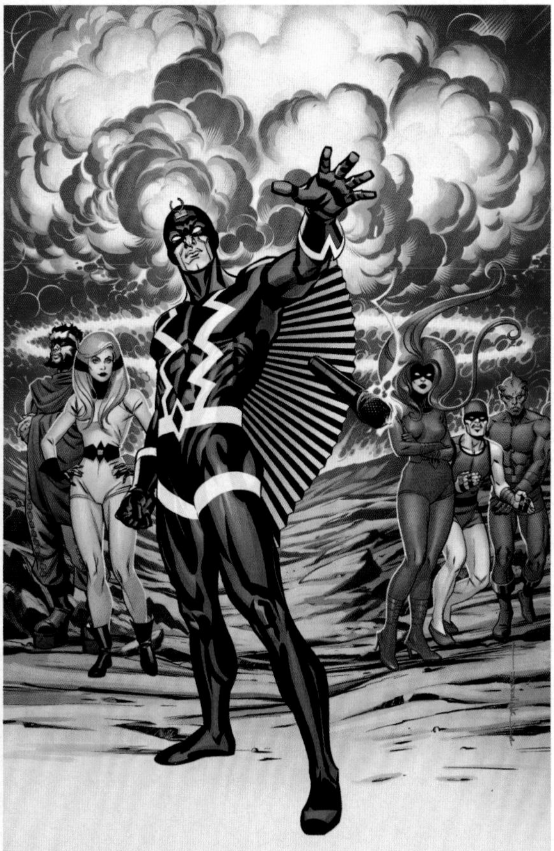

TWO VARIANT BY **BRIAN STELFREEZE** & **LAURA MARTIN**

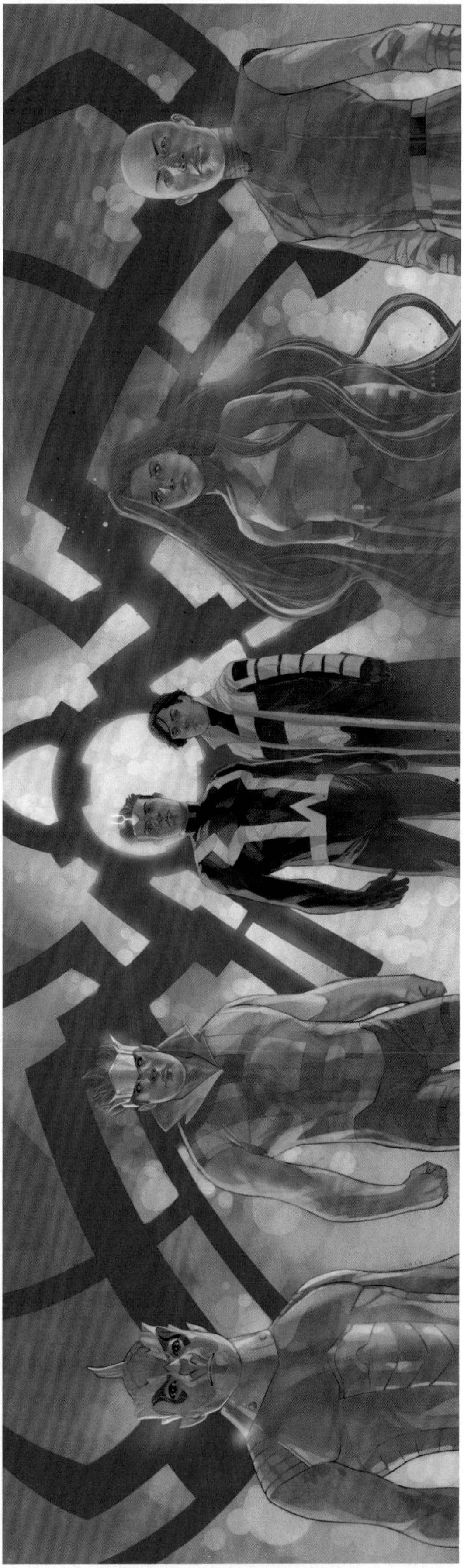

ONE THROUGH **FIVE** COMBINED
CHARACTER VARIANTS BY **PHIL NOTO**

FOUR

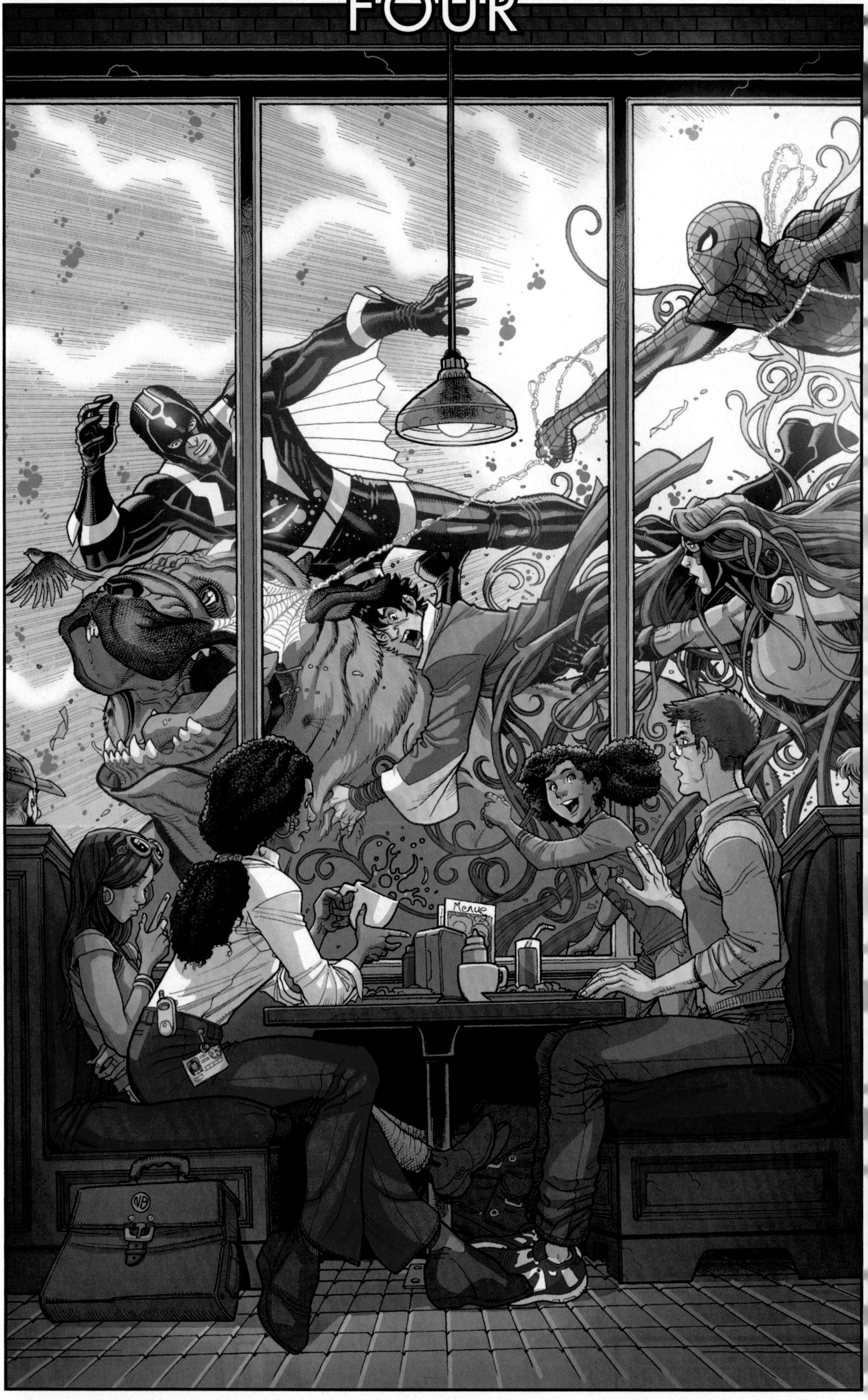

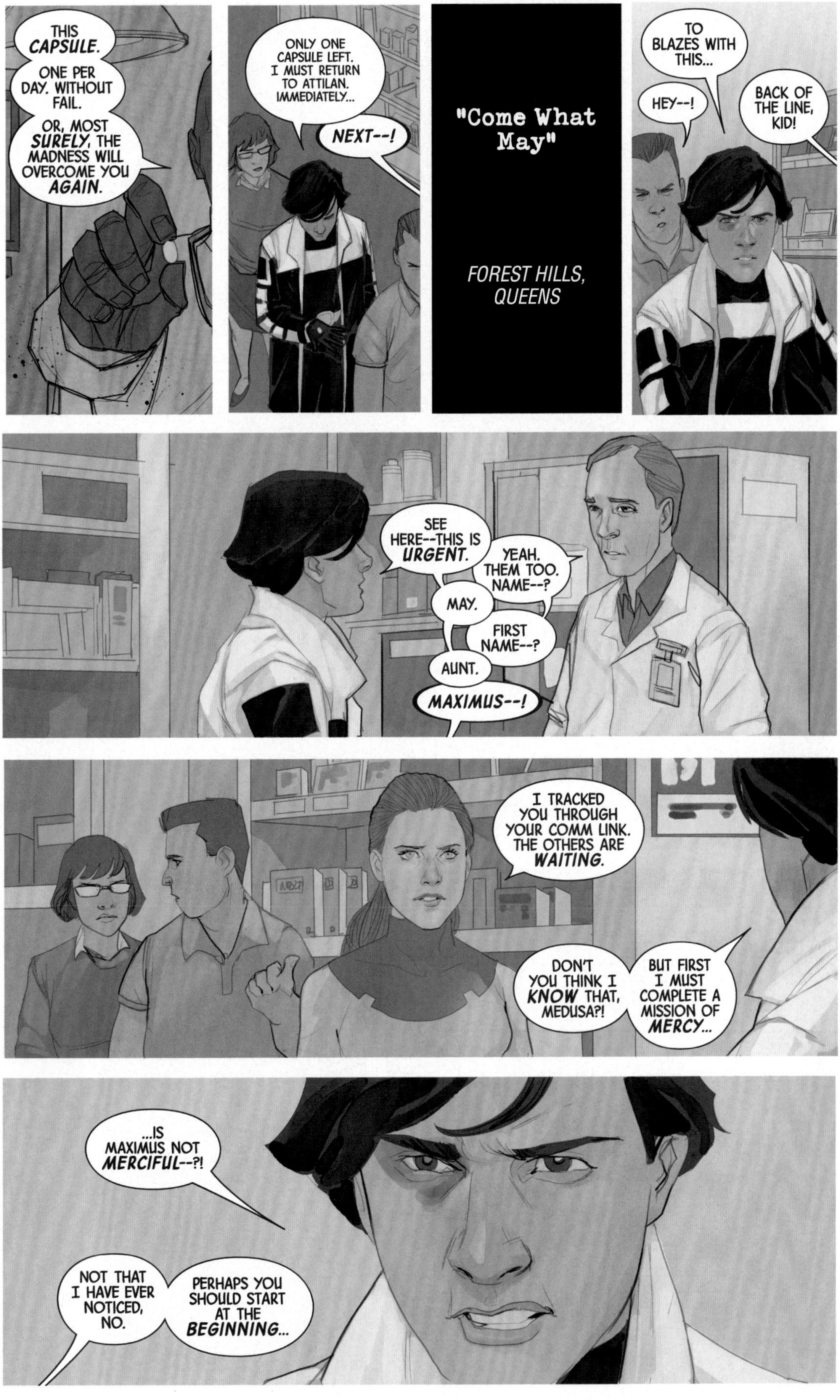

THIS CAPSULE.
ONE PER DAY. WITHOUT FAIL.
OR, MOST SURELY, THE MADNESS WILL OVERCOME YOU AGAIN.
ONLY ONE CAPSULE LEFT. I MUST RETURN TO ATTILAN. IMMEDIATELY...
NEXT--!
"Come What May"
FOREST HILLS, QUEENS
TO BLAZES WITH THIS...
HEY--!
BACK OF THE LINE, KID!
SEE HERE--THIS IS URGENT.
YEAH. THEM TOO. NAME--?
MAY.
FIRST NAME--?
AUNT.
MAXIMUS--!
I TRACKED YOU THROUGH YOUR COMM LINK. THE OTHERS ARE WAITING.
DON'T YOU THINK I KNOW THAT, MEDUSA?!
BUT FIRST I MUST COMPLETE A MISSION OF MERCY...
...IS MAXIMUS NOT MERCIFUL--?!
NOT THAT I HAVE EVER NOTICED, NO.
PERHAPS YOU SHOULD START AT THE BEGINNING...

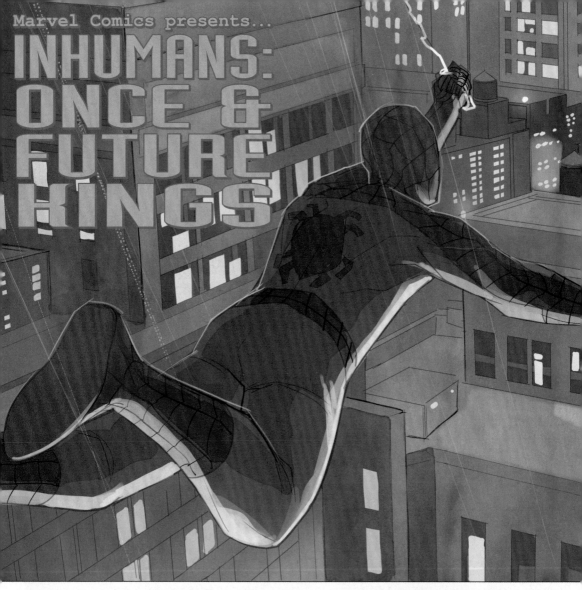

Marvel Comics presents...

INHUMANS: ONCE & FUTURE KINGS

YOU THERE-- *INHUMAN*--

--IN THE NAME OF AGON, YOUR FORMER KING...

...AND I, YOUR *FUTURE* KING...

...I *DEMAND* YOUR SURRENDER.

"Crowns"

MIDTOWN, EARLIER

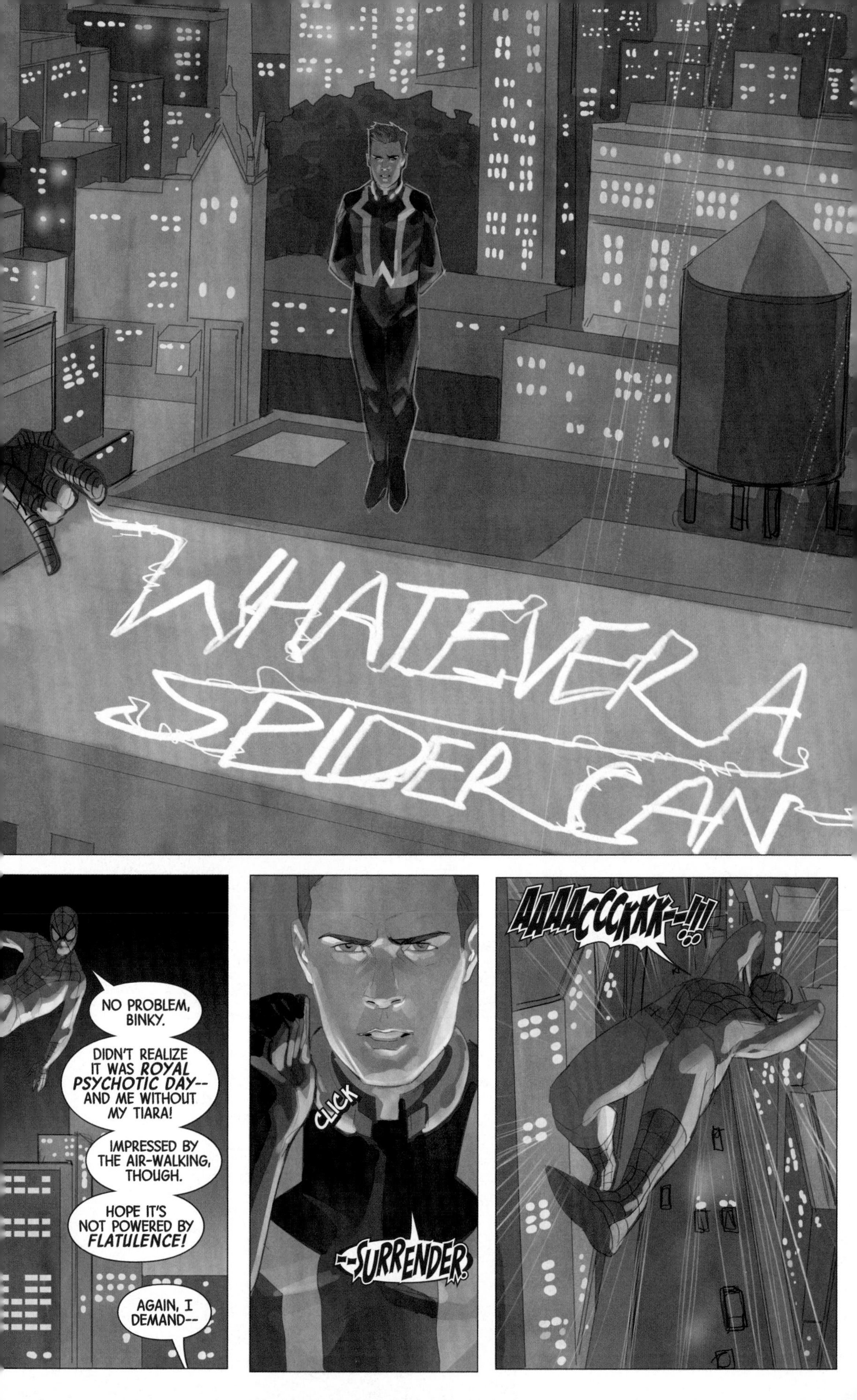
WHATEVER A SPIDER CAN--
NO PROBLEM, BINKY.
DIDN'T REALIZE IT WAS ROYAL PSYCHOTIC DAY-- AND ME WITHOUT MY TIARA!
IMPRESSED BY THE AIR-WALKING, THOUGH.
HOPE IT'S NOT POWERED BY FLATULENCE!
AGAIN, I DEMAND--
CLICK
--SURRENDER.
AAAACCCKKK--!!!

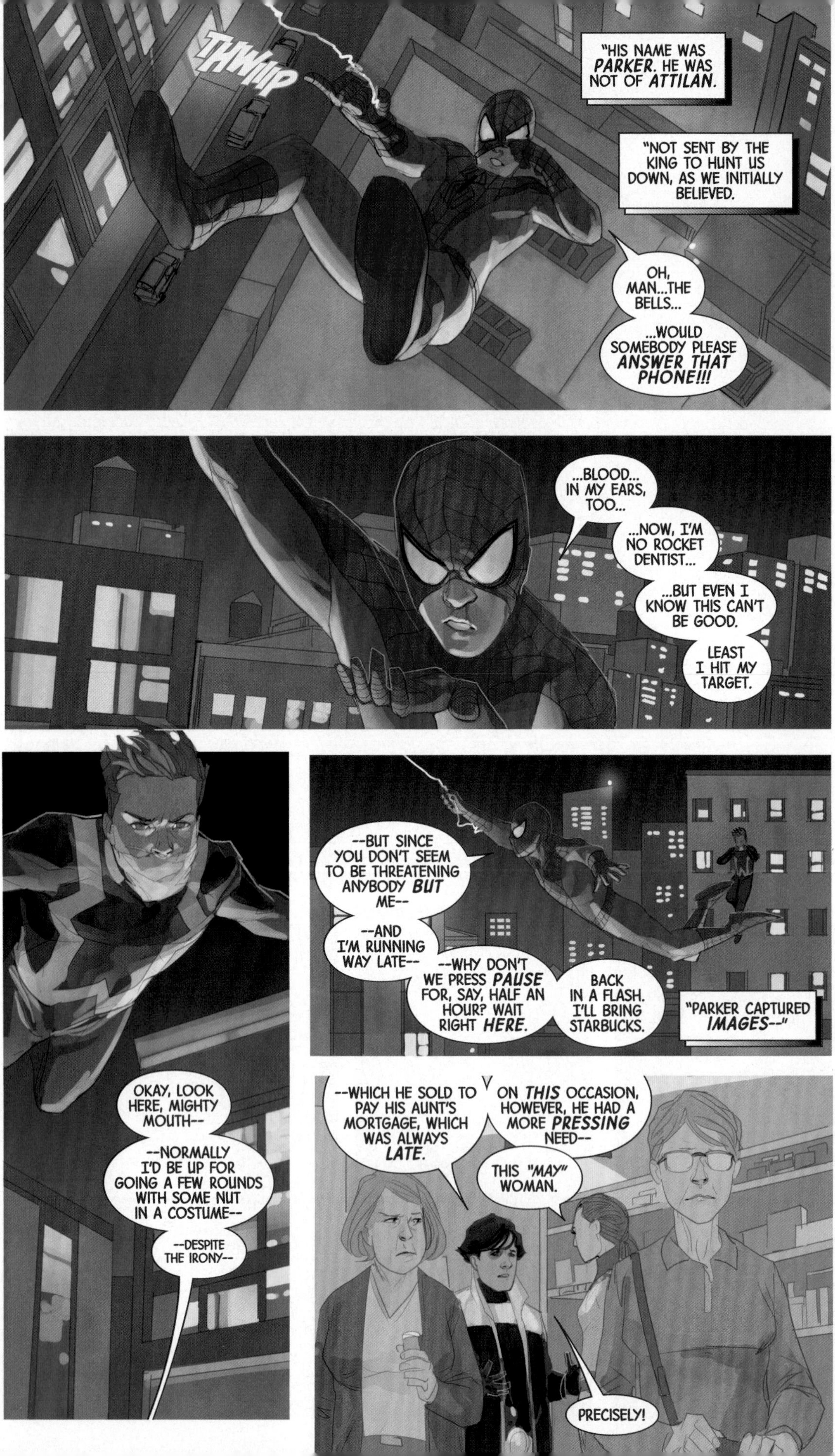
THWIIIP
"HIS NAME WAS PARKER. HE WAS NOT OF ATTILAN.
"NOT SENT BY THE KING TO HUNT US DOWN, AS WE INITIALLY BELIEVED.
OH, MAN...THE BELLS...
...WOULD SOMEBODY PLEASE ANSWER THAT PHONE!!!
...BLOOD... IN MY EARS, TOO...
...NOW, I'M NO ROCKET DENTIST...
...BUT EVEN I KNOW THIS CAN'T BE GOOD.
LEAST I HIT MY TARGET.
OKAY, LOOK HERE, MIGHTY MOUTH--
--NORMALLY I'D BE UP FOR GOING A FEW ROUNDS WITH SOME NUT IN A COSTUME--
--DESPITE THE IRONY--
--BUT SINCE YOU DON'T SEEM TO BE THREATENING ANYBODY BUT ME--
--AND I'M RUNNING WAY LATE--
--WHY DON'T WE PRESS PAUSE FOR, SAY, HALF AN HOUR? WAIT RIGHT HERE.
BACK IN A FLASH. I'LL BRING STARBUCKS.
"PARKER CAPTURED IMAGES--"
--WHICH HE SOLD TO PAY HIS AUNT'S MORTGAGE, WHICH WAS ALWAYS LATE.
ON THIS OCCASION, HOWEVER, HE HAD A MORE PRESSING NEED--
THIS "MAY" WOMAN.
PRECISELY!

"PARKER HAD MERE MINUTES TO DELIVER HIS IMAGES TO HIS EMPLOYER.

"IF HE MISSED HIS DEADLINE, HE WOULD NOT BE COMPENSATED UNTIL THE FOLLOWING WEEK.

MISSED ME! IT'S CALLED "SPIDER-SENSE," YO.

PATENT PENDING.

WH-OOSH

IT'S ACTUALLY MORE LIKE "COCKROACH-SHOE SENSE," BUT I'M PRETTY SURE THAT NAME'S ALREADY TRADEMARKED.

"HIS AUNT NEEDED HER MEDICATION IMMEDIATELY.

THWiiiP

THWiiiP

SO, YOU JUST HANG TIGHT FOR A BIT.

THEN I'LL SET UP MY AUTOMATIC CAMERA AND WE CAN START AGAIN.

"OF COURSE, I KNEW NONE OF THIS AT THE TIME--

"--WHICH IS WHY I ATTACKED HIM."

FOOL!

YOU DARE ATTACK HE WHO SHALL BE KING?!

AAARRGGHHH--!!!

--AND THAT'S NOT A WORD I JUST THROW AROUND--

--WHAT IS IT WITH YOU PEOPLE?! MY... HEAD--!!!

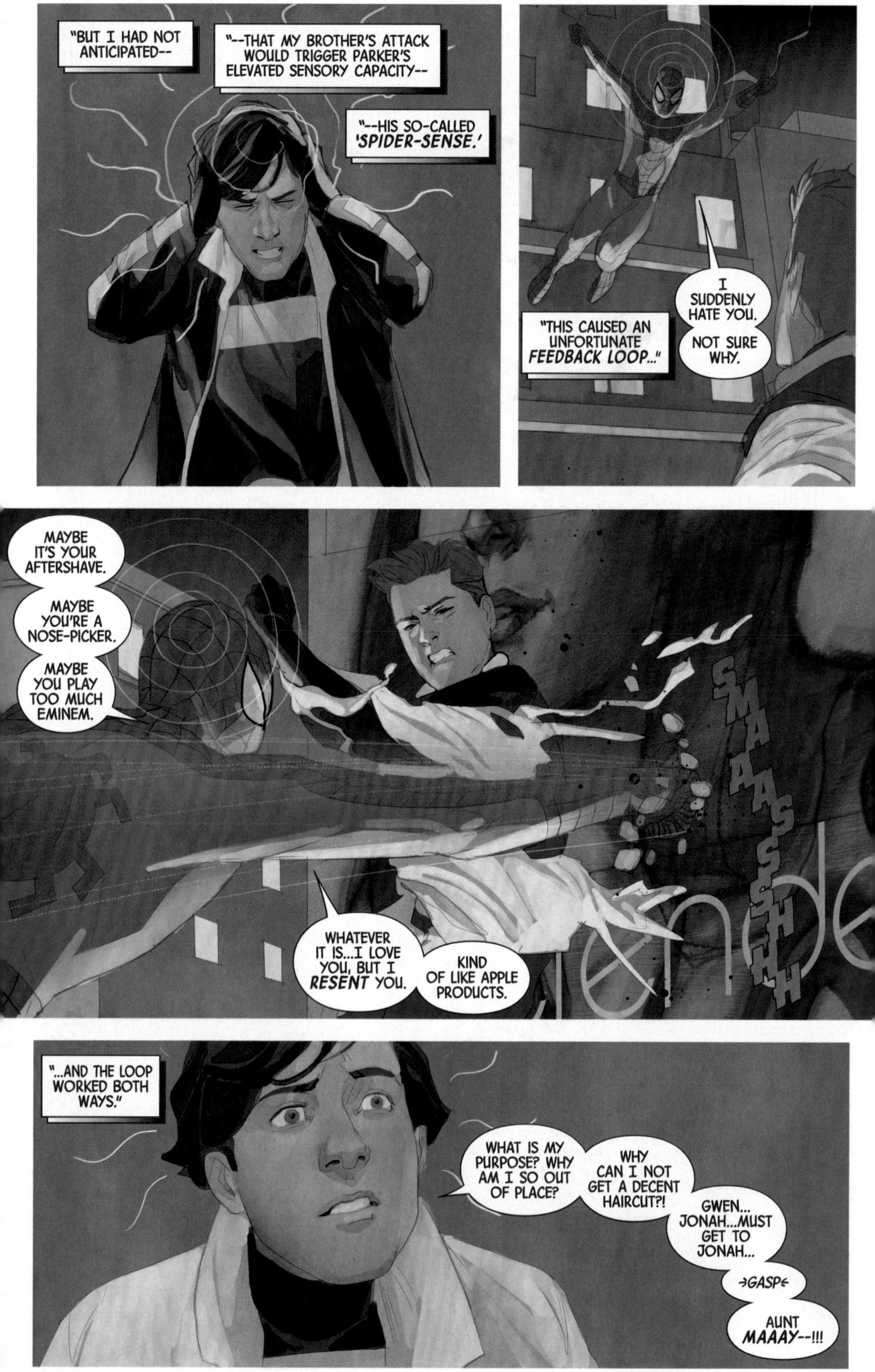
"BUT I HAD NOT ANTICIPATED--
"--THAT MY BROTHER'S ATTACK WOULD TRIGGER PARKER'S ELEVATED SENSORY CAPACITY--
"--HIS SO-CALLED *'SPIDER-SENSE.'*
"THIS CAUSED AN UNFORTUNATE *FEEDBACK LOOP*..."
I SUDDENLY HATE YOU.
NOT SURE WHY.
MAYBE IT'S YOUR AFTERSHAVE.
MAYBE YOU'RE A NOSE-PICKER.
MAYBE YOU PLAY TOO MUCH EMINEM.
SMAAASSSHHH
WHATEVER IT IS...I LOVE YOU, BUT I *RESENT* YOU.
KIND OF LIKE APPLE PRODUCTS.
"...AND THE LOOP WORKED BOTH WAYS."
WHAT IS MY PURPOSE? WHY AM I SO OUT OF PLACE?
WHY CAN I NOT GET A DECENT HAIRCUT?!
GWEN... JONAH...MUST GET TO JONAH...
GASP
AUNT *MAAAY*--!!!

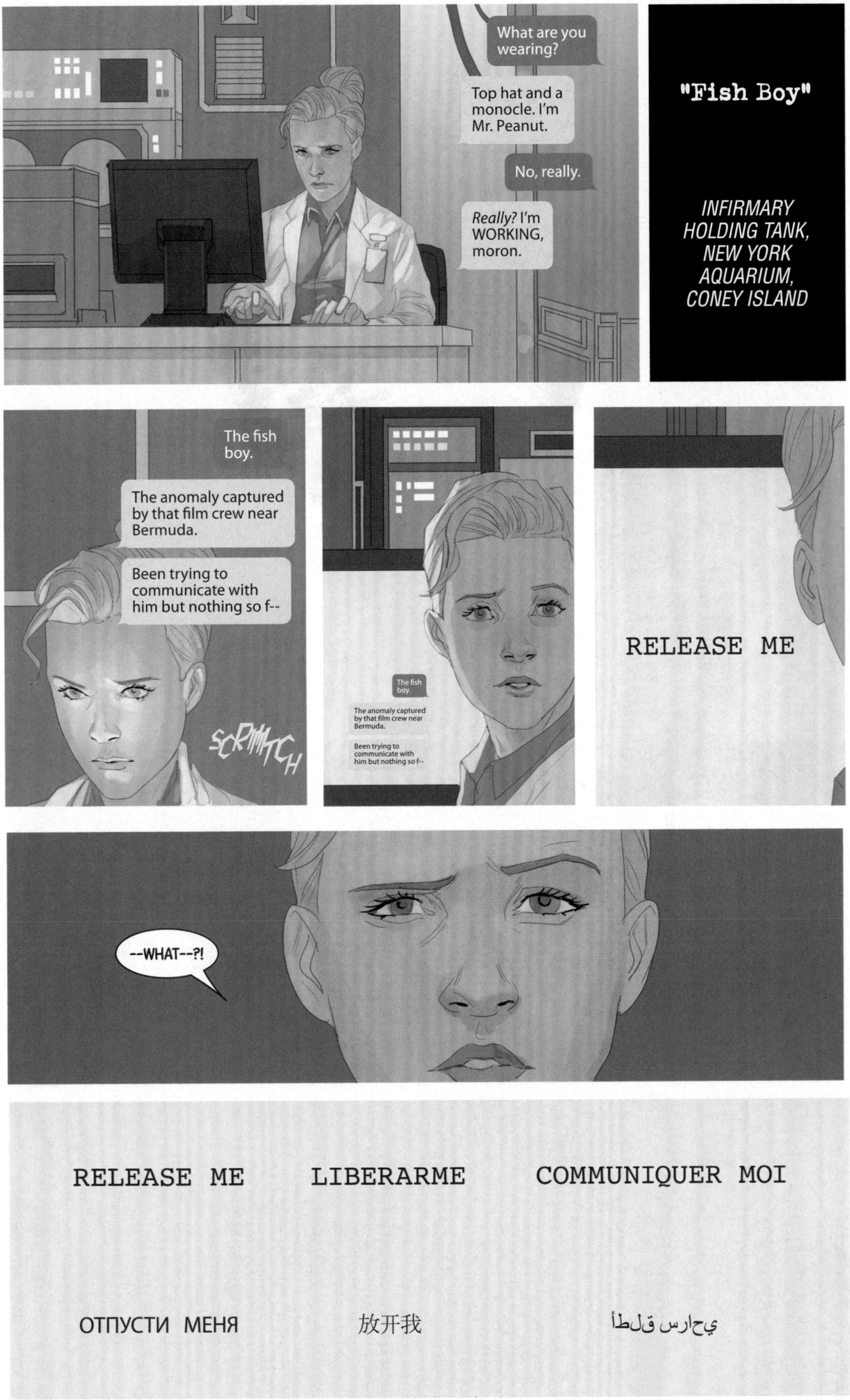
What are you wearing?
Top hat and a monocle. I'm Mr. Peanut.
No, really.
Really? I'm WORKING, moron.
"Fish Boy"
INFIRMARY HOLDING TANK, NEW YORK AQUARIUM, CONEY ISLAND
The fish boy.
The anomaly captured by that film crew near Bermuda.
Been trying to communicate with him but nothing so f--
SCRMTCH
The fish boy.
The anomaly captured by that film crew near Bermuda.
Been trying to communicate with him but nothing so f--
RELEASE ME
--WHAT--?!
RELEASE ME
LIBERARME
COMMUNIQUER MOI
ОТПУСТИ МЕНЯ
放开我
أطلق سراحي

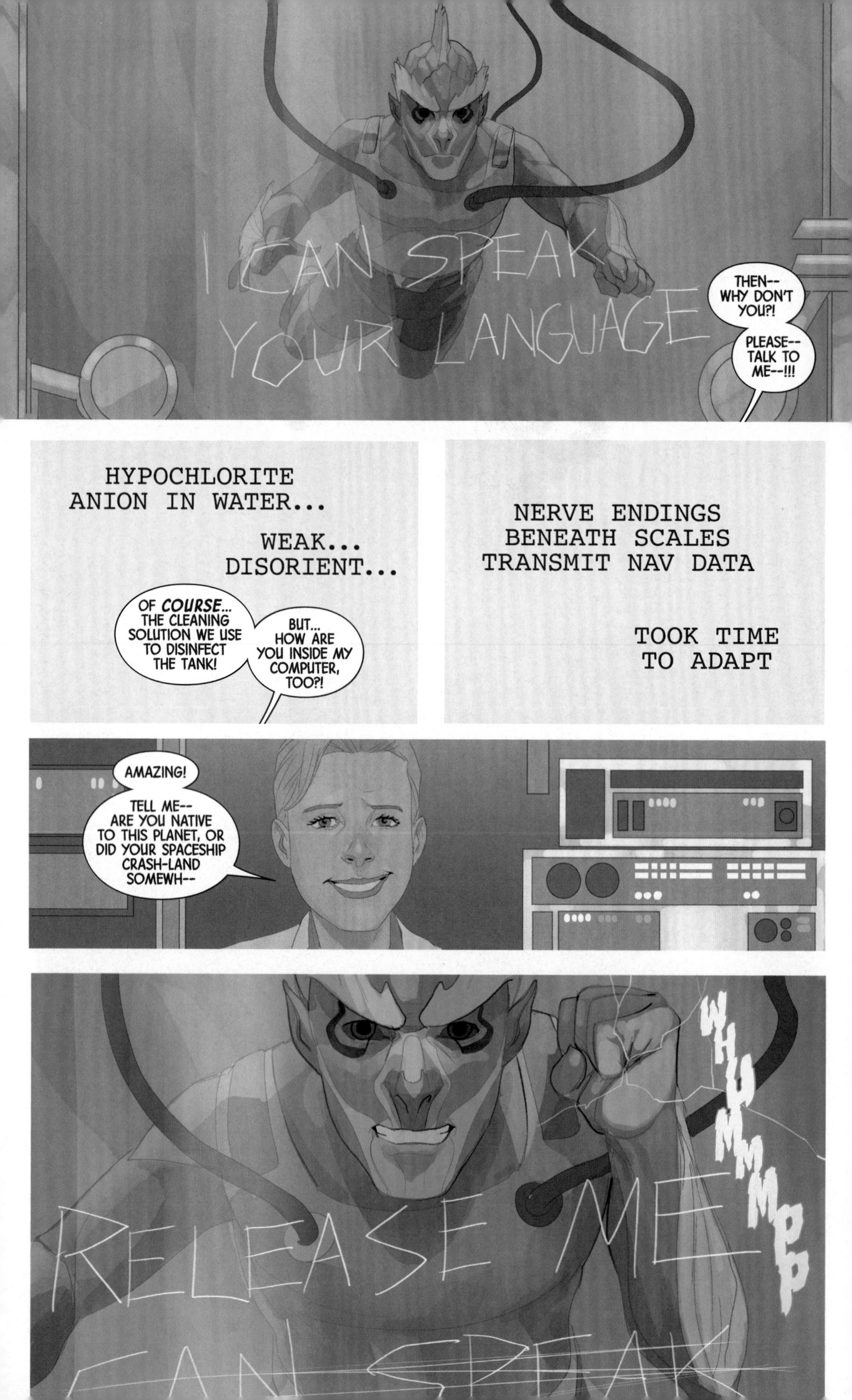
I CAN SPEAK YOUR LANGUAGE
THEN-- WHY DON'T YOU?!
PLEASE-- TALK TO ME--!!!
HYPOCHLORITE ANION IN WATER...
WEAK... DISORIENT...
OF COURSE... THE CLEANING SOLUTION WE USE TO DISINFECT THE TANK!
BUT... HOW ARE YOU INSIDE MY COMPUTER, TOO?!
NERVE ENDINGS BENEATH SCALES TRANSMIT NAV DATA
TOOK TIME TO ADAPT
AMAZING!
TELL ME-- ARE YOU NATIVE TO THIS PLANET, OR DID YOUR SPACESHIP CRASH-LAND SOMEWH--
WHUMMMPP
RELEASE ME
CAN SPEAK

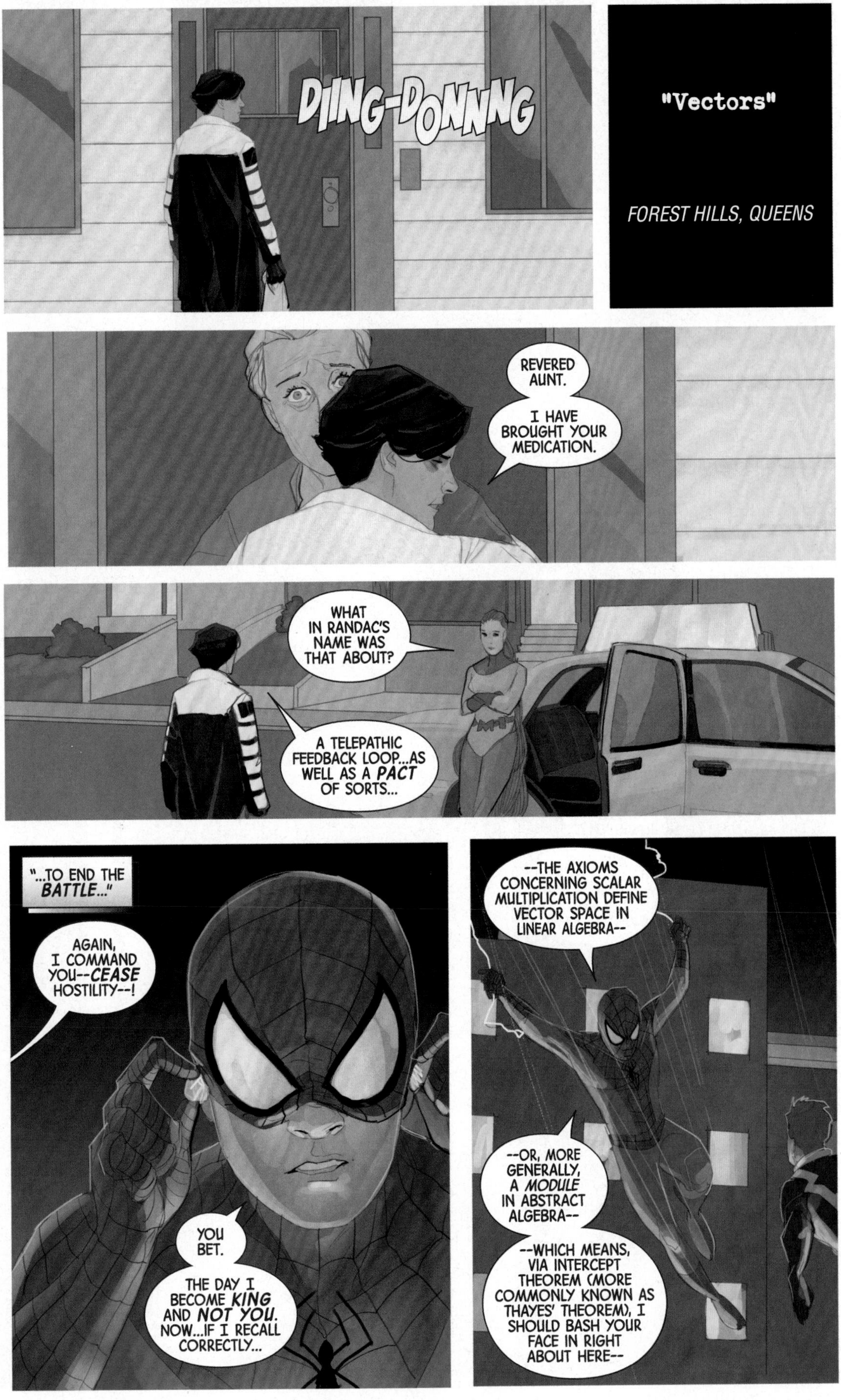
DIING-DONNNG
"Vectors"
FOREST HILLS, QUEENS
REVERED AUNT.
I HAVE BROUGHT YOUR MEDICATION.
WHAT IN RANDAC'S NAME WAS THAT ABOUT?
A TELEPATHIC FEEDBACK LOOP...AS WELL AS A *PACT* OF SORTS...
"...TO END THE *BATTLE*..."
AGAIN, I COMMAND YOU--*CEASE* HOSTILITY--!
YOU BET.
THE DAY I BECOME *KING* AND *NOT YOU*. NOW...IF I RECALL CORRECTLY...
--THE AXIOMS CONCERNING SCALAR MULTIPLICATION DEFINE VECTOR SPACE IN LINEAR ALGEBRA--
--OR, MORE GENERALLY, A *MODULE* IN ABSTRACT ALGEBRA--
--WHICH MEANS, VIA INTERCEPT THEOREM (MORE COMMONLY KNOWN AS THAYES' THEOREM), I SHOULD BASH YOUR FACE IN RIGHT ABOUT HERE--

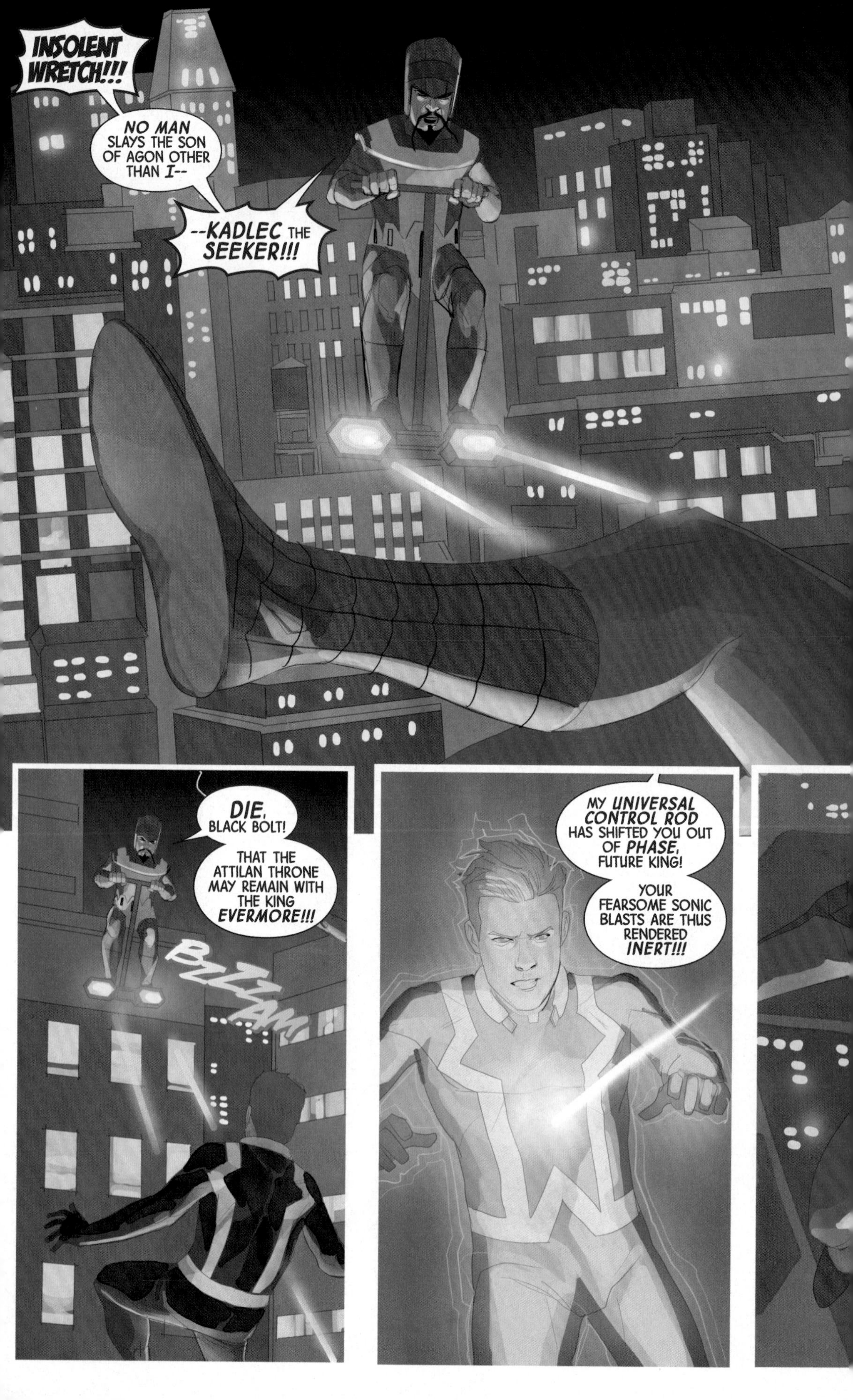
INSOLENT WRETCH!!!
NO MAN SLAYS THE SON OF AGON OTHER THAN I--
--KADLEC THE SEEKER!!!
DIE, BLACK BOLT!
THAT THE ATTILAN THRONE MAY REMAIN WITH THE KING EVERMORE!!!
BZZZAM!
MY UNIVERSAL CONTROL ROD HAS SHIFTED YOU OUT OF PHASE, FUTURE KING!
YOUR FEARSOME SONIC BLASTS ARE THUS RENDERED INERT!!!

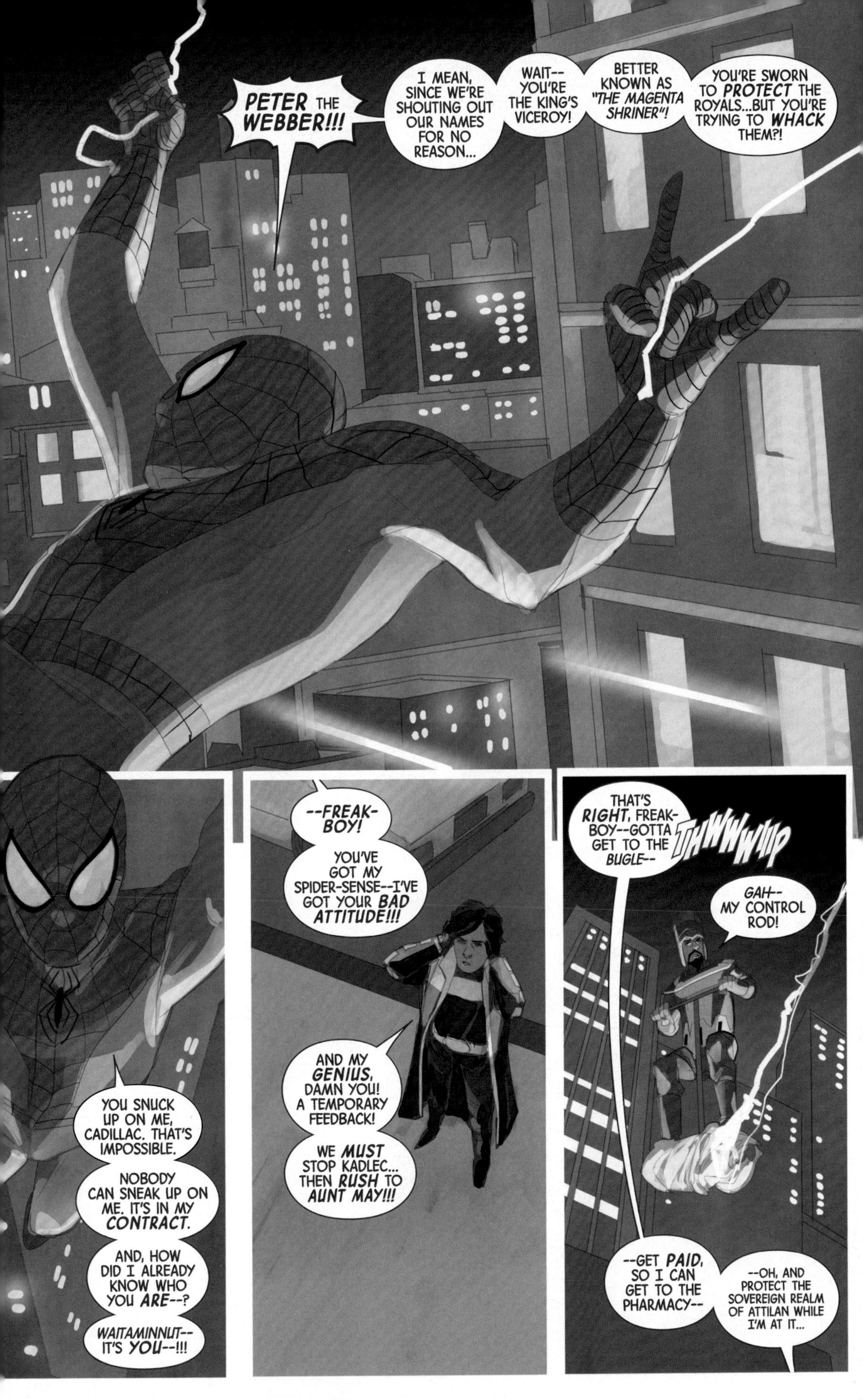
PETER THE WEBBER!!!
I MEAN, SINCE WE'RE SHOUTING OUT OUR NAMES FOR NO REASON...
WAIT-- YOU'RE THE KING'S VICEROY!
BETTER KNOWN AS "THE MAGENTA SHRINER"!
YOU'RE SWORN TO PROTECT THE ROYALS...BUT YOU'RE TRYING TO WHACK THEM?!
YOU SNUCK UP ON ME, CADILLAC. THAT'S IMPOSSIBLE.
NOBODY CAN SNEAK UP ON ME. IT'S IN MY CONTRACT.
AND, HOW DID I ALREADY KNOW WHO YOU ARE--?
WAITAMINNUT-- IT'S YOU--!!!
--FREAK-BOY!
YOU'VE GOT MY SPIDER-SENSE--I'VE GOT YOUR BAD ATTITUDE!!!
AND MY GENIUS, DAMN YOU! A TEMPORARY FEEDBACK!
WE MUST STOP KADLEC... THEN RUSH TO AUNT MAY!!!
THAT'S RIGHT, FREAK-BOY--GOTTA GET TO THE BUGLE--
THWWWIIP
GAH-- MY CONTROL ROD!
--GET PAID, SO I CAN GET TO THE PHARMACY--
--OH, AND PROTECT THE SOVEREIGN REALM OF ATTILAN WHILE I'M AT IT...

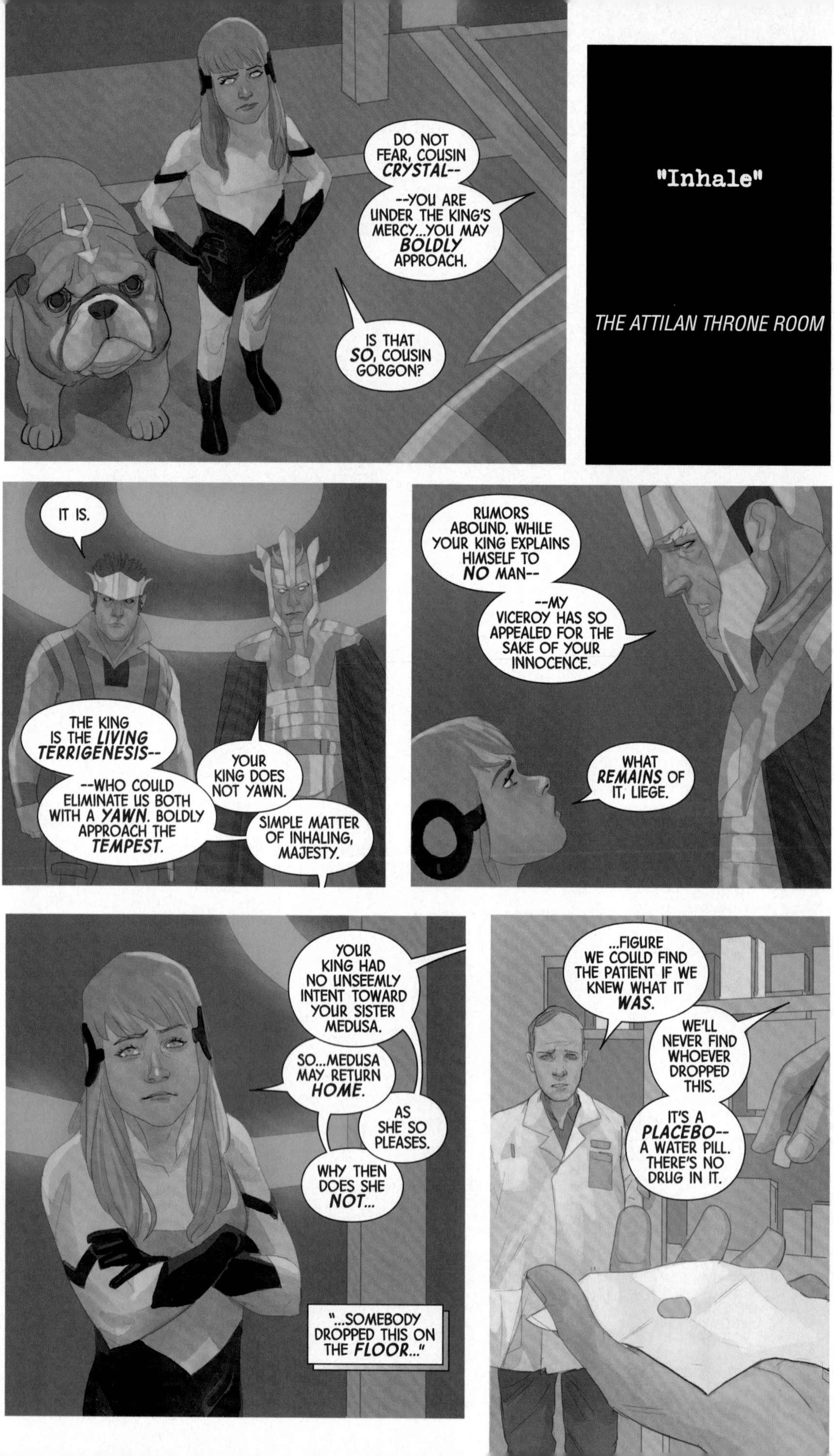
DO NOT FEAR, COUSIN CRYSTAL--
--YOU ARE UNDER THE KING'S MERCY...YOU MAY BOLDLY APPROACH.
IS THAT SO, COUSIN GORGON?
"Inhale"
THE ATTILAN THRONE ROOM
IT IS.
THE KING IS THE LIVING TERRIGENESIS--
--WHO COULD ELIMINATE US BOTH WITH A YAWN. BOLDLY APPROACH THE TEMPEST.
YOUR KING DOES NOT YAWN.
SIMPLE MATTER OF INHALING, MAJESTY.
RUMORS ABOUND. WHILE YOUR KING EXPLAINS HIMSELF TO NO MAN--
--MY VICEROY HAS SO APPEALED FOR THE SAKE OF YOUR INNOCENCE.
WHAT REMAINS OF IT, LIEGE.
YOUR KING HAD NO UNSEEMLY INTENT TOWARD YOUR SISTER MEDUSA.
SO...MEDUSA MAY RETURN HOME.
AS SHE SO PLEASES.
WHY THEN DOES SHE NOT...
"...SOMEBODY DROPPED THIS ON THE FLOOR..."
...FIGURE WE COULD FIND THE PATIENT IF WE KNEW WHAT IT WAS.
WE'LL NEVER FIND WHOEVER DROPPED THIS.
IT'S A PLACEBO-- A WATER PILL. THERE'S NO DRUG IN IT.

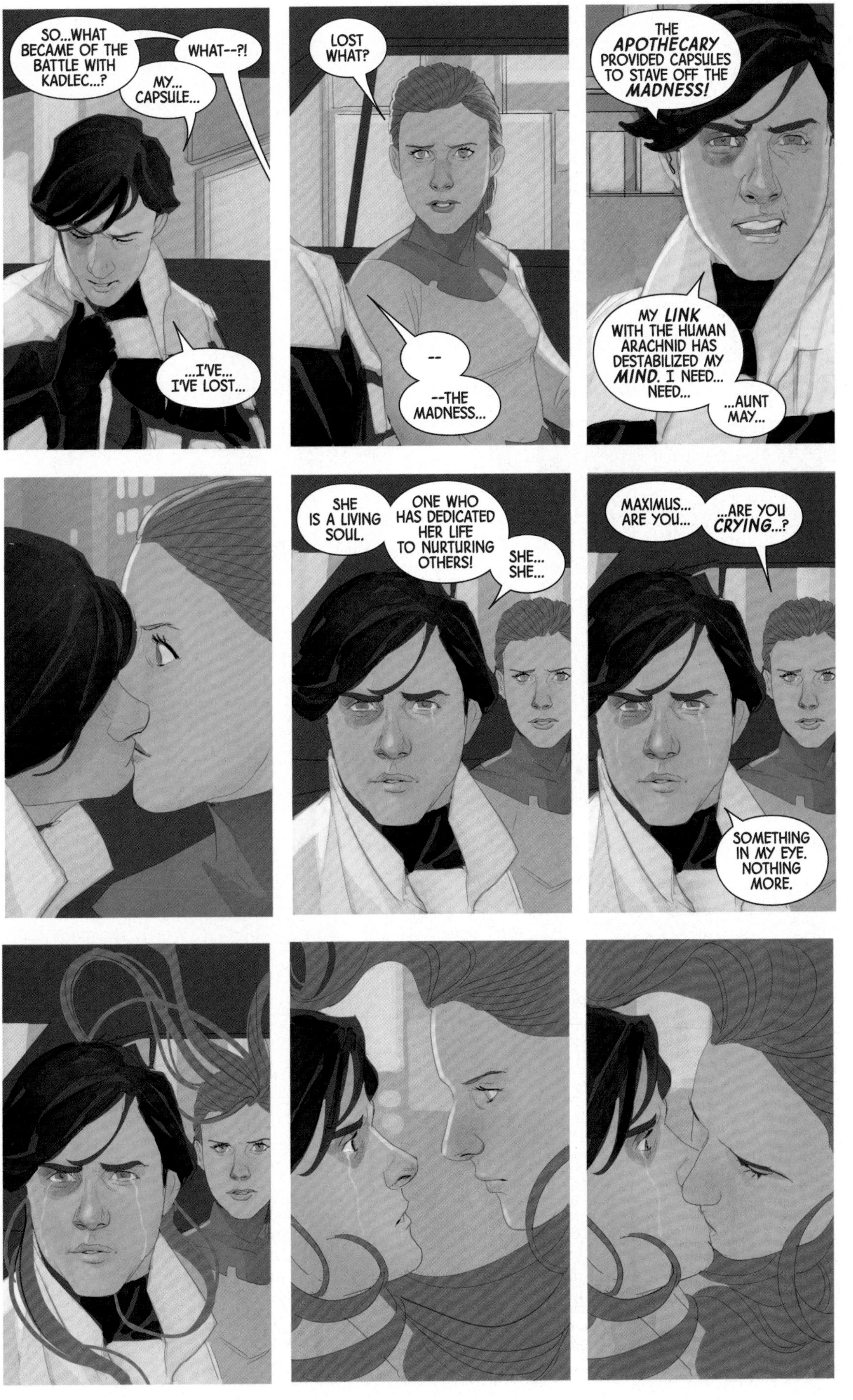
SO...WHAT BECAME OF THE BATTLE WITH KADLEC...?
MY... CAPSULE...
WHAT--?!
...I'VE... I'VE LOST...
LOST WHAT?
--
--THE MADNESS...
THE APOTHECARY PROVIDED CAPSULES TO STAVE OFF THE MADNESS!
MY LINK WITH THE HUMAN ARACHNID HAS DESTABILIZED MY MIND. I NEED... NEED...
...AUNT MAY...
SHE IS A LIVING SOUL.
ONE WHO HAS DEDICATED HER LIFE TO NURTURING OTHERS!
SHE... SHE...
MAXIMUS... ARE YOU...
...ARE YOU CRYING...?
SOMETHING IN MY EYE. NOTHING MORE.

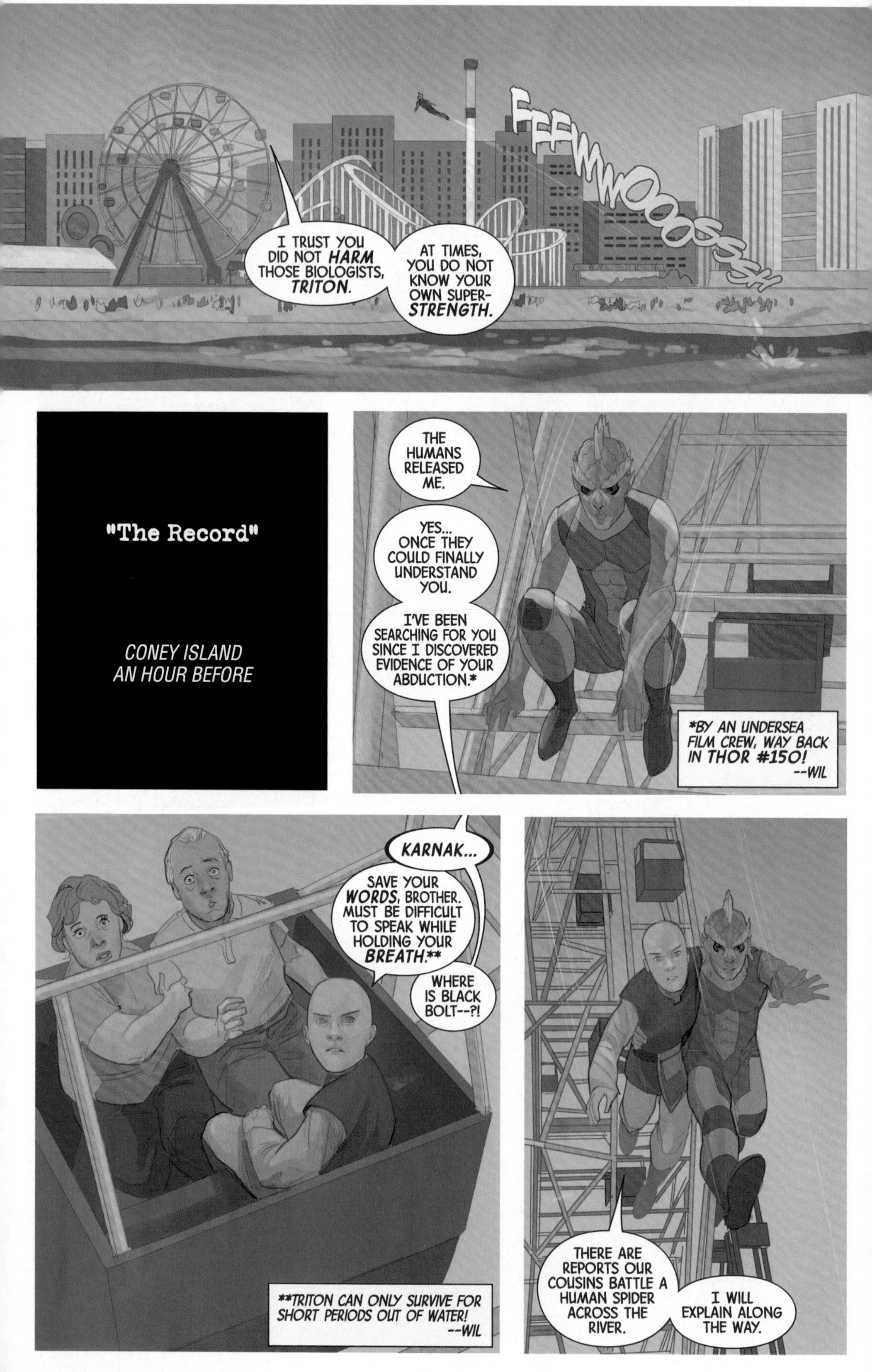
FFFWWOOOSSSSH
I TRUST YOU DID NOT HARM THOSE BIOLOGISTS, TRITON.
AT TIMES, YOU DO NOT KNOW YOUR OWN SUPER-STRENGTH.
"The Record"
CONEY ISLAND AN HOUR BEFORE
THE HUMANS RELEASED ME.
YES... ONCE THEY COULD FINALLY UNDERSTAND YOU.
I'VE BEEN SEARCHING FOR YOU SINCE I DISCOVERED EVIDENCE OF YOUR ABDUCTION.*
*BY AN UNDERSEA FILM CREW, WAY BACK IN THOR #150! --WIL
KARNAK...
SAVE YOUR WORDS, BROTHER. MUST BE DIFFICULT TO SPEAK WHILE HOLDING YOUR BREATH.**
WHERE IS BLACK BOLT--?!
**TRITON CAN ONLY SURVIVE FOR SHORT PERIODS OUT OF WATER! --WIL
THERE ARE REPORTS OUR COUSINS BATTLE A HUMAN SPIDER ACROSS THE RIVER.
I WILL EXPLAIN ALONG THE WAY.

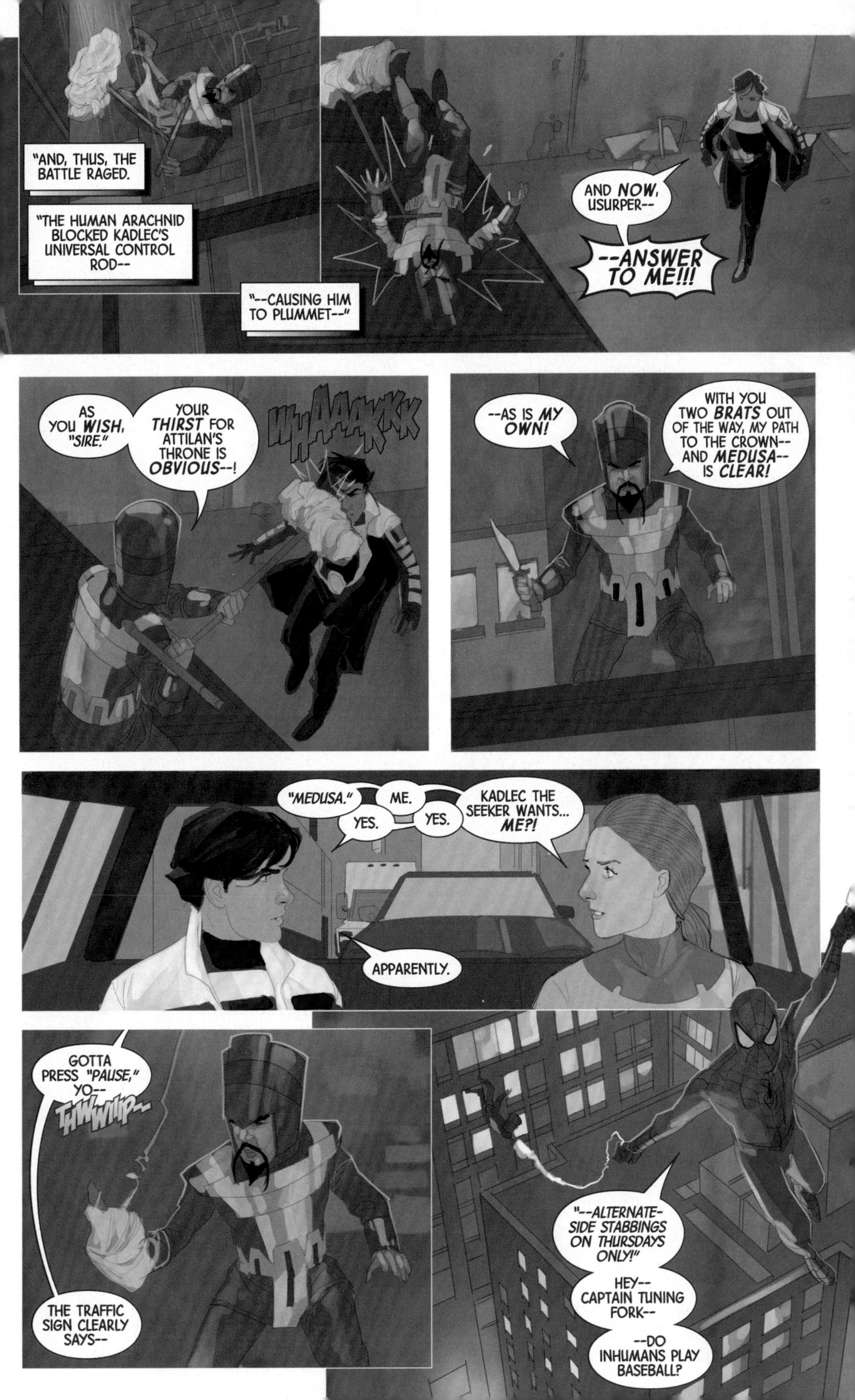
"AND, THUS, THE BATTLE RAGED.
"THE HUMAN ARACHNID BLOCKED KADLEC'S UNIVERSAL CONTROL ROD--
"--CAUSING HIM TO PLUMMET--"
AND NOW, USURPER--
--ANSWER TO ME!!!
AS YOU WISH, "SIRE."
YOUR THIRST FOR ATTILAN'S THRONE IS OBVIOUS--!
WHAAAKKK
--AS IS MY OWN!
WITH YOU TWO BRATS OUT OF THE WAY, MY PATH TO THE CROWN-- AND MEDUSA-- IS CLEAR!
"MEDUSA."
YES.
ME.
YES.
KADLEC THE SEEKER WANTS... ME?!
APPARENTLY.
GOTTA PRESS "PAUSE," YO--
THWWHIP--
THE TRAFFIC SIGN CLEARLY SAYS--
"--ALTERNATE-SIDE STABBINGS ON THURSDAYS ONLY!"
HEY-- CAPTAIN TUNING FORK--
--DO INHUMANS PLAY BASEBALL?

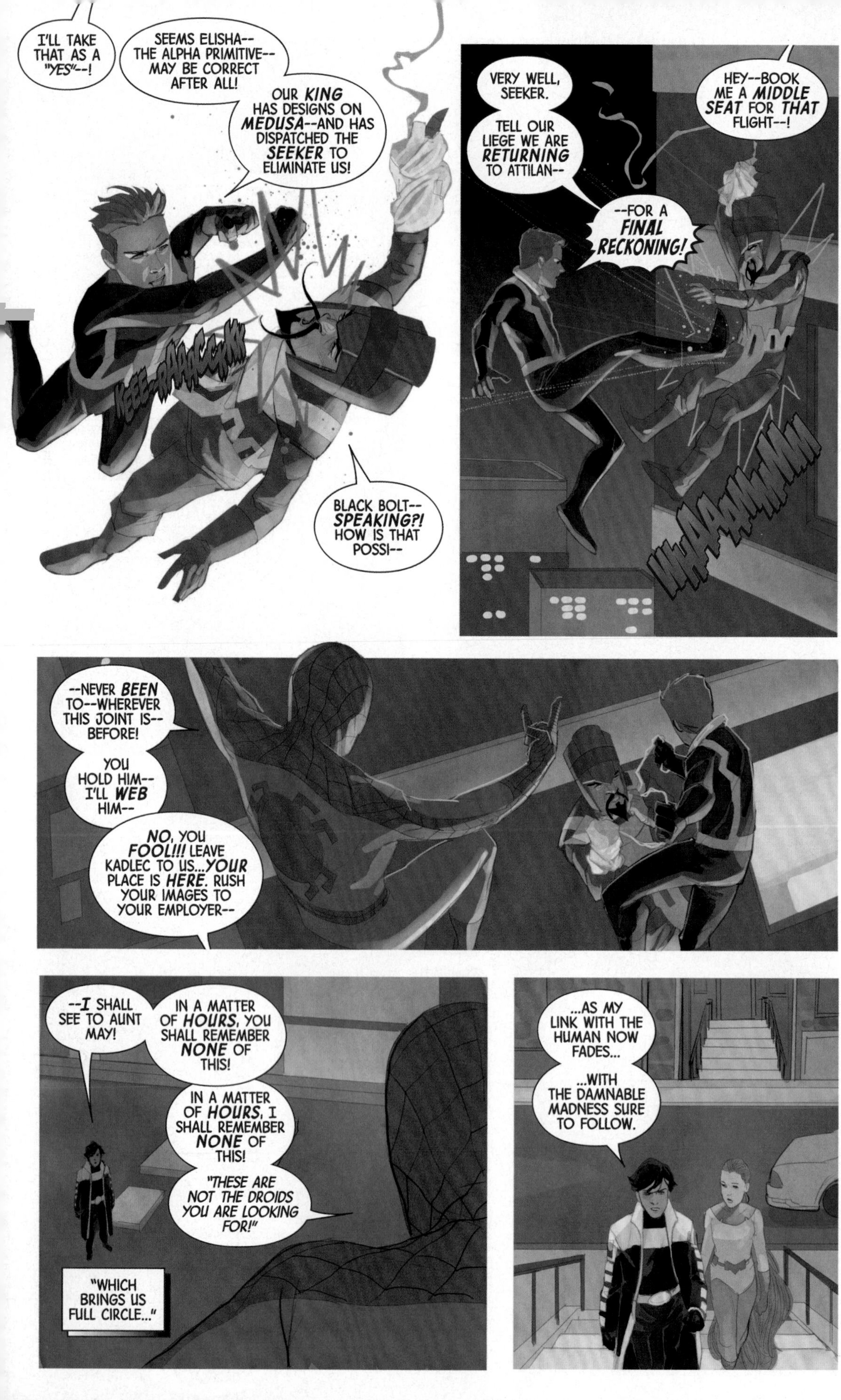
I'LL TAKE THAT AS A "YES"--!
SEEMS ELISHA-- THE ALPHA PRIMITIVE-- MAY BE CORRECT AFTER ALL!
OUR KING HAS DESIGNS ON MEDUSA--AND HAS DISPATCHED THE SEEKER TO ELIMINATE US!
BLACK BOLT-- SPEAKING?! HOW IS THAT POSSI--
VERY WELL, SEEKER.
TELL OUR LIEGE WE ARE RETURNING TO ATTILAN--
--FOR A FINAL RECKONING!
HEY--BOOK ME A MIDDLE SEAT FOR THAT FLIGHT--!
--NEVER BEEN TO--WHEREVER THIS JOINT IS-- BEFORE!
YOU HOLD HIM-- I'LL WEB HIM--
NO, YOU FOOL!!! LEAVE KADLEC TO US...YOUR PLACE IS HERE. RUSH YOUR IMAGES TO YOUR EMPLOYER--
--I SHALL SEE TO AUNT MAY!
IN A MATTER OF HOURS, YOU SHALL REMEMBER NONE OF THIS!
IN A MATTER OF HOURS, I SHALL REMEMBER NONE OF THIS!
"THESE ARE NOT THE DROIDS YOU ARE LOOKING FOR!"
"WHICH BRINGS US FULL CIRCLE..."
...AS MY LINK WITH THE HUMAN NOW FADES...
...WITH THE DAMNABLE MADNESS SURE TO FOLLOW.

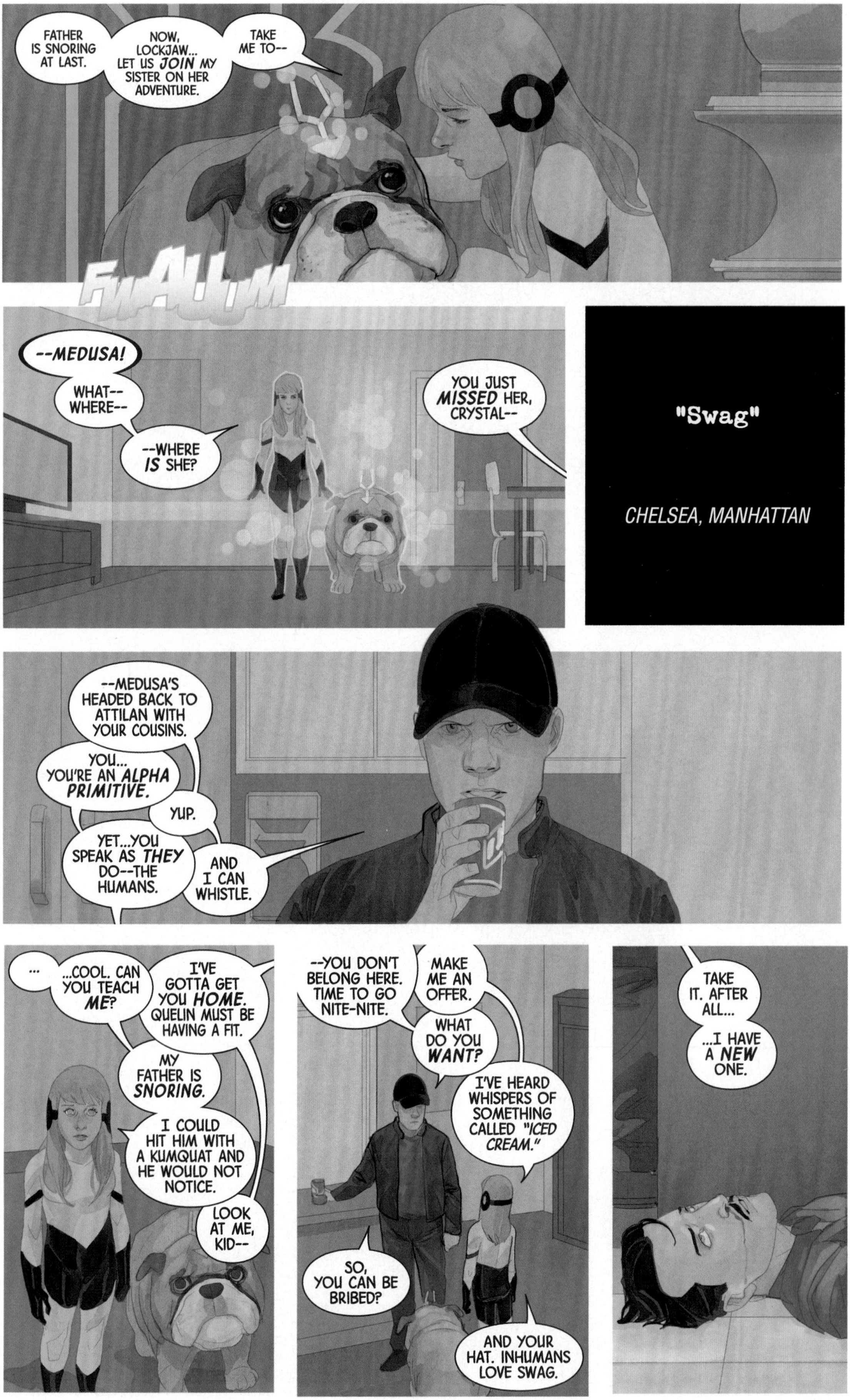
FATHER IS SNORING AT LAST.
NOW, LOCKJAW... LET US JOIN MY SISTER ON HER ADVENTURE.
TAKE ME TO--
FWAUUM
--MEDUSA!
WHAT-- WHERE--
--WHERE IS SHE?
YOU JUST MISSED HER, CRYSTAL--
"Swag"
CHELSEA, MANHATTAN
--MEDUSA'S HEADED BACK TO ATTILAN WITH YOUR COUSINS.
YOU... YOU'RE AN ALPHA PRIMITIVE.
YUP.
YET...YOU SPEAK AS THEY DO--THE HUMANS.
AND I CAN WHISTLE.
...
...COOL. CAN YOU TEACH ME?
I'VE GOTTA GET YOU HOME. QUELIN MUST BE HAVING A FIT.
MY FATHER IS SNORING.
I COULD HIT HIM WITH A KUMQUAT AND HE WOULD NOT NOTICE.
LOOK AT ME, KID--
--YOU DON'T BELONG HERE. TIME TO GO NITE-NITE.
MAKE ME AN OFFER.
WHAT DO YOU WANT?
I'VE HEARD WHISPERS OF SOMETHING CALLED "ICED CREAM."
SO, YOU CAN BE BRIBED?
AND YOUR HAT. INHUMANS LOVE SWAG.
TAKE IT. AFTER ALL...
...I HAVE A NEW ONE.

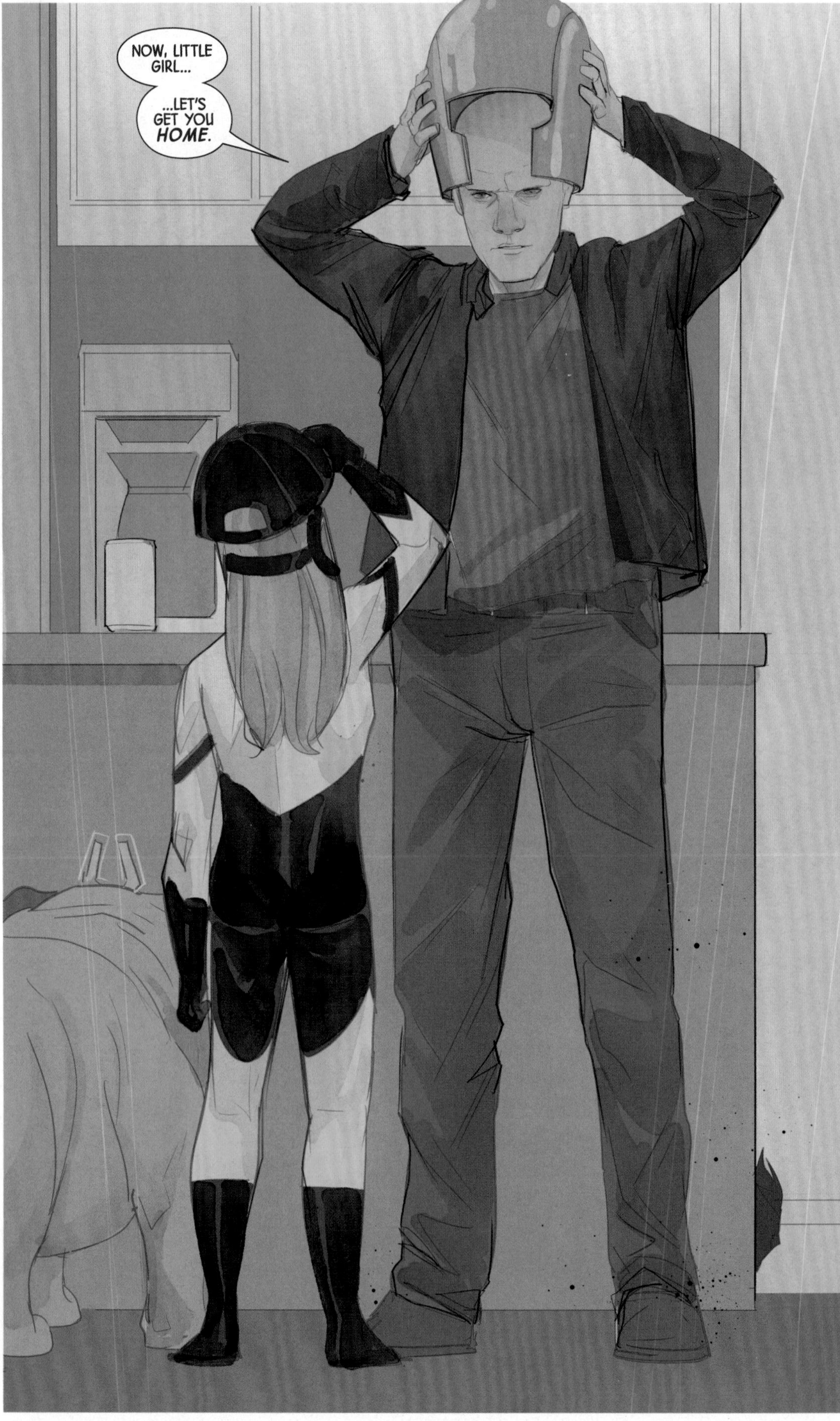
NOW, LITTLE GIRL...
...LET'S GET YOU HOME.

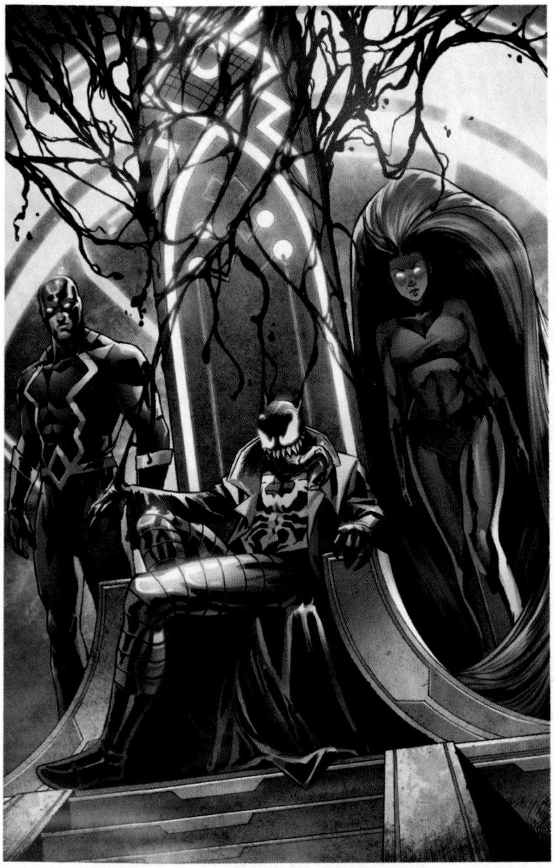

TWO VENOMIZED VILLAINS VARIANT BY
DJIBRIL MORISSETTE-PHAN & **DONO SÁNCHEZ-ALMARA**

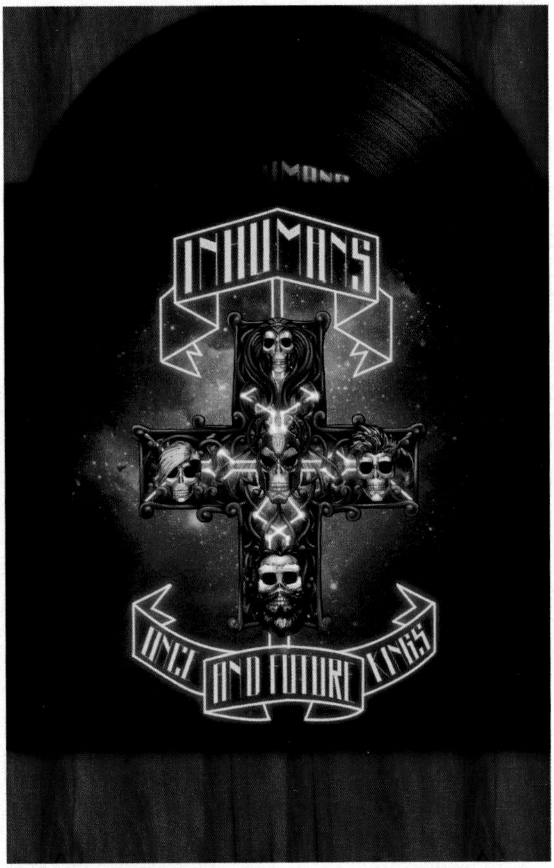
INHUMANS
ONCE AND FUTURE KINGS

TWO ROCK-N-ROLL VARIANT BY **DAMION SCOTT**

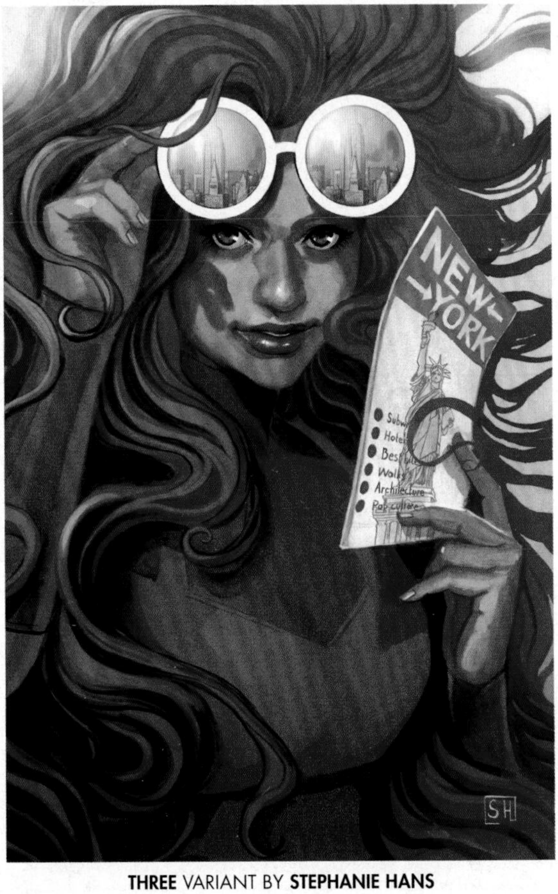
NEW YORK
Architecture
Pop culture
SH

THREE VARIANT BY **STEPHANIE HANS**

FIVE

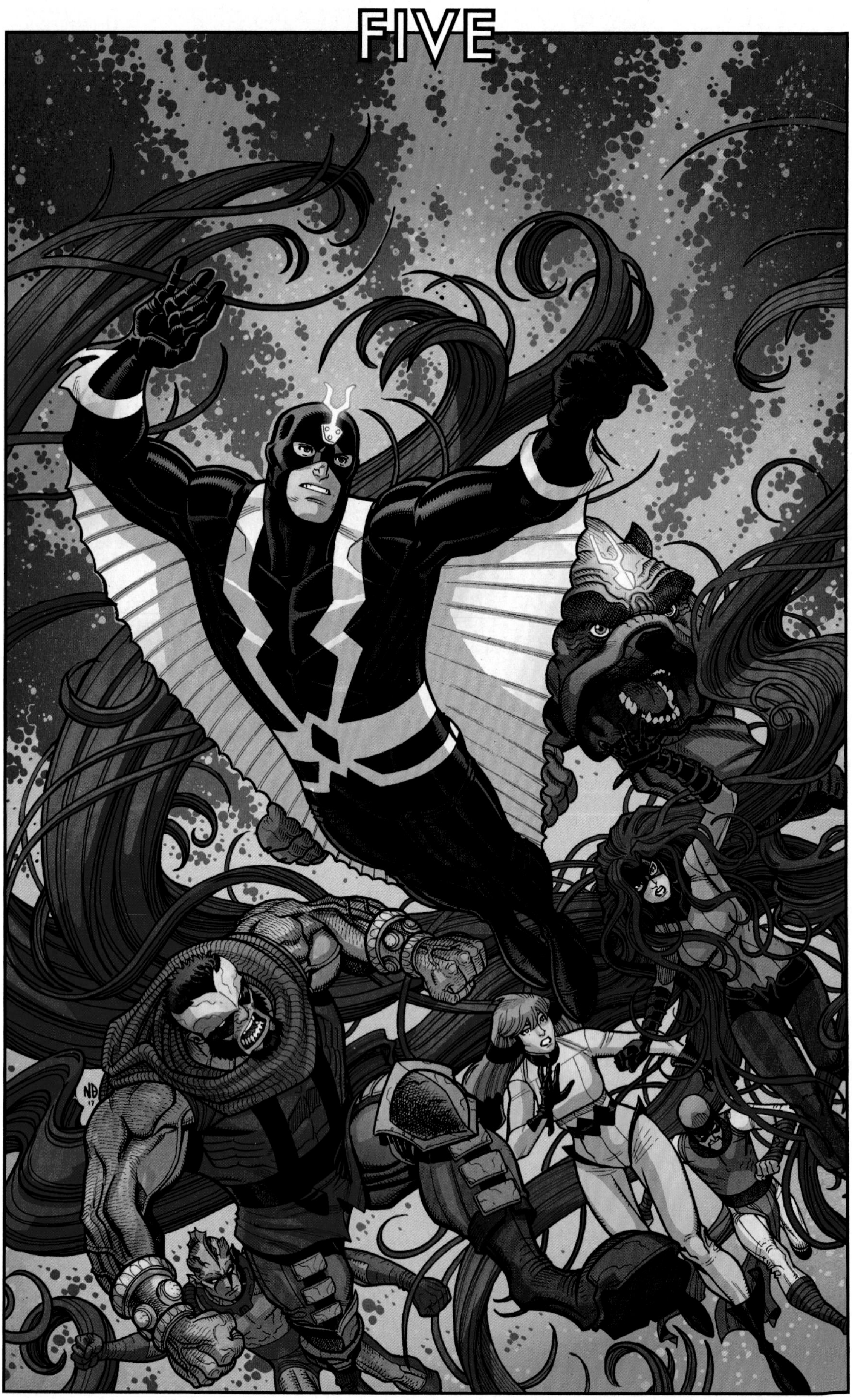

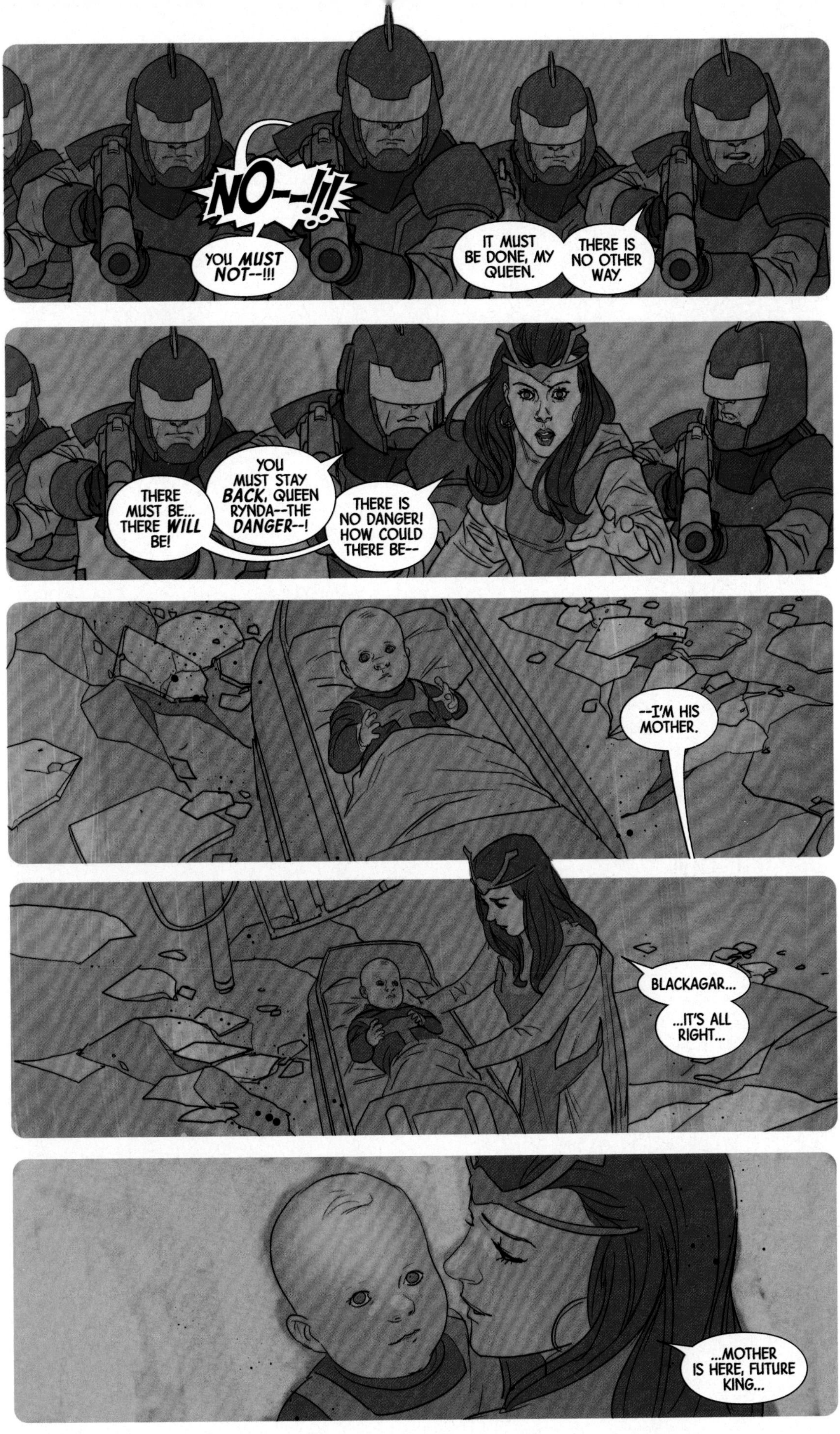
NO--!!!
YOU MUST NOT--!!!
IT MUST BE DONE, MY QUEEN.
THERE IS NO OTHER WAY.
THERE MUST BE... THERE WILL BE!
YOU MUST STAY BACK, QUEEN RYNDA--THE DANGER--!
THERE IS NO DANGER! HOW COULD THERE BE--
--I'M HIS MOTHER.
BLACKAGAR...
...IT'S ALL RIGHT...
...MOTHER IS HERE, FUTURE KING...

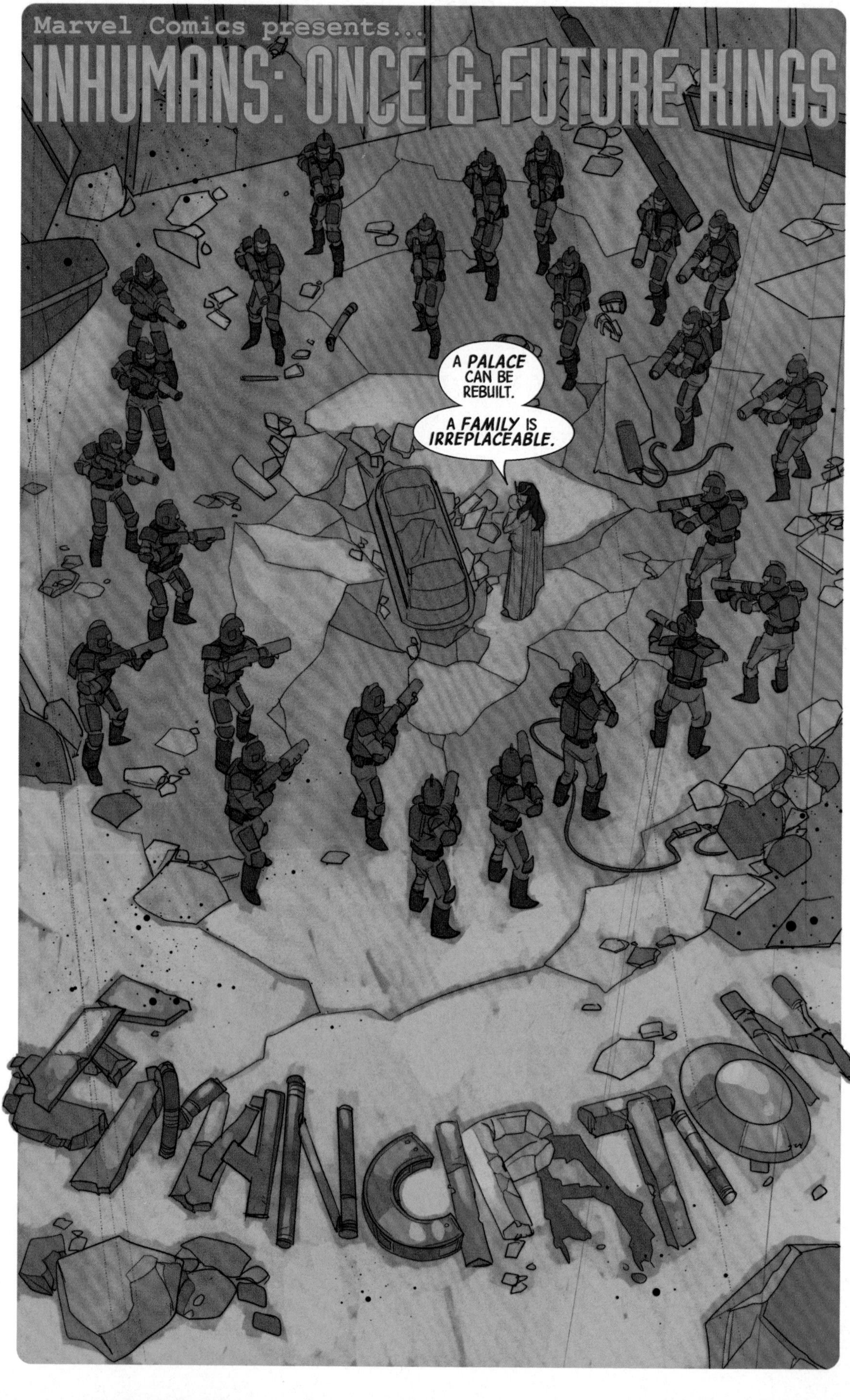
Marvel Comics presents...
INHUMANS: ONCE & FUTURE KINGS
A PALACE CAN BE REBUILT.
A FAMILY IS IRREPLACEABLE.
EMANCIPATION

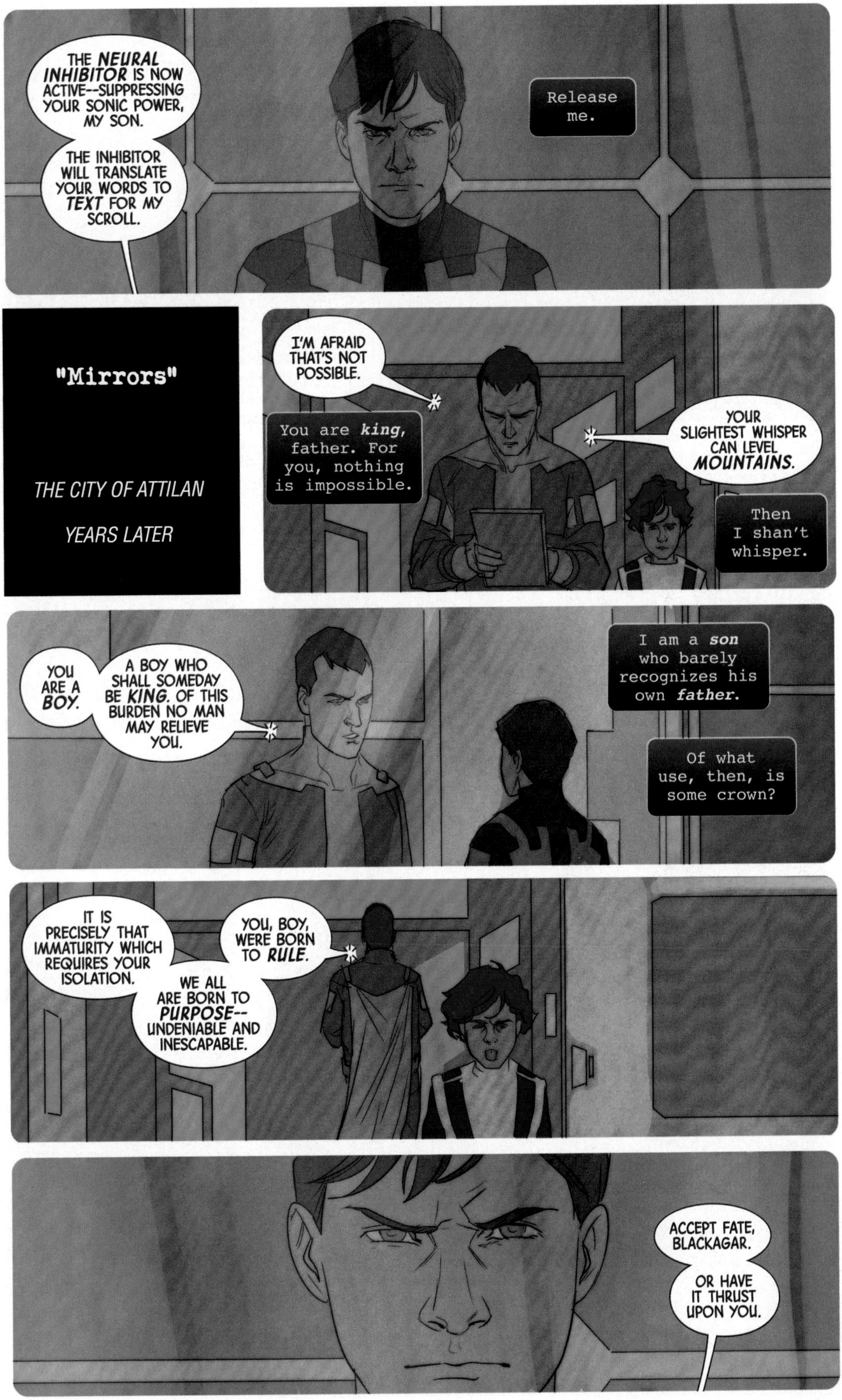
THE NEURAL INHIBITOR IS NOW ACTIVE--SUPPRESSING YOUR SONIC POWER, MY SON.
THE INHIBITOR WILL TRANSLATE YOUR WORDS TO TEXT FOR MY SCROLL.
Release me.
"Mirrors"
THE CITY OF ATTILAN
YEARS LATER
I'M AFRAID THAT'S NOT POSSIBLE.
You are king, father. For you, nothing is impossible.
YOUR SLIGHTEST WHISPER CAN LEVEL MOUNTAINS.
Then I shan't whisper.
YOU ARE A BOY.
A BOY WHO SHALL SOMEDAY BE KING. OF THIS BURDEN NO MAN MAY RELIEVE YOU.
I am a son who barely recognizes his own father.
Of what use, then, is some crown?
IT IS PRECISELY THAT IMMATURITY WHICH REQUIRES YOUR ISOLATION.
YOU, BOY, WERE BORN TO RULE.
WE ALL ARE BORN TO PURPOSE--UNDENIABLE AND INESCAPABLE.
ACCEPT FATE, BLACKAGAR.
OR HAVE IT THRUST UPON YOU.

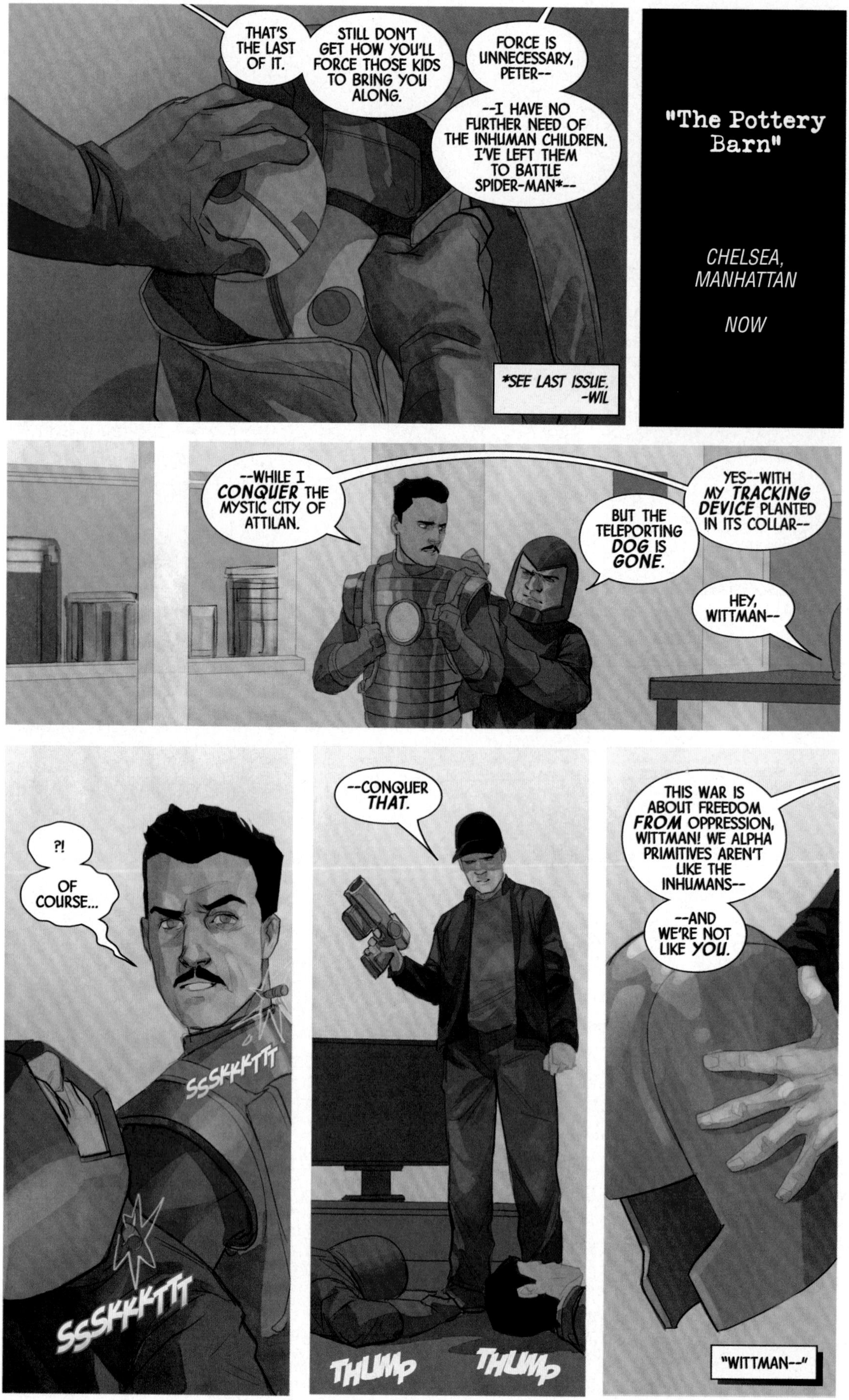

THAT'S THE LAST OF IT.
STILL DON'T GET HOW YOU'LL FORCE THOSE KIDS TO BRING YOU ALONG.
FORCE IS UNNECESSARY, PETER--
--I HAVE NO FURTHER NEED OF THE INHUMAN CHILDREN. I'VE LEFT THEM TO BATTLE SPIDER-MAN*--
*SEE LAST ISSUE. -WIL
"The Pottery Barn"
CHELSEA, MANHATTAN
NOW
--WHILE I CONQUER THE MYSTIC CITY OF ATTILAN.
BUT THE TELEPORTING DOG IS GONE.
YES--WITH MY TRACKING DEVICE PLANTED IN ITS COLLAR--
HEY, WITTMAN--
?!
OF COURSE...
SSSKKKTTT
SSSKKKTTT
--CONQUER THAT.
THUMP
THUMP
THIS WAR IS ABOUT FREEDOM FROM OPPRESSION, WITTMAN! WE ALPHA PRIMITIVES AREN'T LIKE THE INHUMANS--
--AND WE'RE NOT LIKE YOU.
"WITTMAN--"

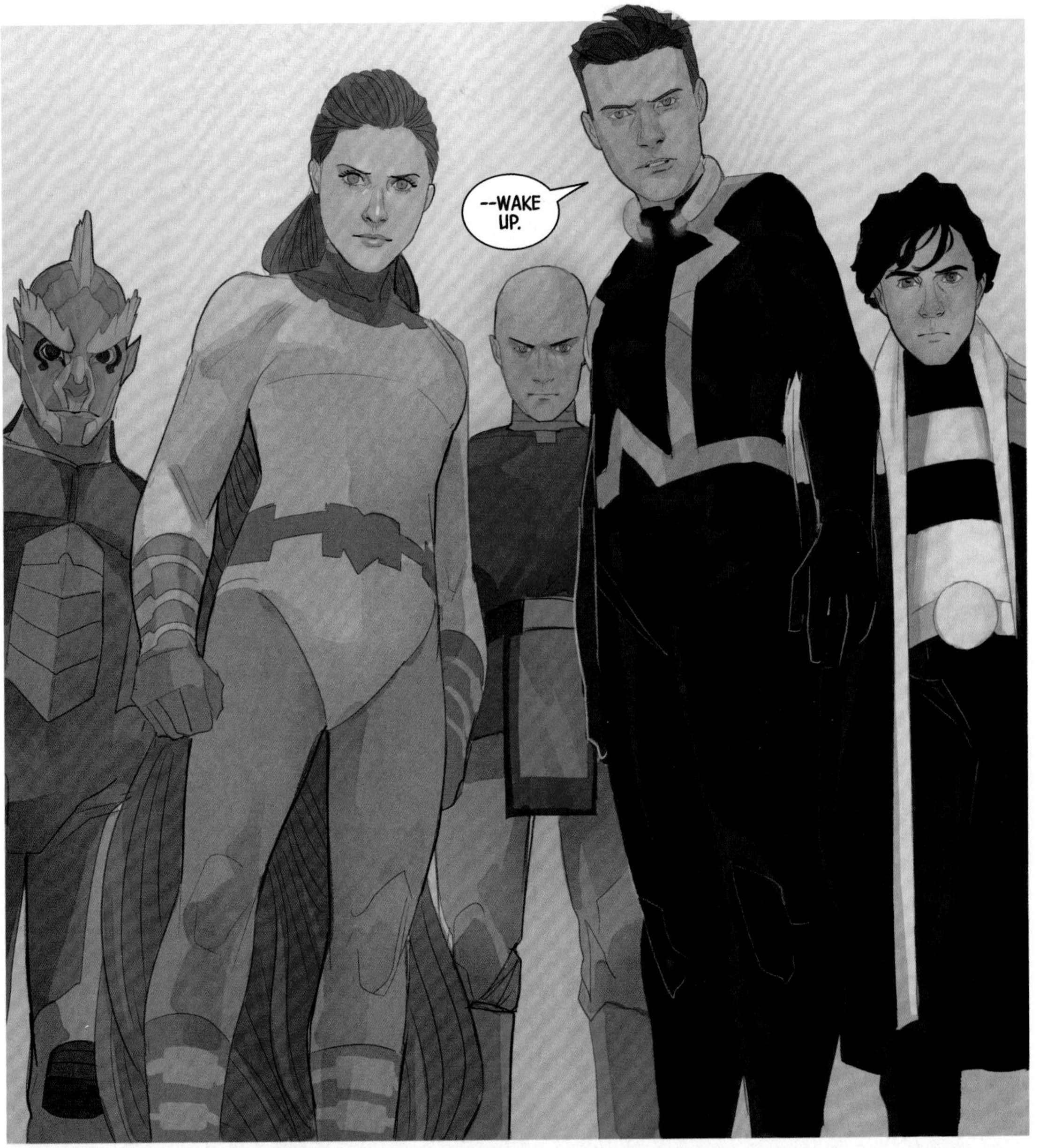
--WAKE UP.

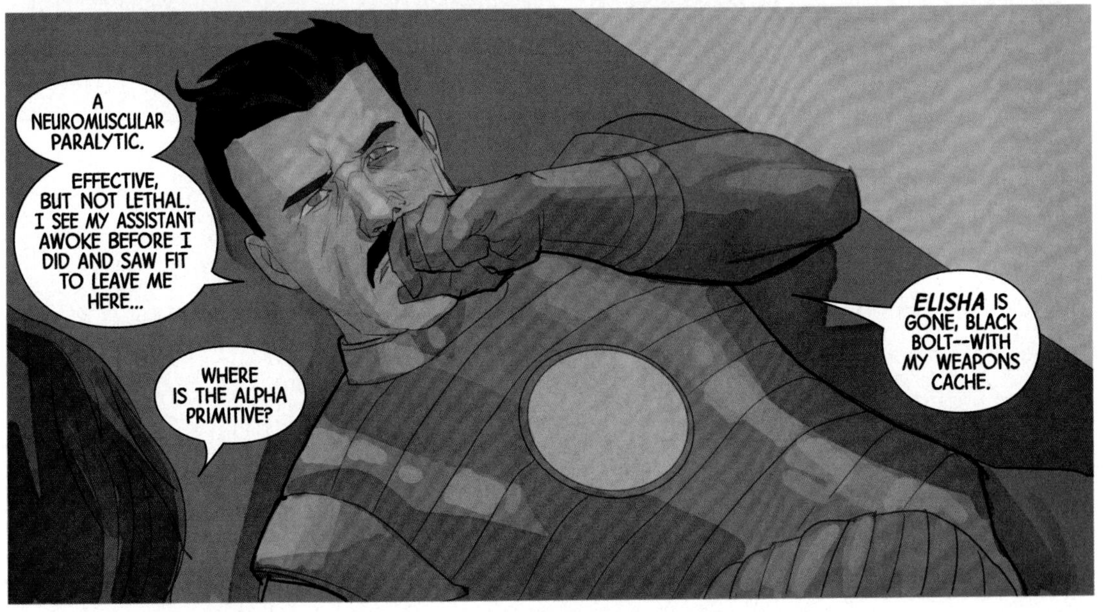
A NEUROMUSCULAR PARALYTIC.
EFFECTIVE, BUT NOT LETHAL. I SEE MY ASSISTANT AWOKE BEFORE I DID AND SAW FIT TO LEAVE ME HERE...
WHERE IS THE ALPHA PRIMITIVE?
ELISHA IS GONE, BLACK BOLT--WITH MY WEAPONS CACHE.

TRITON?

WATER.

THIS *"ELISHA"* IS THE ENHANCED ALPHA PRIMITIVE...?

HEADED FOR ATTILAN, ONE PRESUMES.

WITH THE WEAPONS YOU DEVELOPED FOR US.

IF THEY ACTUALLY *WERE* FOR US--

--WITTMAN HAD INSISTED ON ACCOMPANYING US HOME TO ATTILAN... WITH WEAPONS TO DEFEND AGAINST THE MAD KING...

...WEAPONS THAT COULD EASILY BE TURNED AGAINST *US.*

IT'S WHAT I WOULD DO...

YES, MAXIMUS. FOR THERE IS NONE MORE CRAVEN.

IT IS THE *MADNESS,* KARNAK, NOT A CHOICE--AN *AFFLICTION.*

THE *FEVER* THAT LED HIM INTO AN ALLIANCE WITH THE *KREE**--

**IN THE SILVER AGE OF *AVENGERS* (1963) #95. --WIL*

"--AND CAUSED THE *DEATH* OF A *KING.*"

MOTHER... FATHER...

...WHAT HAVE I...

...WHAT HAVE *YOU* DONE, BROTHER?!

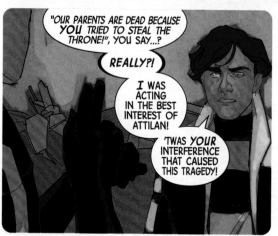

"OUR PARENTS ARE DEAD BECAUSE *YOU* TRIED TO STEAL THE THRONE!", YOU SAY...?

REALLY?!

I WAS ACTING IN THE BEST INTEREST OF ATTILAN!

'TWAS *YOUR* INTERFERENCE THAT CAUSED THIS TRAGEDY!

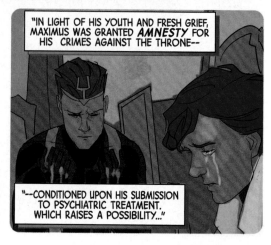

"IN LIGHT OF HIS YOUTH AND FRESH GRIEF, MAXIMUS WAS GRANTED *AMNESTY* FOR HIS CRIMES AGAINST THE THRONE--

"--CONDITIONED UPON HIS SUBMISSION TO PSYCHIATRIC TREATMENT. WHICH RAISES A POSSIBILITY..."

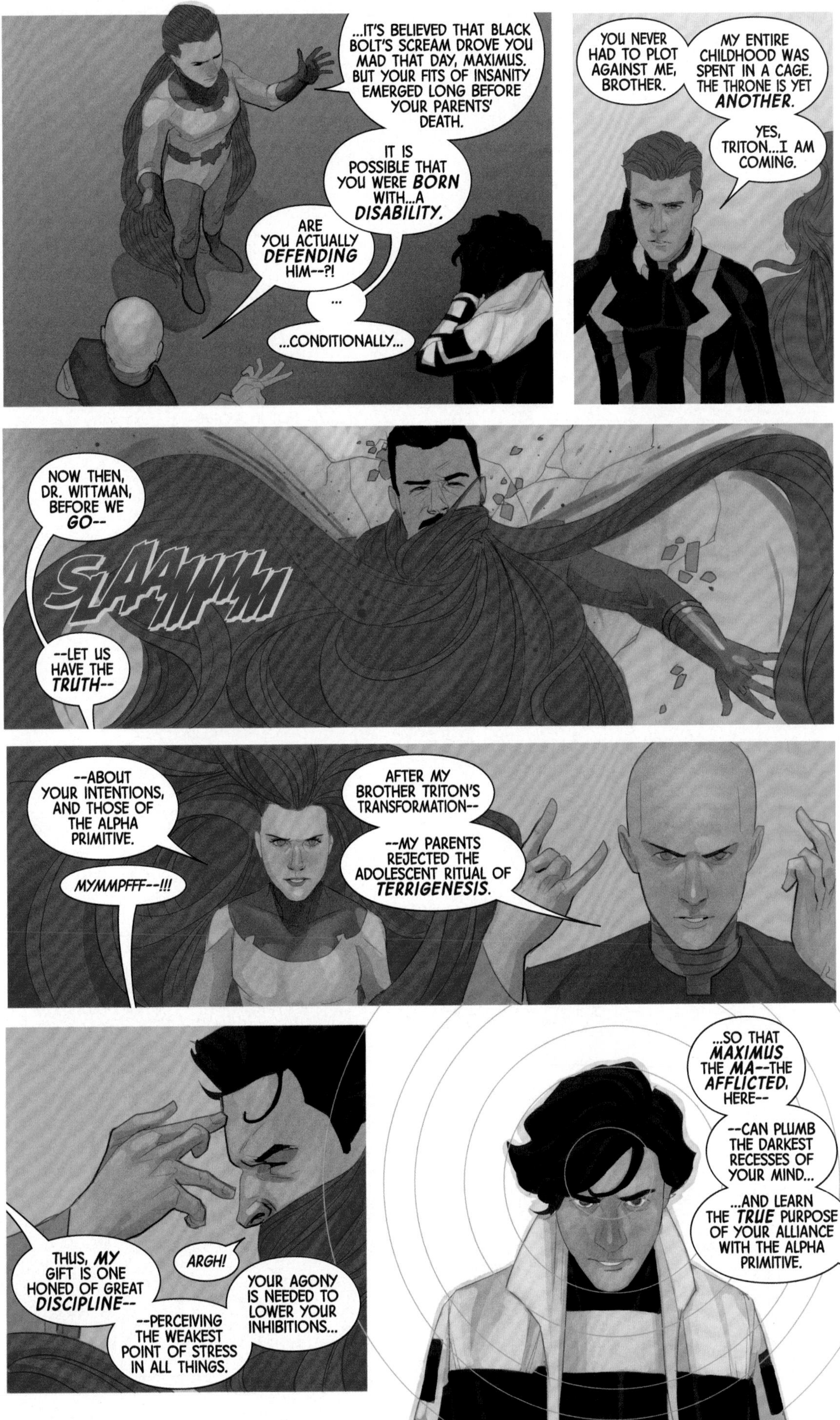

...IT'S BELIEVED THAT BLACK BOLT'S SCREAM DROVE YOU MAD THAT DAY, MAXIMUS. BUT YOUR FITS OF INSANITY EMERGED LONG BEFORE YOUR PARENTS' DEATH.
IT IS POSSIBLE THAT YOU WERE BORN WITH...A DISABILITY.
ARE YOU ACTUALLY DEFENDING HIM--?!
...
...CONDITIONALLY...
YOU NEVER HAD TO PLOT AGAINST ME, BROTHER.
MY ENTIRE CHILDHOOD WAS SPENT IN A CAGE. THE THRONE IS YET ANOTHER.
YES, TRITON...I AM COMING.
NOW THEN, DR. WITTMAN, BEFORE WE GO--
SLAAMMM
--LET US HAVE THE TRUTH--
--ABOUT YOUR INTENTIONS, AND THOSE OF THE ALPHA PRIMITIVE.
MYMMPFFF--!!!
AFTER MY BROTHER TRITON'S TRANSFORMATION--
--MY PARENTS REJECTED THE ADOLESCENT RITUAL OF TERRIGENESIS.
THUS, MY GIFT IS ONE HONED OF GREAT DISCIPLINE--
--PERCEIVING THE WEAKEST POINT OF STRESS IN ALL THINGS.
ARGH!
YOUR AGONY IS NEEDED TO LOWER YOUR INHIBITIONS...
...SO THAT MAXIMUS THE MA--THE AFFLICTED, HERE--
--CAN PLUMB THE DARKEST RECESSES OF YOUR MIND...
...AND LEARN THE TRUE PURPOSE OF YOUR ALLIANCE WITH THE ALPHA PRIMITIVE.

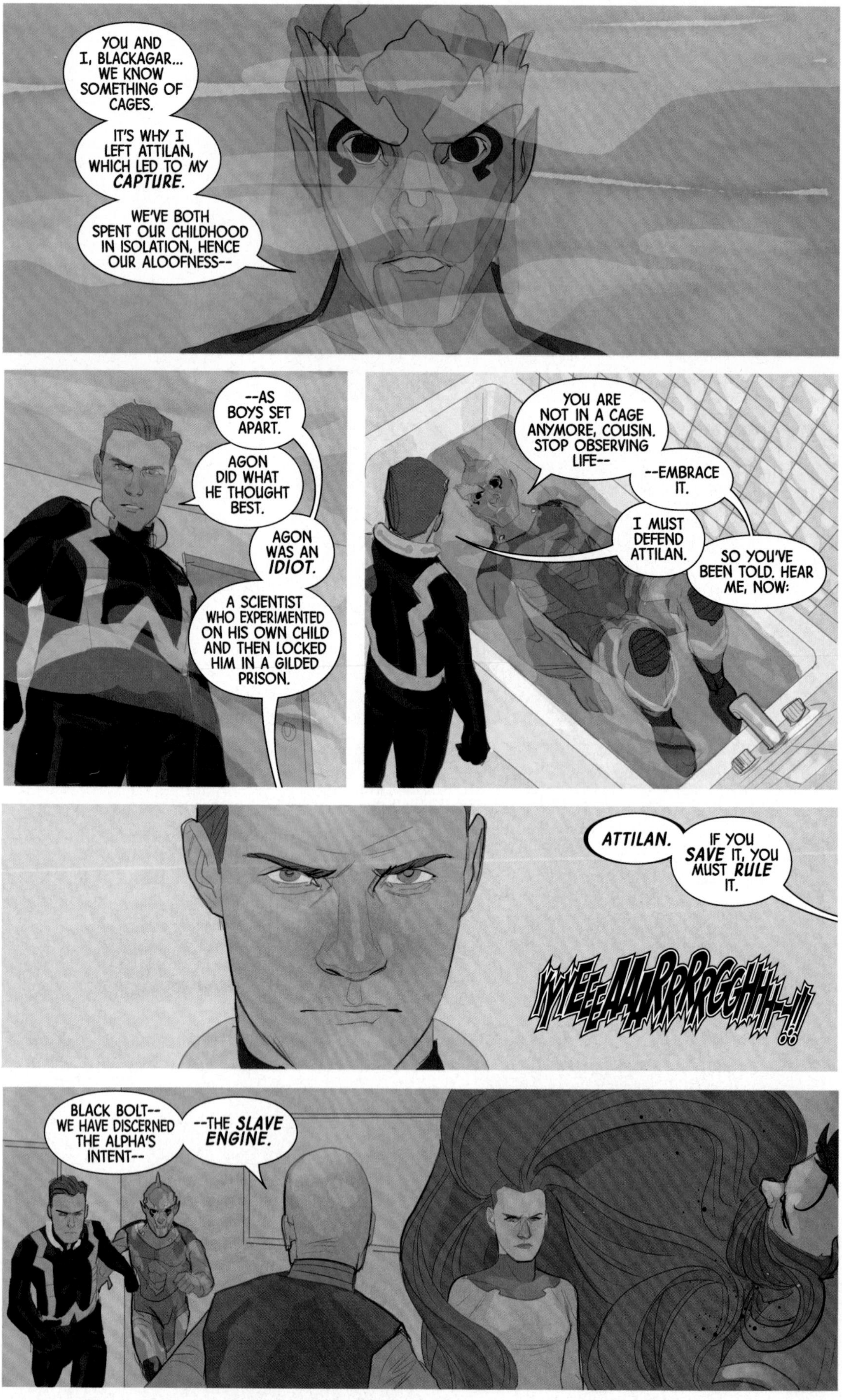
YOU AND I, BLACKAGAR... WE KNOW SOMETHING OF CAGES.
IT'S WHY I LEFT ATTILAN, WHICH LED TO MY *CAPTURE*.
WE'VE BOTH SPENT OUR CHILDHOOD IN ISOLATION, HENCE OUR ALOOFNESS--
--AS BOYS SET APART.
AGON DID WHAT HE THOUGHT BEST.
AGON WAS AN *IDIOT*.
A SCIENTIST WHO EXPERIMENTED ON HIS OWN CHILD AND THEN LOCKED HIM IN A GILDED PRISON.
YOU ARE NOT IN A CAGE ANYMORE, COUSIN. STOP OBSERVING LIFE--
--EMBRACE IT.
I MUST DEFEND ATTILAN.
SO YOU'VE BEEN TOLD. HEAR ME, NOW:
ATTILAN.
IF YOU *SAVE* IT, YOU MUST *RULE* IT.
YYEEEAAARRRRGGHHH--!!
BLACK BOLT-- WE HAVE DISCERNED THE ALPHA'S INTENT--
--THE *SLAVE ENGINE.*

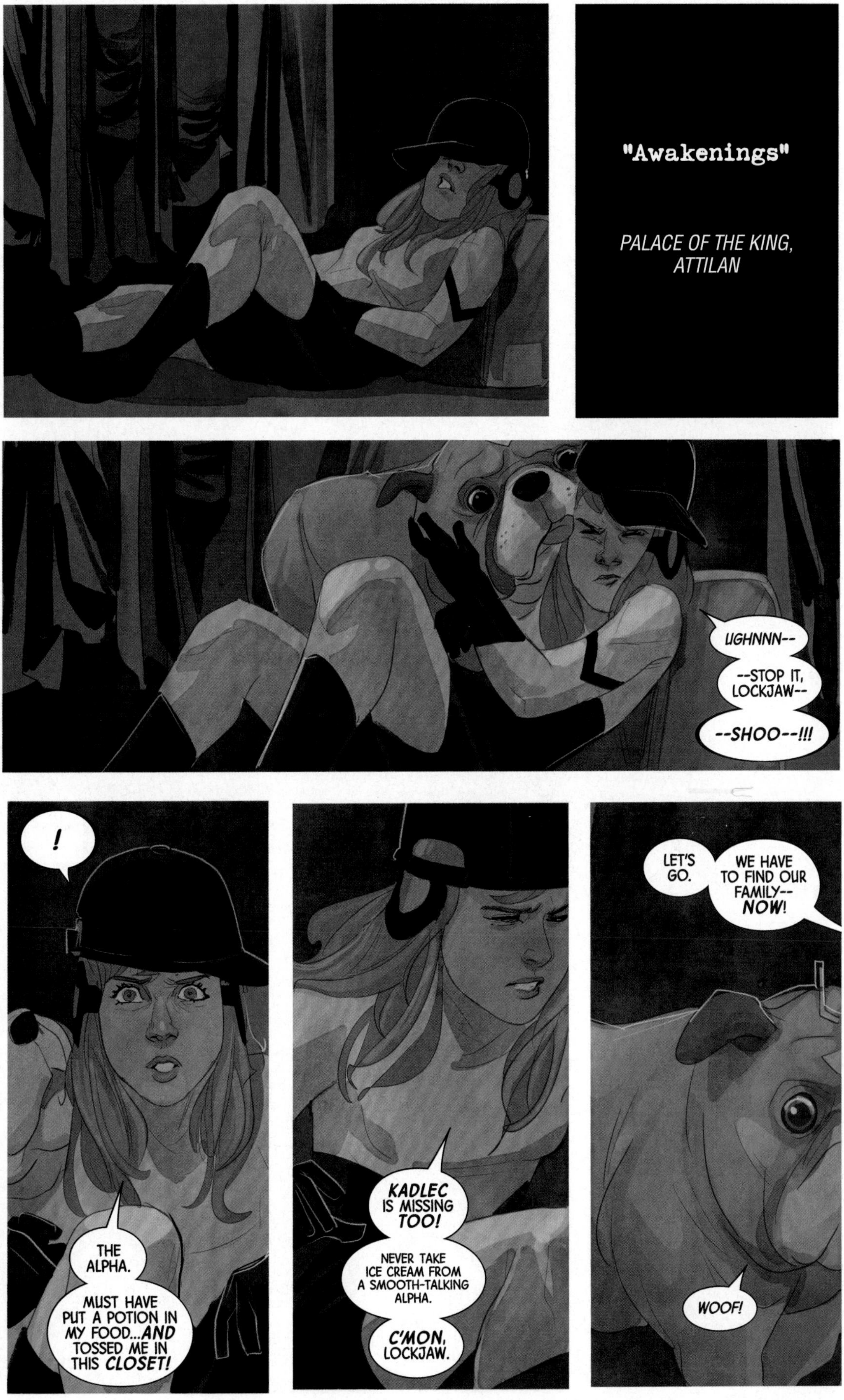
"Awakenings"
PALACE OF THE KING, ATTILAN
UGHNNN--
--STOP IT, LOCKJAW--
--SHOO--!!!
!
THE ALPHA.
MUST HAVE PUT A POTION IN MY FOOD...AND TOSSED ME IN THIS CLOSET!
KADLEC IS MISSING TOO!
NEVER TAKE ICE CREAM FROM A SMOOTH-TALKING ALPHA.
C'MON, LOCKJAW.
LET'S GO.
WE HAVE TO FIND OUR FAMILY--NOW!
WOOF!

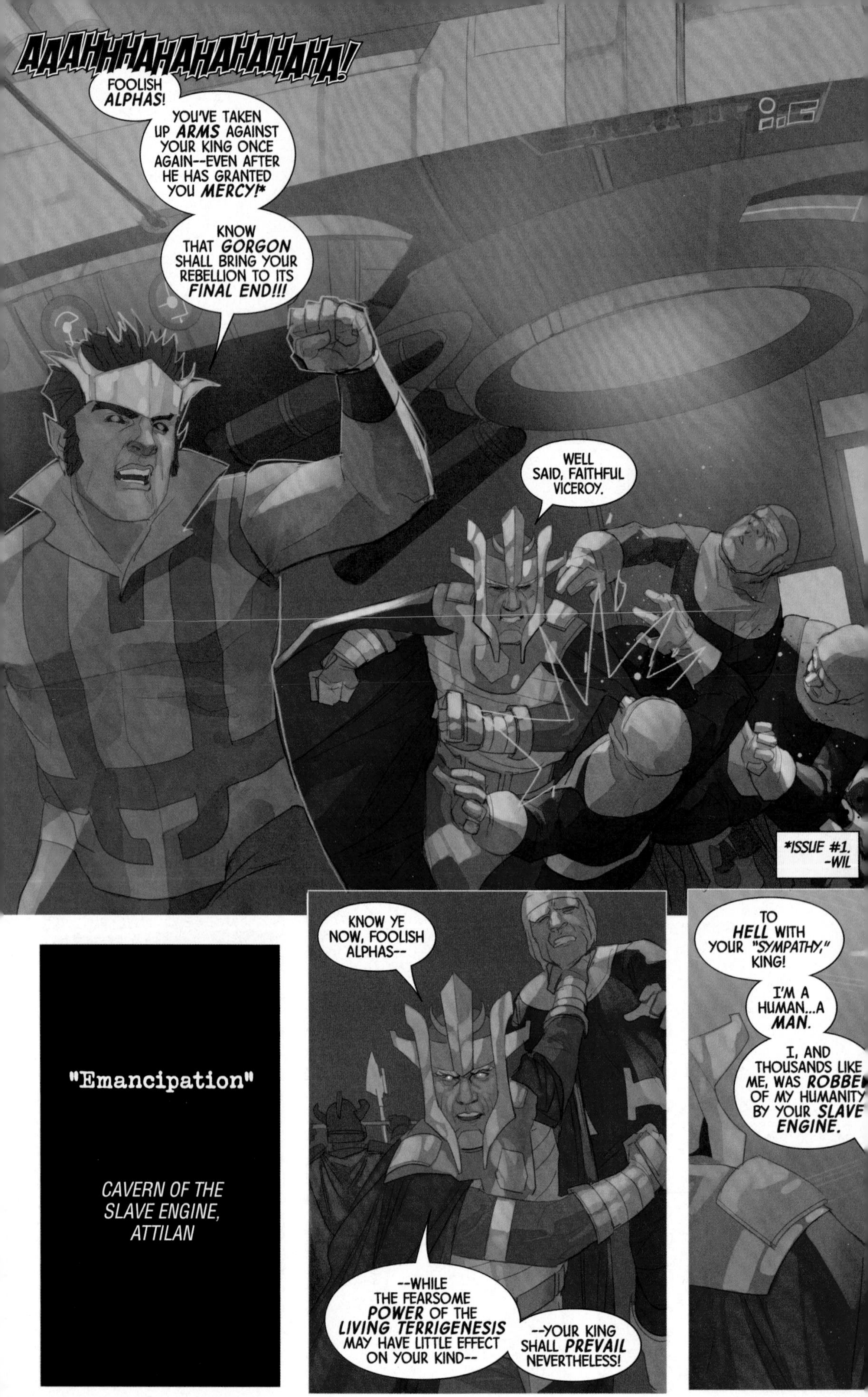
AAAHHHAHAHAHAHAHA!
FOOLISH ALPHAS!
YOU'VE TAKEN UP ARMS AGAINST YOUR KING ONCE AGAIN--EVEN AFTER HE HAS GRANTED YOU MERCY!*
KNOW THAT GORGON SHALL BRING YOUR REBELLION TO ITS FINAL END!!!
WELL SAID, FAITHFUL VICEROY.
*ISSUE #1. -WIL
"Emancipation"
CAVERN OF THE SLAVE ENGINE, ATTILAN
KNOW YE NOW, FOOLISH ALPHAS--
--WHILE THE FEARSOME POWER OF THE LIVING TERRIGENESIS MAY HAVE LITTLE EFFECT ON YOUR KIND--
--YOUR KING SHALL PREVAIL NEVERTHELESS!
TO HELL WITH YOUR "SYMPATHY," KING!
I'M A HUMAN...A MAN.
I, AND THOUSANDS LIKE ME, WAS ROBBE
OF MY HUMANITY BY YOUR SLAVE ENGINE.

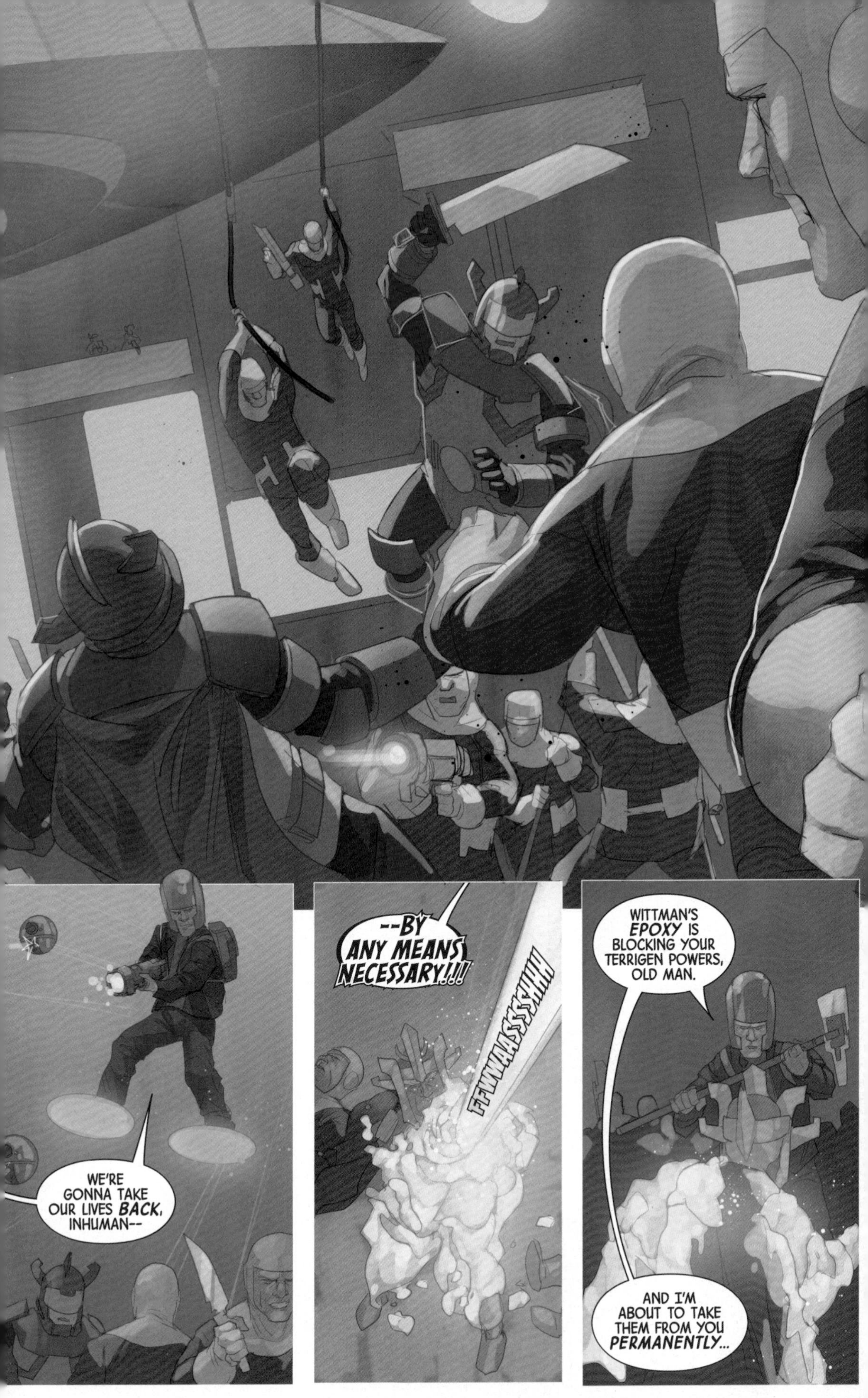
WE'RE GONNA TAKE OUR LIVES BACK, INHUMAN--
--BY ANY MEANS NECESSARY!!!
FFWAASSSHHH
WITTMAN'S EPOXY IS BLOCKING YOUR TERRIGEN POWERS, OLD MAN.
AND I'M ABOUT TO TAKE THEM FROM YOU PERMANENTLY...

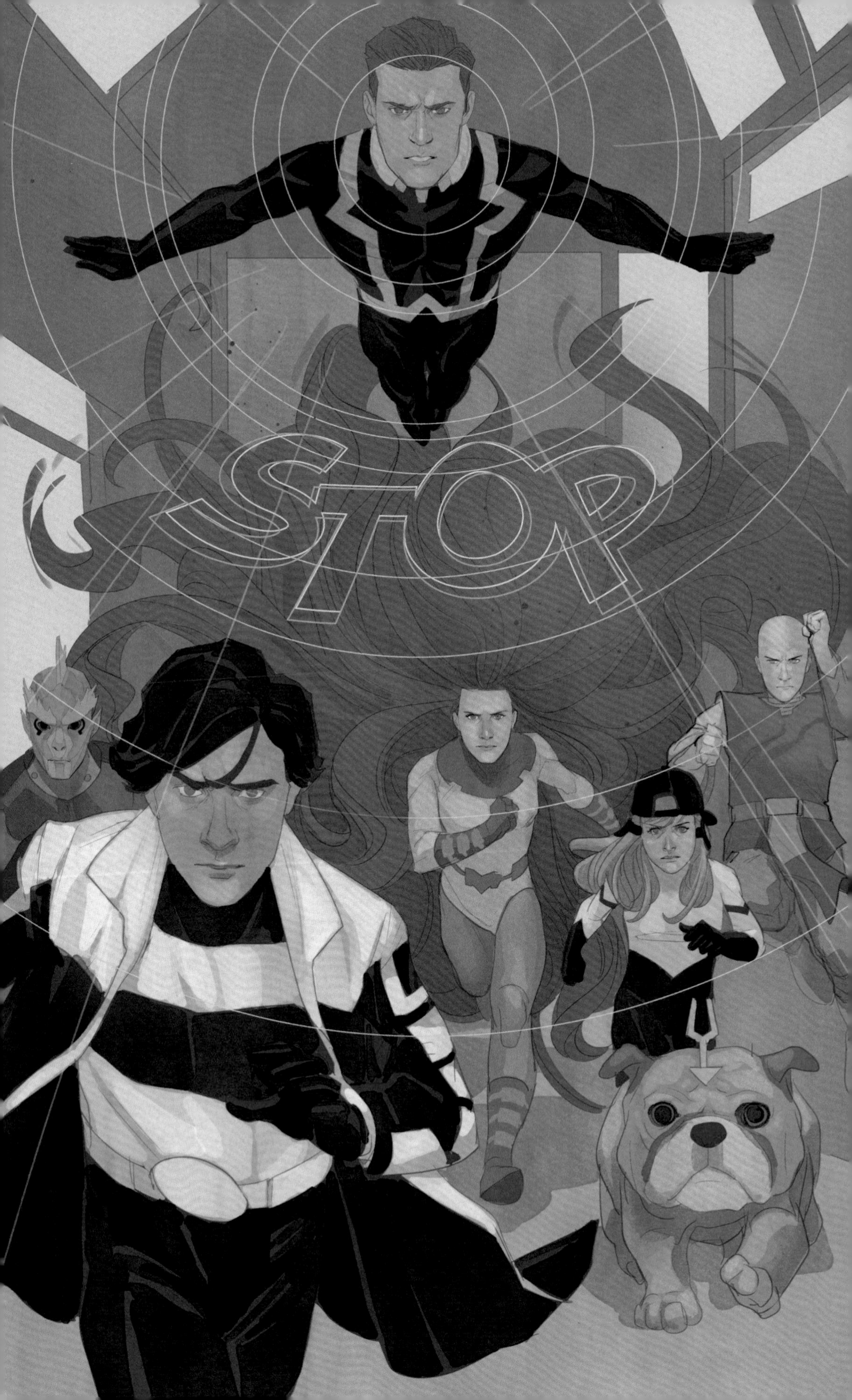
STOP

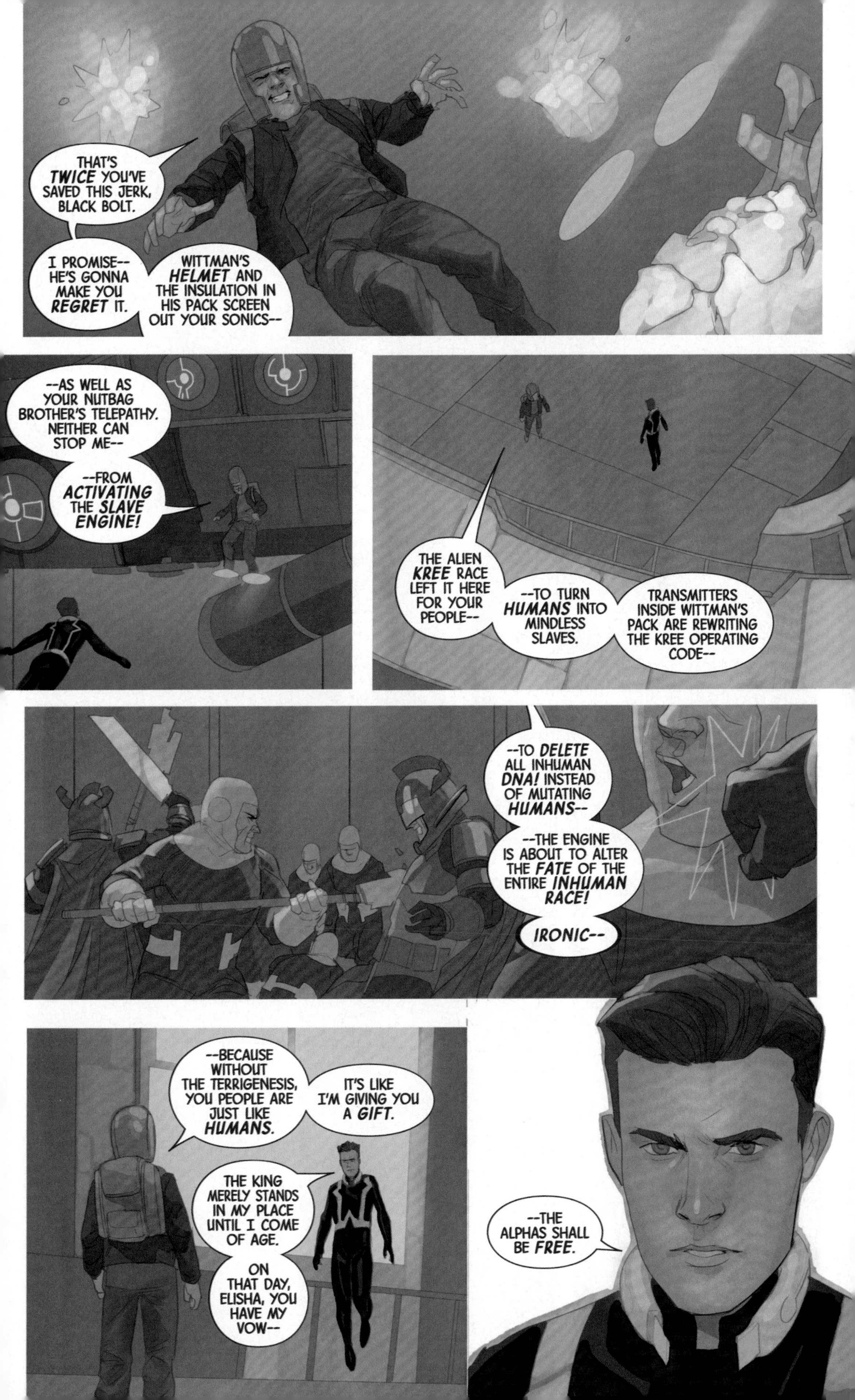
THAT'S TWICE YOU'VE SAVED THIS JERK, BLACK BOLT.
I PROMISE-- HE'S GONNA MAKE YOU REGRET IT.
WITTMAN'S HELMET AND THE INSULATION IN HIS PACK SCREEN OUT YOUR SONICS--
--AS WELL AS YOUR NUTBAG BROTHER'S TELEPATHY. NEITHER CAN STOP ME--
--FROM ACTIVATING THE SLAVE ENGINE!
THE ALIEN KREE RACE LEFT IT HERE FOR YOUR PEOPLE--
--TO TURN HUMANS INTO MINDLESS SLAVES.
TRANSMITTERS INSIDE WITTMAN'S PACK ARE REWRITING THE KREE OPERATING CODE--
--TO DELETE ALL INHUMAN DNA! INSTEAD OF MUTATING HUMANS--
--THE ENGINE IS ABOUT TO ALTER THE FATE OF THE ENTIRE INHUMAN RACE!
IRONIC--
--BECAUSE WITHOUT THE TERRIGENESIS, YOU PEOPLE ARE JUST LIKE HUMANS.
IT'S LIKE I'M GIVING YOU A GIFT.
THE KING MERELY STANDS IN MY PLACE UNTIL I COME OF AGE.
ON THAT DAY, ELISHA, YOU HAVE MY VOW--
--THE ALPHAS SHALL BE FREE.

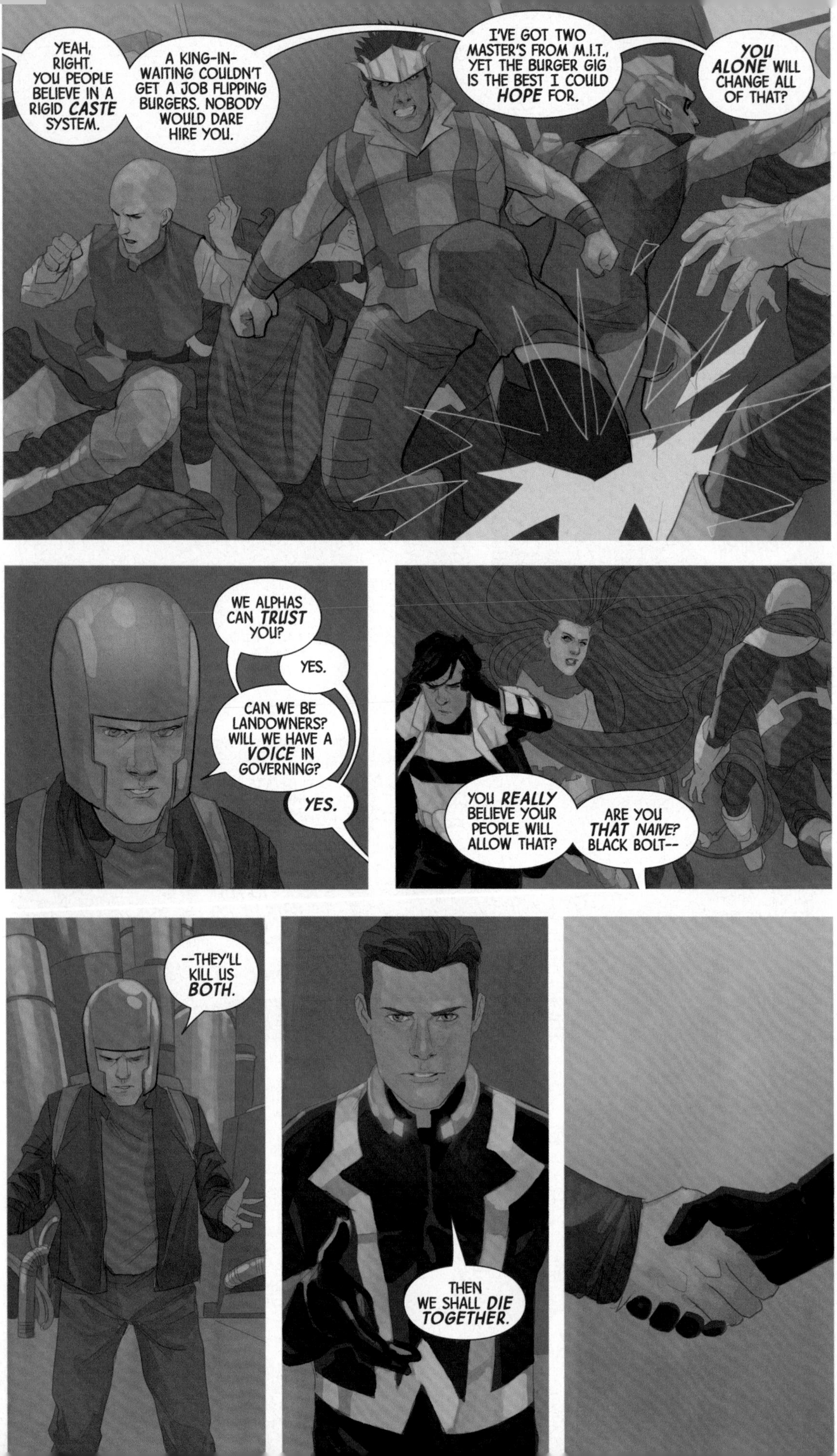
YEAH, RIGHT. YOU PEOPLE BELIEVE IN A RIGID *CASTE* SYSTEM.
A KING-IN-WAITING COULDN'T GET A JOB FLIPPING BURGERS. NOBODY WOULD DARE HIRE YOU.
I'VE GOT TWO MASTER'S FROM M.I.T., YET THE BURGER GIG IS THE BEST I COULD *HOPE* FOR.
YOU ALONE WILL CHANGE ALL OF THAT?
WE ALPHAS CAN *TRUST* YOU?
YES.
CAN WE BE LANDOWNERS? WILL WE HAVE A *VOICE* IN GOVERNING?
YES.
YOU *REALLY* BELIEVE YOUR PEOPLE WILL ALLOW THAT?
ARE YOU *THAT NAIVE?* BLACK BOLT--
--THEY'LL KILL US *BOTH.*
THEN WE SHALL *DIE TOGETHER.*

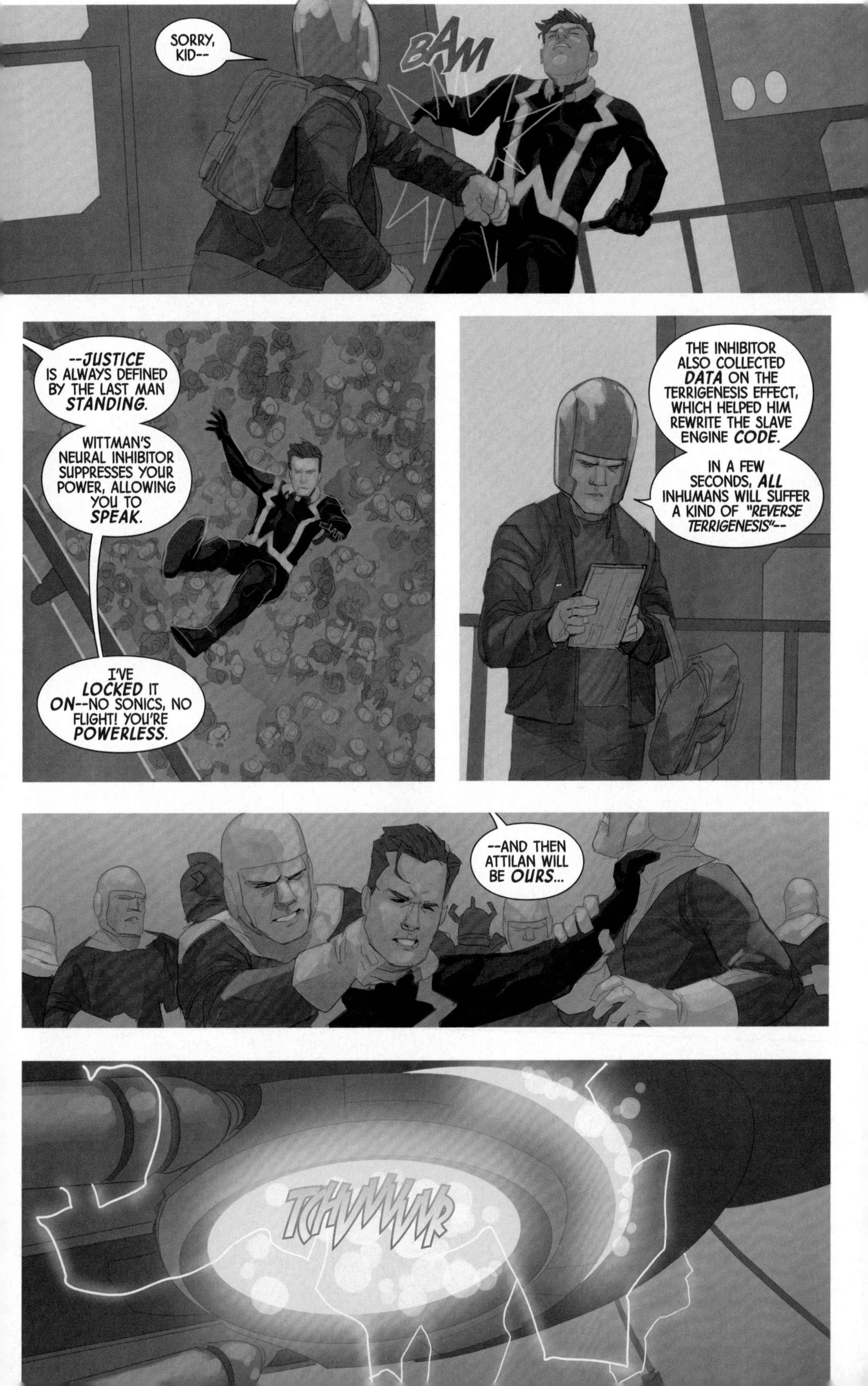
SORRY, KID--
BAM
--JUSTICE IS ALWAYS DEFINED BY THE LAST MAN STANDING.
WITTMAN'S NEURAL INHIBITOR SUPPRESSES YOUR POWER, ALLOWING YOU TO SPEAK.
I'VE LOCKED IT ON--NO SONICS, NO FLIGHT! YOU'RE POWERLESS.
THE INHIBITOR ALSO COLLECTED DATA ON THE TERRIGENESIS EFFECT, WHICH HELPED HIM REWRITE THE SLAVE ENGINE CODE.
IN A FEW SECONDS, ALL INHUMANS WILL SUFFER A KIND OF "REVERSE TERRIGENESIS"--
--AND THEN ATTILAN WILL BE OURS...
TCHMMMR

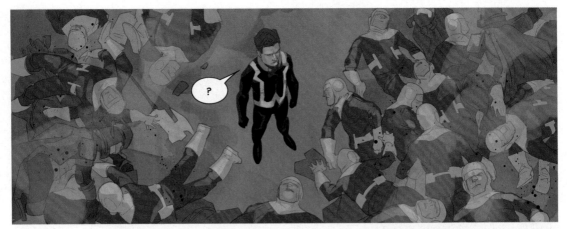

BLACK BOLT--ARE YOU--

MY BROTHER LIVES, MEDUSA--

--THANKS TO *MY* GENIUS. HAVING ACCESSED WITTMAN'S MIND--

--I WAS ABLE TO IMPLANT AN EXECUTABLE FILE INTO BLACK BOLT'S NEURAL INHIBITOR SYSTEM--

--WHICH *OVERWROTE* ELISHA'S CODE TO *STUN* ALL ALPHA PRIMITIVES IN RANGE WHEN ACTIVATED.

NEED I SAY-- IT WOULD NEVER HAVE *COME* TO THIS HAD THE KING LISTENED TO ME IN THE FIRST PLACE...

PERHAPS, YOUNG MAXIMUS--

--YOUR KING IS NOT SO WISE AS HE IS *AGED.*

CLEARLY, DESPITE OUR TRADITIONS, THE ISSUE OF THE ALPHAS MUST BE REVISITED.

PERHAPS IT IS NOW TIME BLACK BOLT *LED* THE WAY.

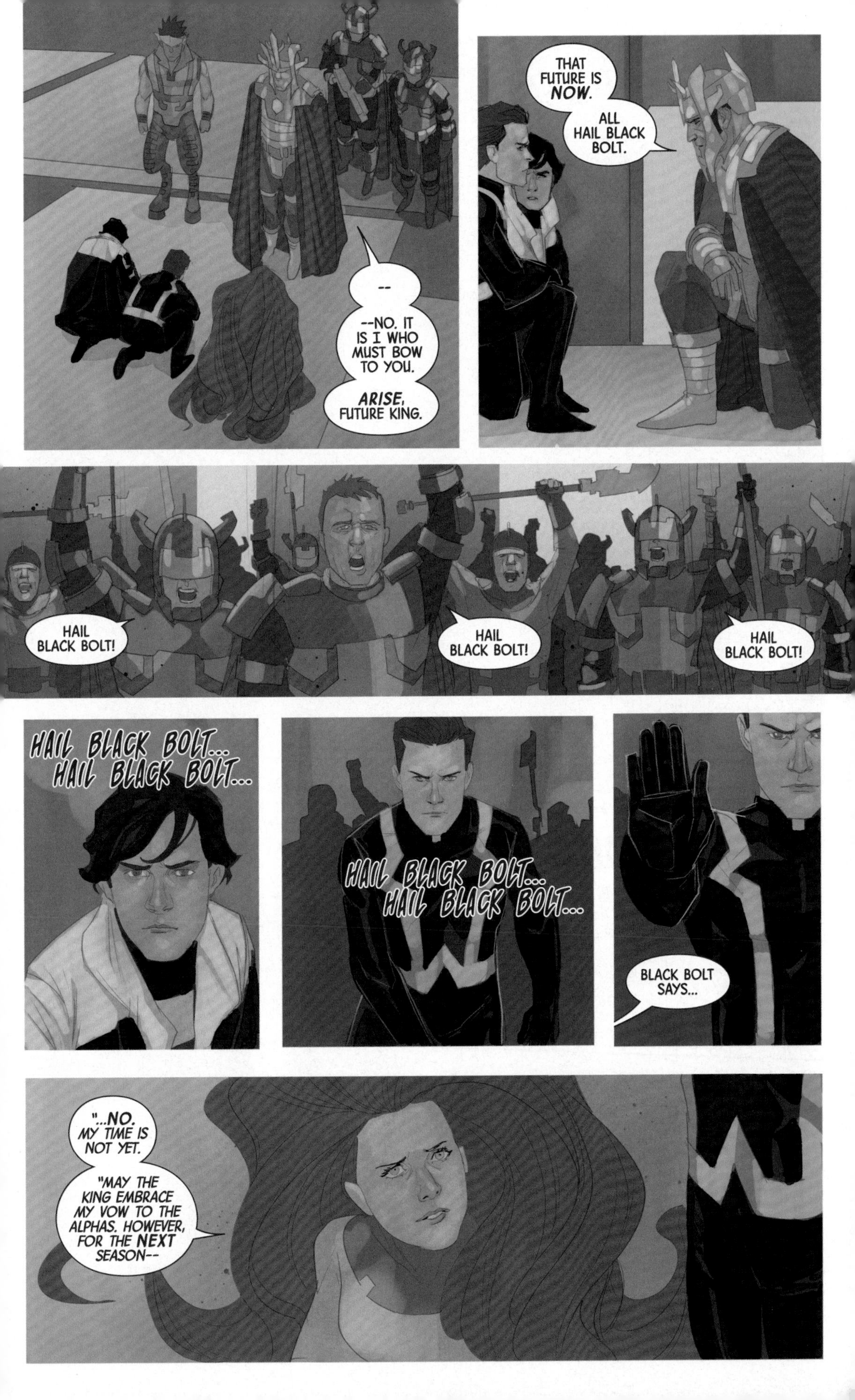
--
--NO. IT IS I WHO MUST BOW TO YOU.
ARISE, FUTURE KING.
THAT FUTURE IS NOW.
ALL HAIL BLACK BOLT.
HAIL BLACK BOLT!
HAIL BLACK BOLT!
HAIL BLACK BOLT!
HAIL BLACK BOLT... HAIL BLACK BOLT...
HAIL BLACK BOLT... HAIL BLACK BOLT...
BLACK BOLT SAYS...
"...NO. MY TIME IS NOT YET.
"MAY THE KING EMBRACE MY VOW TO THE ALPHAS. HOWEVER, FOR THE NEXT SEASON--

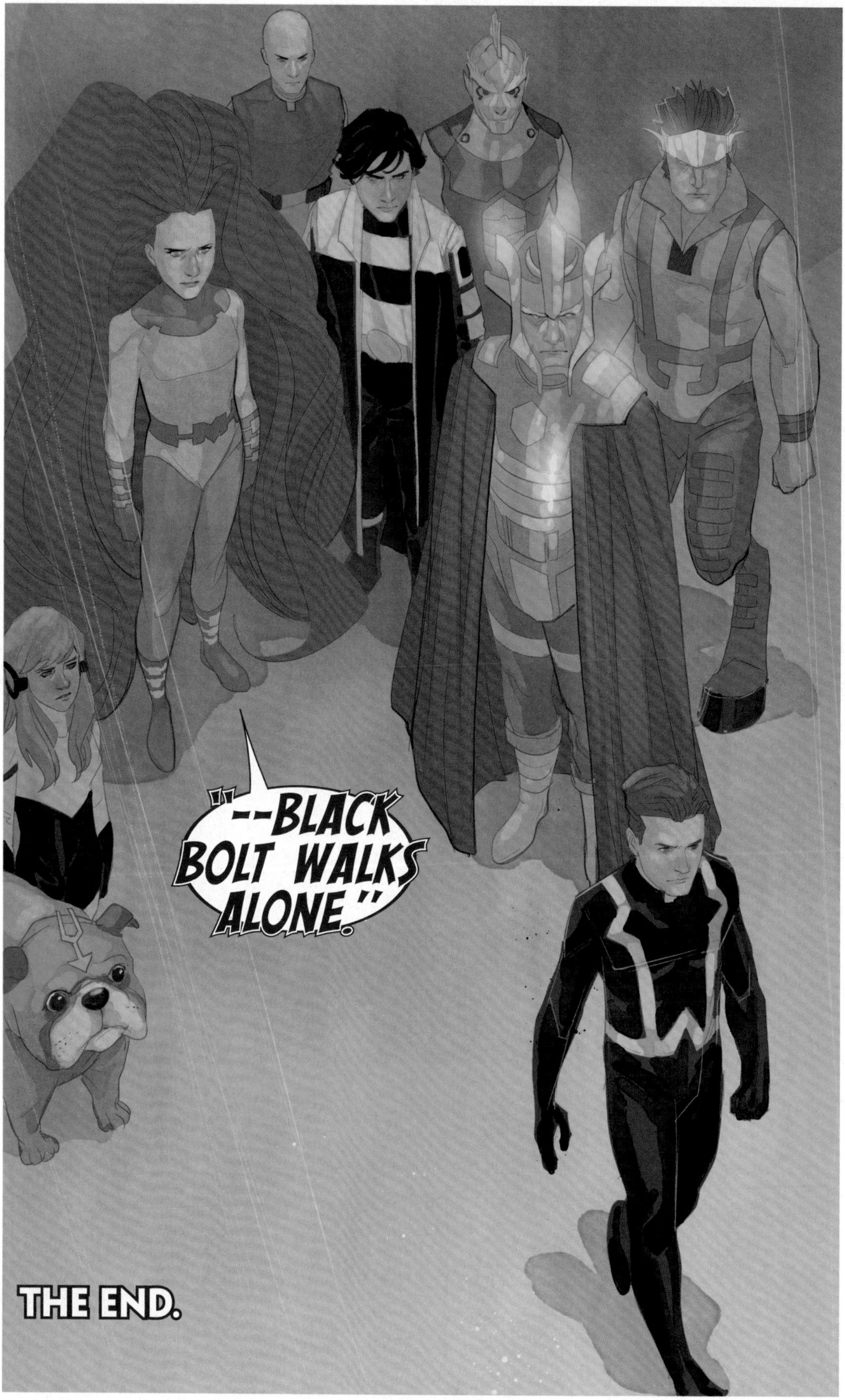
"--BLACK BOLT WALKS ALONE."
THE END.

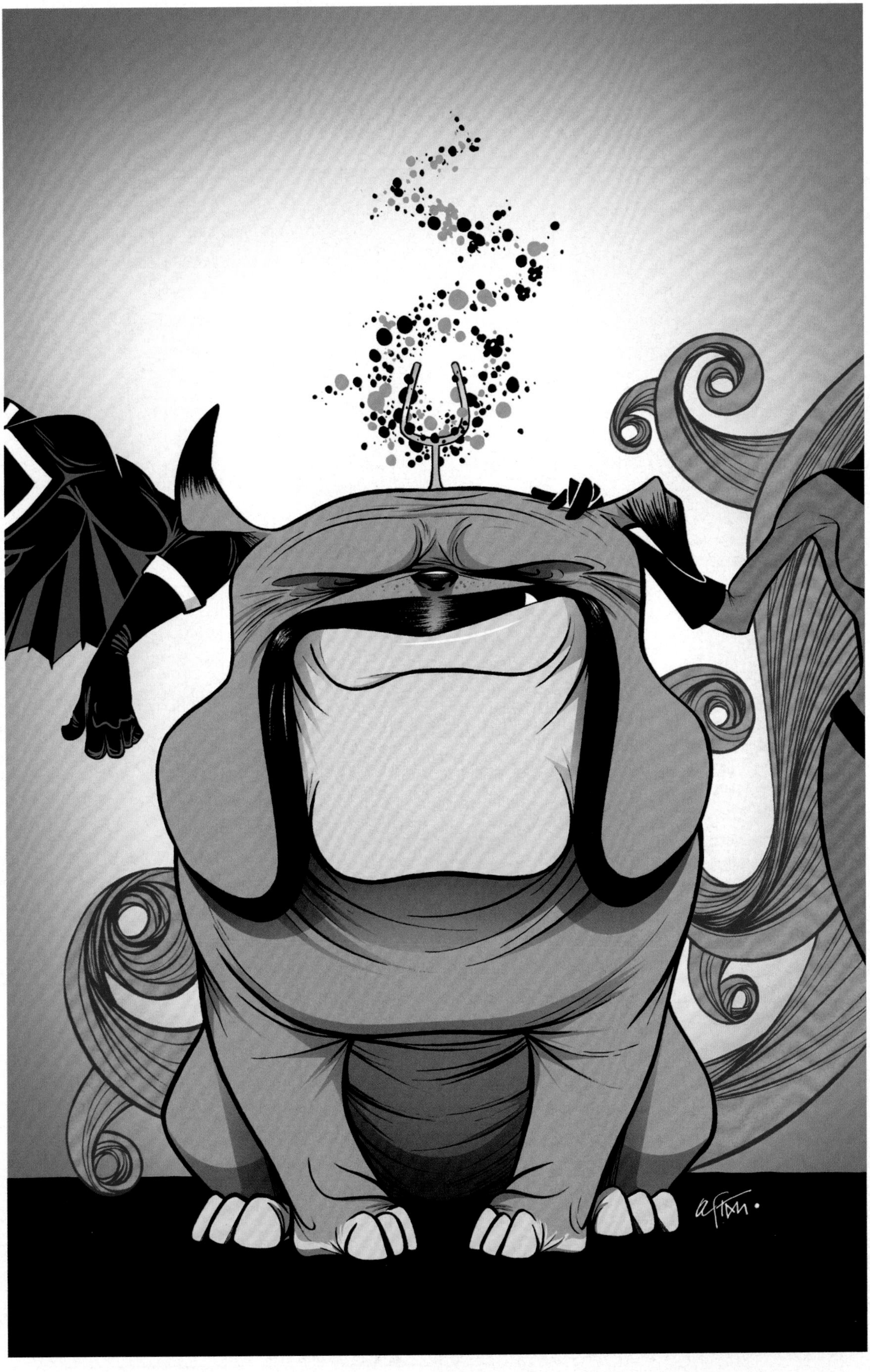

ONE VARIANT BY **GUSTAVO DUARTE**

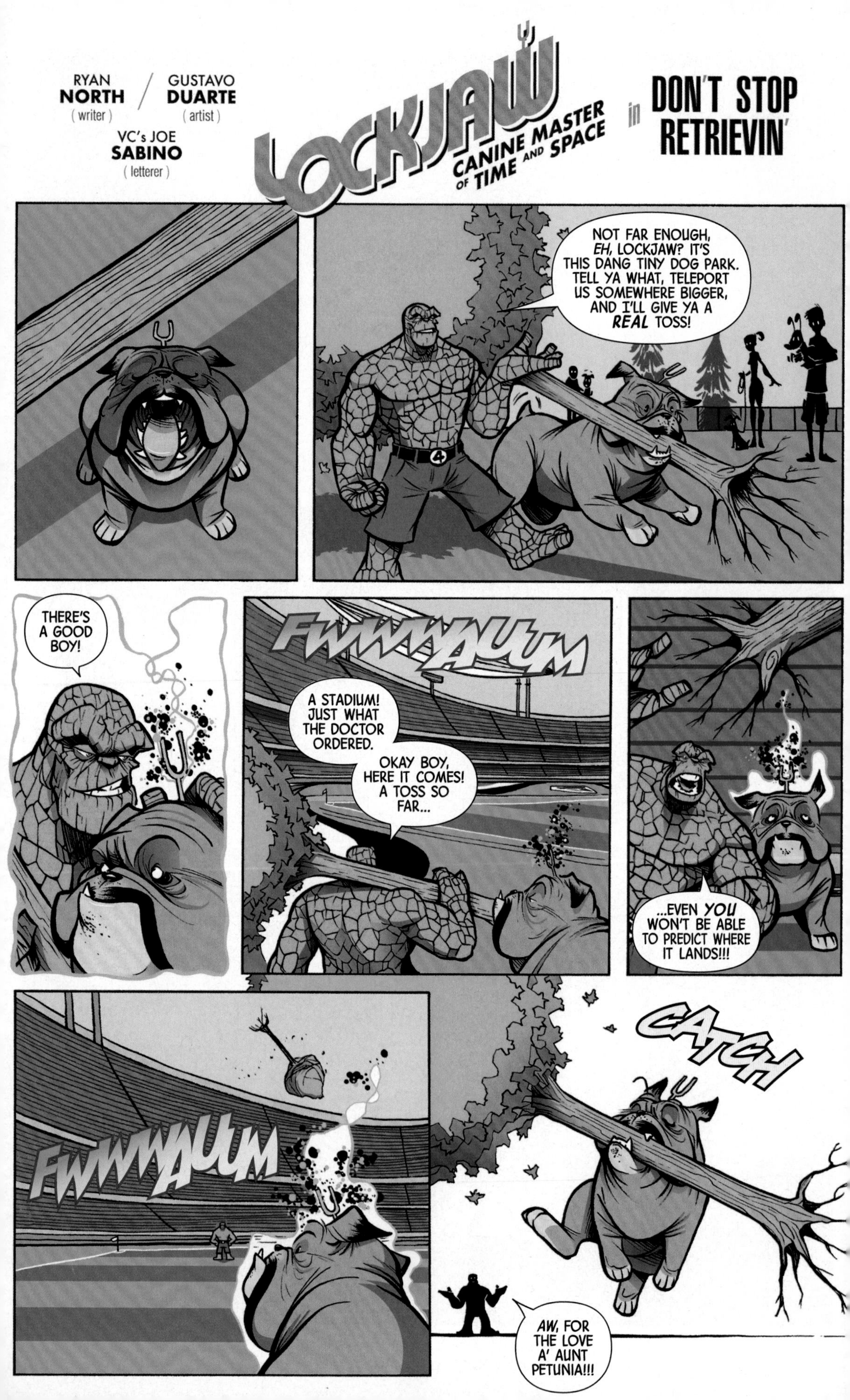
RYAN NORTH (writer) / GUSTAVO DUARTE (artist)
VC's JOE SABINO (letterer)
LOCKJAW CANINE MASTER OF TIME AND SPACE in DON'T STOP RETRIEVIN'
NOT FAR ENOUGH, EH, LOCKJAW? IT'S THIS DANG TINY DOG PARK. TELL YA WHAT, TELEPORT US SOMEWHERE BIGGER, AND I'LL GIVE YA A REAL TOSS!
THERE'S A GOOD BOY!
FWWWAUUM
A STADIUM! JUST WHAT THE DOCTOR ORDERED.
OKAY BOY, HERE IT COMES! A TOSS SO FAR...
...EVEN YOU WON'T BE ABLE TO PREDICT WHERE IT LANDS!!!
FWWWAUUM
CATCH
AW, FOR THE LOVE A' AUNT PETUNIA!!!

STILL TOO EASY, HUH? ALL RIGHT BUD, NO HOLDIN' BACK. I'M GONNA GIVE YA THE MAX POWER MEGATHROW. BUT WE'RE GONNA NEED TONS A' ROOM.
TAKE US TO THE TOP O' MOUNT EVEREST OR SOMETHIN', WILL YA?
FWWWAUUUM
PERFECT! NOW WATCH CLOSELY, LOCKJAW, BECAUSE...
IT'S...
...FETCHIN' TIME!!!
WELL?
EVEREST
SMAK!
GAH!
THE END

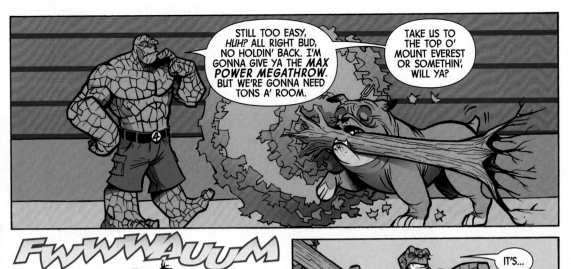

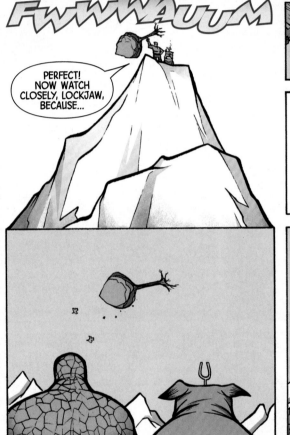

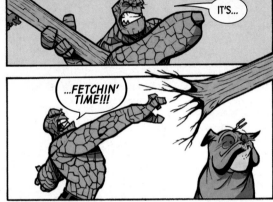

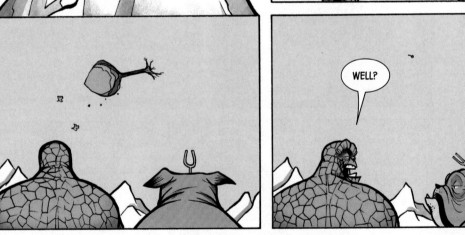

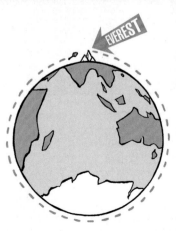

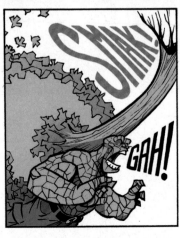

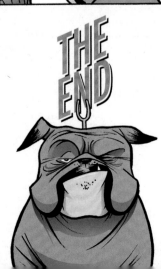

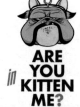

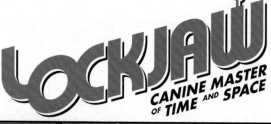

RYAN NORTH
(writer)
GUSTAVO DUARTE
(artist)
VC's JOE SABINO
(letterer)

LOCKJAW CANINE MASTER OF TIME AND SPACE in ARE YOU KITTEN ME?

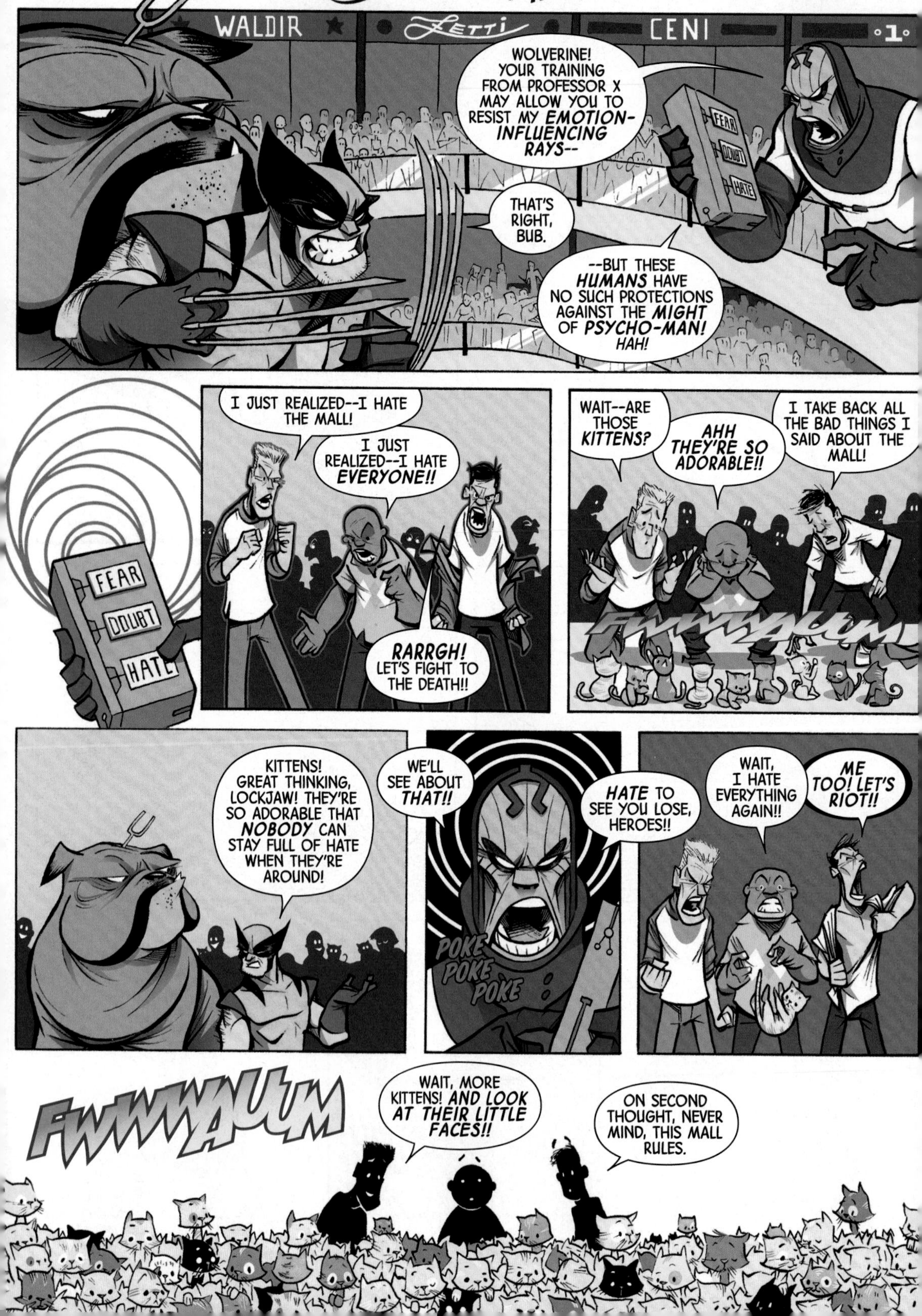

WALDIR
LETTI
CENI
1
WOLVERINE! YOUR TRAINING FROM PROFESSOR X MAY ALLOW YOU TO RESIST MY EMOTION-INFLUENCING RAYS--
THAT'S RIGHT, BUB.
--BUT THESE HUMANS HAVE NO SUCH PROTECTIONS AGAINST THE MIGHT OF PSYCHO-MAN! HAH!
FEAR
DOUBT
HATE
I JUST REALIZED--I HATE THE MALL!
I JUST REALIZED--I HATE EVERYONE!!
RARRGH! LET'S FIGHT TO THE DEATH!!
WAIT--ARE THOSE KITTENS?
AHH THEY'RE SO ADORABLE!!
I TAKE BACK ALL THE BAD THINGS I SAID ABOUT THE MALL!
FWWAUM
KITTENS! GREAT THINKING, LOCKJAW! THEY'RE SO ADORABLE THAT NOBODY CAN STAY FULL OF HATE WHEN THEY'RE AROUND!
WE'LL SEE ABOUT THAT!!
POKE POKE POKE
HATE TO SEE YOU LOSE, HEROES!!
WAIT, I HATE EVERYTHING AGAIN!!
ME TOO! LET'S RIOT!!
FWWAUM
WAIT, MORE KITTENS! AND LOOK AT THEIR LITTLE FACES!!
ON SECOND THOUGHT, NEVER MIND, THIS MALL RULES.

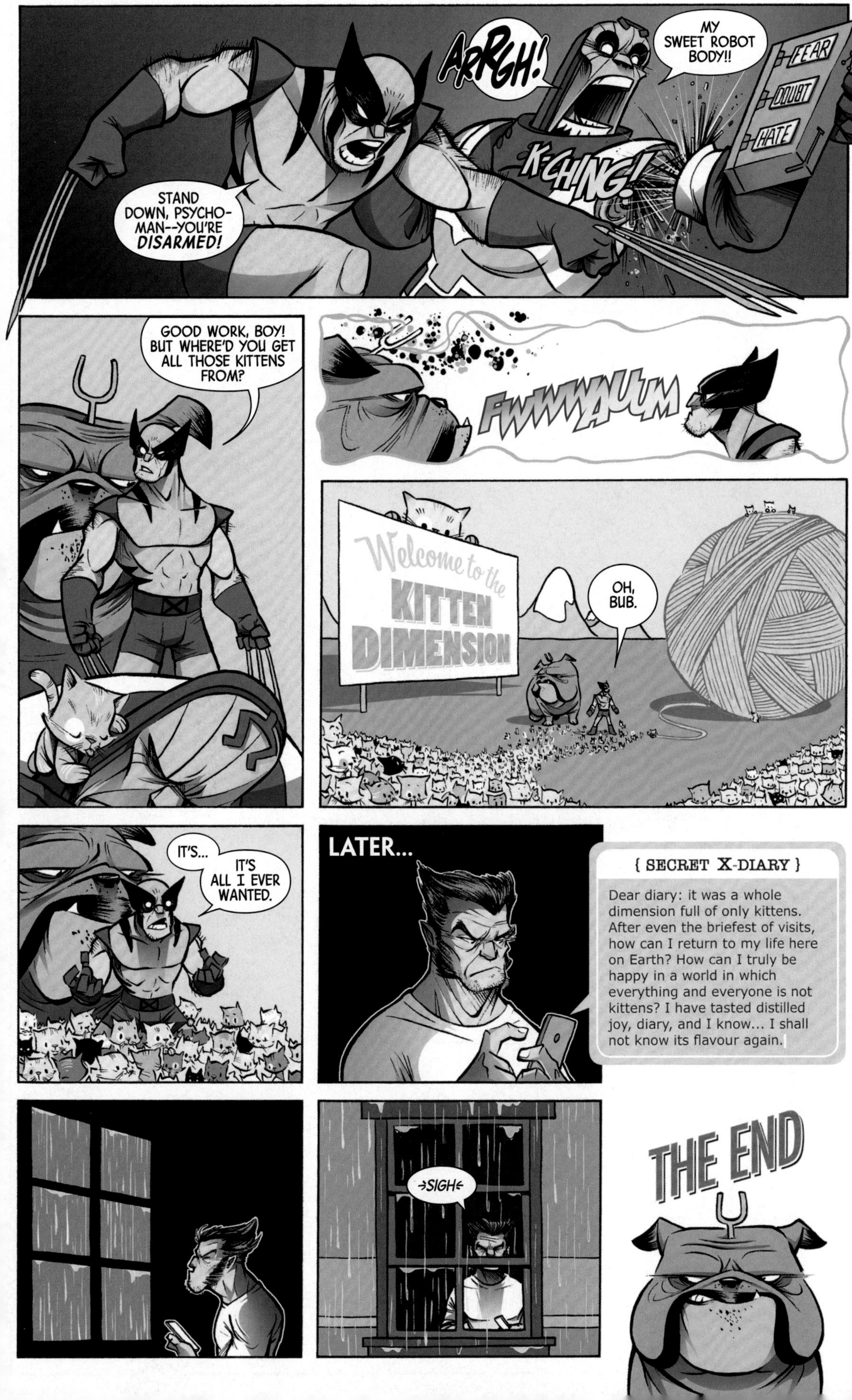
ARRGH!
MY SWEET ROBOT BODY!!
FEAR
DOUBT
HATE
K-CHING!
STAND DOWN, PSYCHO-MAN--YOU'RE DISARMED!
GOOD WORK, BOY! BUT WHERE'D YOU GET ALL THOSE KITTENS FROM?
FWWAUUM
Welcome to the KITTEN DIMENSION
OH, BUB.
IT'S...
IT'S ALL I EVER WANTED.
LATER...
{ SECRET X-DIARY }
Dear diary: it was a whole dimension full of only kittens. After even the briefest of visits, how can I return to my life here on Earth? How can I truly be happy in a world in which everything and everyone is not kittens? I have tasted distilled joy, diary, and I know... I shall not know its flavour again.
SIGH
THE END

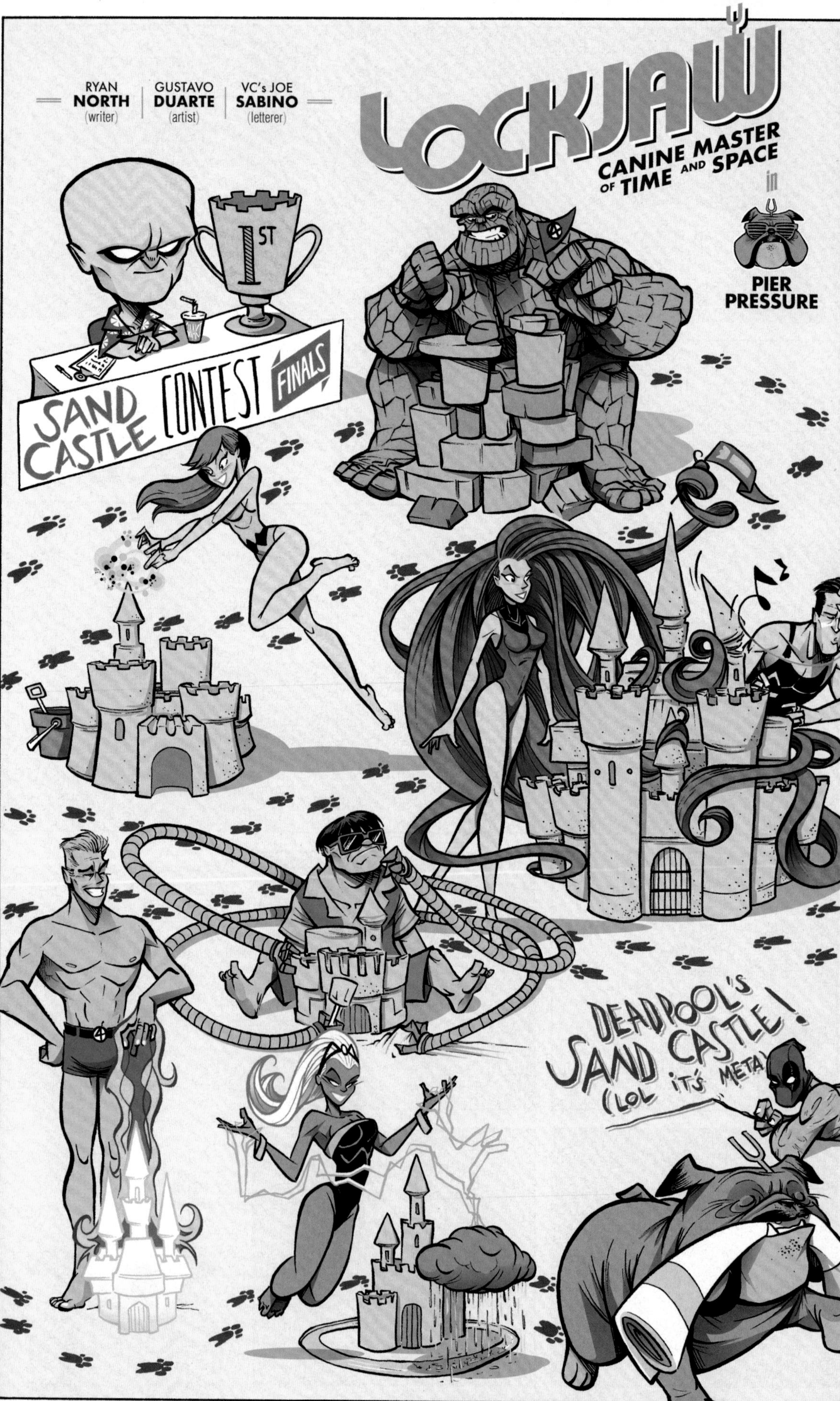
RYAN NORTH (writer)
GUSTAVO DUARTE (artist)
VC's JOE SABINO (letterer)
LOCKJAW
CANINE MASTER OF TIME AND SPACE
in
PIER PRESSURE
1ST
SAND CASTLE CONTEST FINALS
DEADPOOL'S SAND CASTLE! (LOL IT'S META)

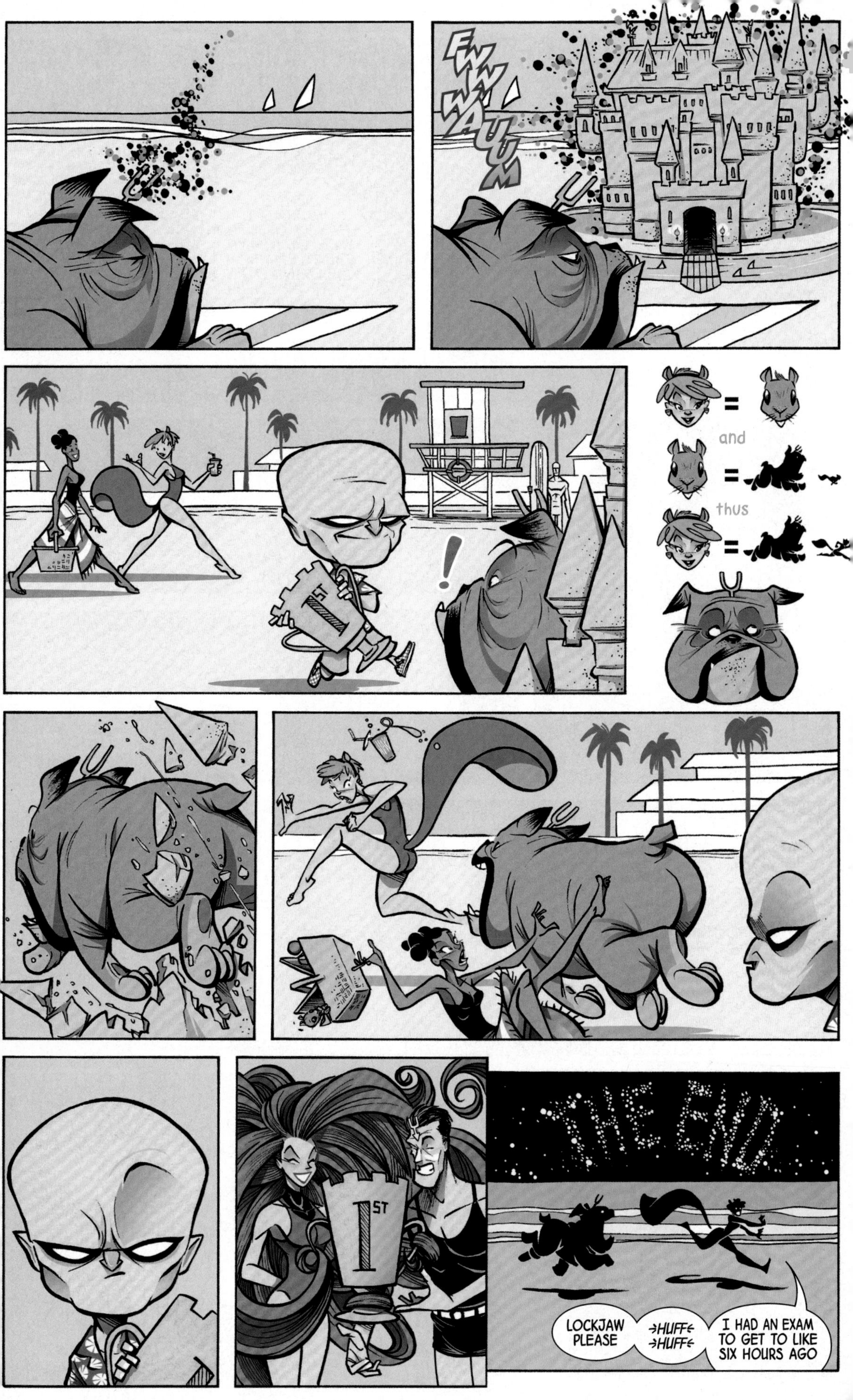
FWWAUUM
and
thus
1ST
THE END
LOCKJAW PLEASE
HUFF HUFF
I HAD AN EXAM TO GET TO LIKE SIX HOURS AGO

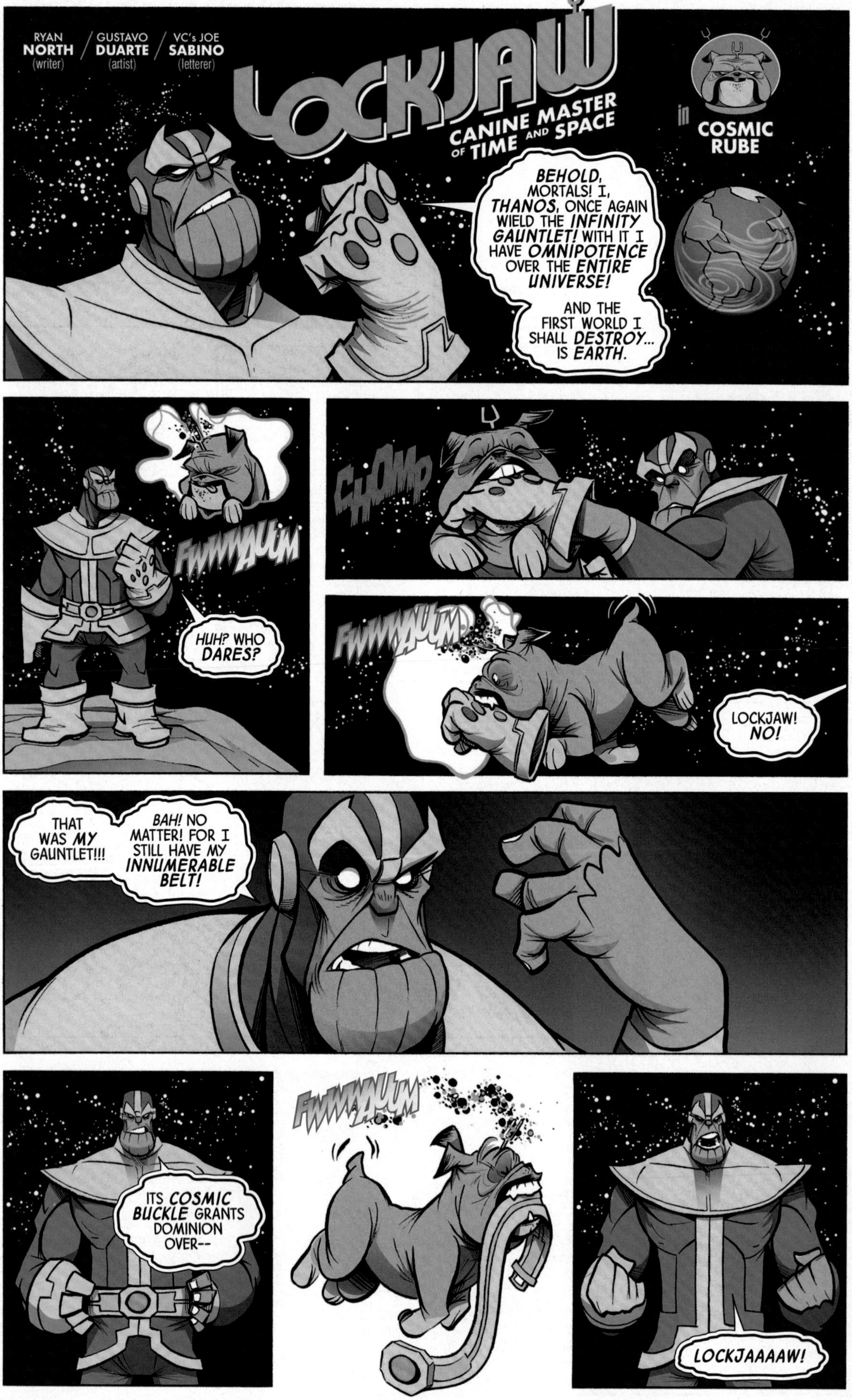
RYAN NORTH (writer) / GUSTAVO DUARTE (artist) / VC's JOE SABINO (letterer)
LOCKJAW
CANINE MASTER OF TIME AND SPACE
in
COSMIC RUBE
BEHOLD, MORTALS! I, THANOS, ONCE AGAIN WIELD THE INFINITY GAUNTLET! WITH IT I HAVE OMNIPOTENCE OVER THE ENTIRE UNIVERSE!
AND THE FIRST WORLD I SHALL DESTROY... IS EARTH.
FWMAUM
HUH? WHO DARES?
CHOMP
FWMAUM
LOCKJAW! NO!
THAT WAS MY GAUNTLET!!!
BAH! NO MATTER! FOR I STILL HAVE MY INNUMERABLE BELT!
ITS COSMIC BUCKLE GRANTS DOMINION OVER--
FWMAUM
LOCKJAAAAW!

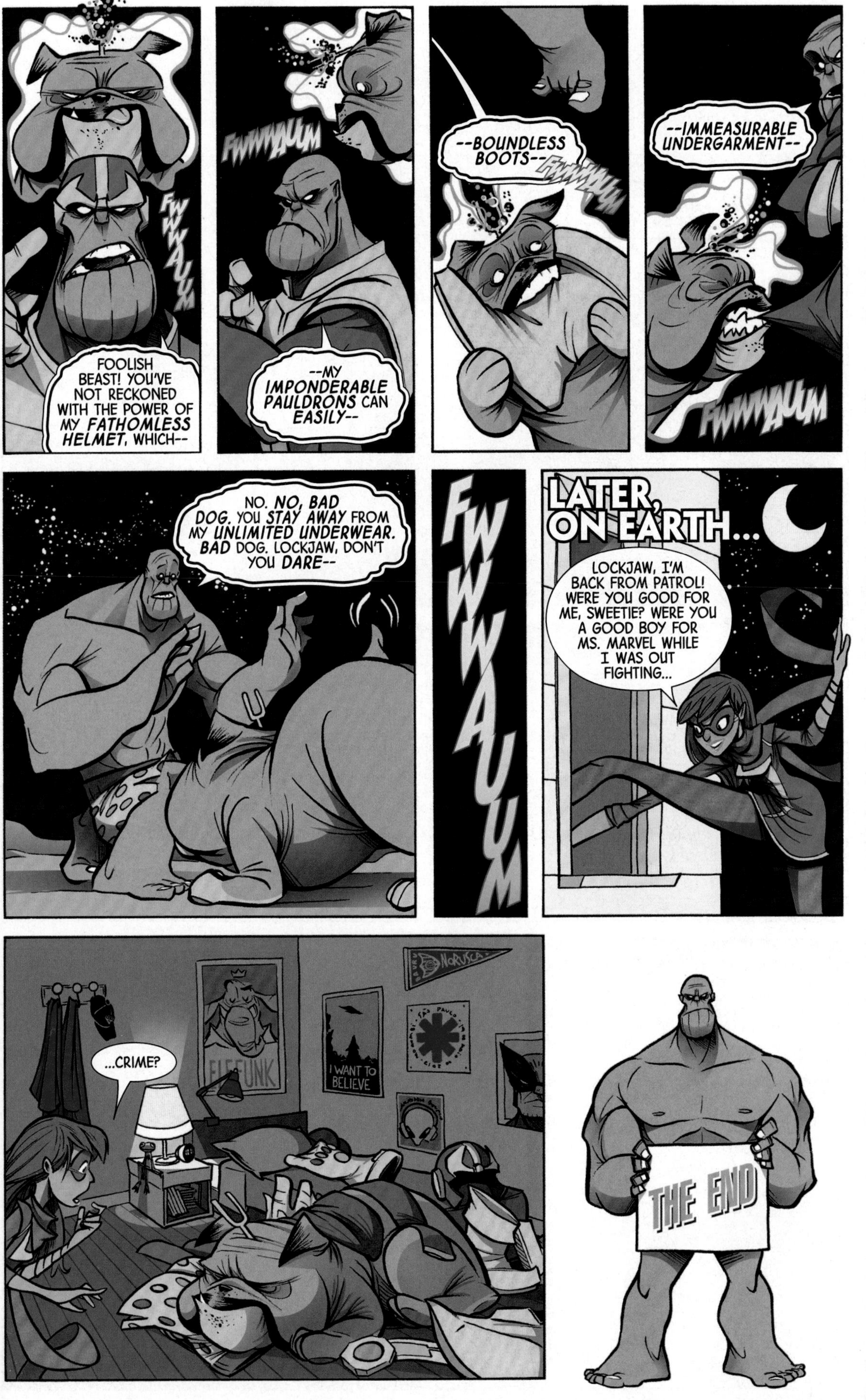
FWWAUUM
FOOLISH BEAST! YOU'VE NOT RECKONED WITH THE POWER OF MY FATHOMLESS HELMET, WHICH--
FWWAUUM
--MY IMPONDERABLE PAULDRONS CAN EASILY--
--BOUNDLESS BOOTS--
FWWAUUM
--IMMEASURABLE UNDERGARMENT--
FWWAUUM
NO. NO, BAD DOG. YOU STAY AWAY FROM MY UNLIMITED UNDERWEAR. BAD DOG. LOCKJAW, DON'T YOU DARE--
FWWAUUM
LATER, ON EARTH...
LOCKJAW, I'M BACK FROM PATROL! WERE YOU GOOD FOR ME, SWEETIE? WERE YOU A GOOD BOY FOR MS. MARVEL WHILE I WAS OUT FIGHTING...
...CRIME?
ELEFUNK
I WANT TO BELIEVE
THE END

RYAN **NORTH**
(writer)
GUSTAVO **DUARTE**
(artist)
VC's JOE **SABINO**
(letterer)

LOCKJAW
CANINE MASTER OF TIME AND SPACE in A CHRISTMAS PERIL

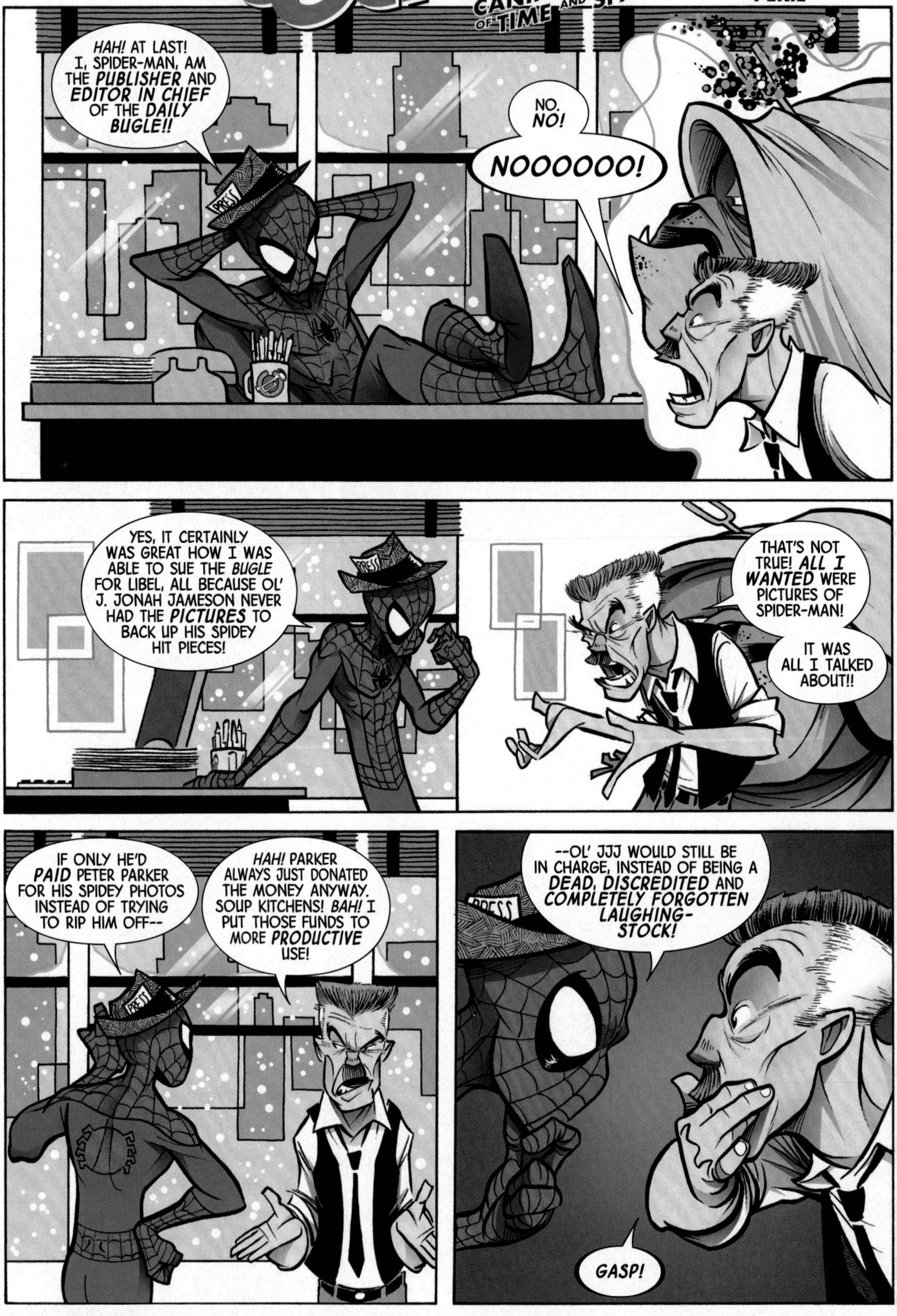
HAH! AT LAST! I, SPIDER-MAN, AM THE PUBLISHER AND EDITOR IN CHIEF OF THE DAILY BUGLE!!
PRESS
NO. NO!
NOOOOOO!
YES, IT CERTAINLY WAS GREAT HOW I WAS ABLE TO SUE THE BUGLE FOR LIBEL, ALL BECAUSE OL' J. JONAH JAMESON NEVER HAD THE PICTURES TO BACK UP HIS SPIDEY HIT PIECES!
THAT'S NOT TRUE! ALL I WANTED WERE PICTURES OF SPIDER-MAN!
IT WAS ALL I TALKED ABOUT!!
IF ONLY HE'D PAID PETER PARKER FOR HIS SPIDEY PHOTOS INSTEAD OF TRYING TO RIP HIM OFF--
HAH! PARKER ALWAYS JUST DONATED THE MONEY ANYWAY. SOUP KITCHENS! BAH! I PUT THOSE FUNDS TO MORE PRODUCTIVE USE!
--OL' JJJ WOULD STILL BE IN CHARGE, INSTEAD OF BEING A DEAD, DISCREDITED AND COMPLETELY FORGOTTEN LAUGHING-STOCK!
GASP!

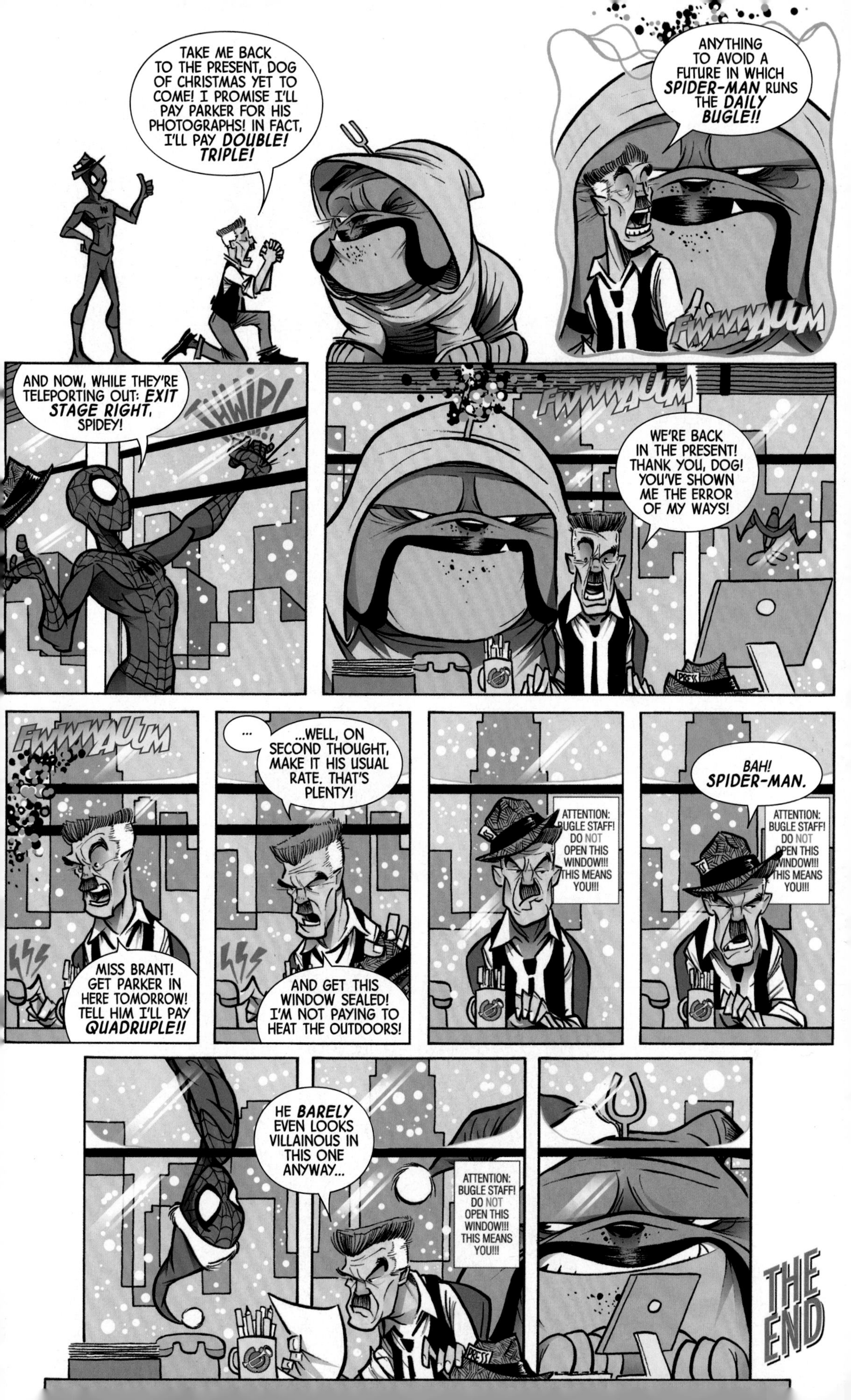
TAKE ME BACK TO THE PRESENT, DOG OF CHRISTMAS YET TO COME! I PROMISE I'LL PAY PARKER FOR HIS PHOTOGRAPHS! IN FACT, I'LL PAY DOUBLE! TRIPLE!
ANYTHING TO AVOID A FUTURE IN WHICH SPIDER-MAN RUNS THE DAILY BUGLE!!
FWWWAUUM
AND NOW, WHILE THEY'RE TELEPORTING OUT: EXIT STAGE RIGHT, SPIDEY!
THWIP!
FWWWAUUM
WE'RE BACK IN THE PRESENT! THANK YOU, DOG! YOU'VE SHOWN ME THE ERROR OF MY WAYS!
FWWWAUUM
MISS BRANT! GET PARKER IN HERE TOMORROW! TELL HIM I'LL PAY QUADRUPLE!!
...
...WELL, ON SECOND THOUGHT, MAKE IT HIS USUAL RATE. THAT'S PLENTY!
AND GET THIS WINDOW SEALED! I'M NOT PAYING TO HEAT THE OUTDOORS!
ATTENTION: BUGLE STAFF! DO NOT OPEN THIS WINDOW!!! THIS MEANS YOU!!!
BAH! SPIDER-MAN.
ATTENTION: BUGLE STAFF! DO NOT OPEN THIS WINDOW!!! THIS MEANS YOU!!!
HE BARELY EVEN LOOKS VILLAINOUS IN THIS ONE ANYWAY...
ATTENTION: BUGLE STAFF! DO NOT OPEN THIS WINDOW!!! THIS MEANS YOU!!!
THE END

CHARACTER DESIGNS BY **PHIL NOTO**

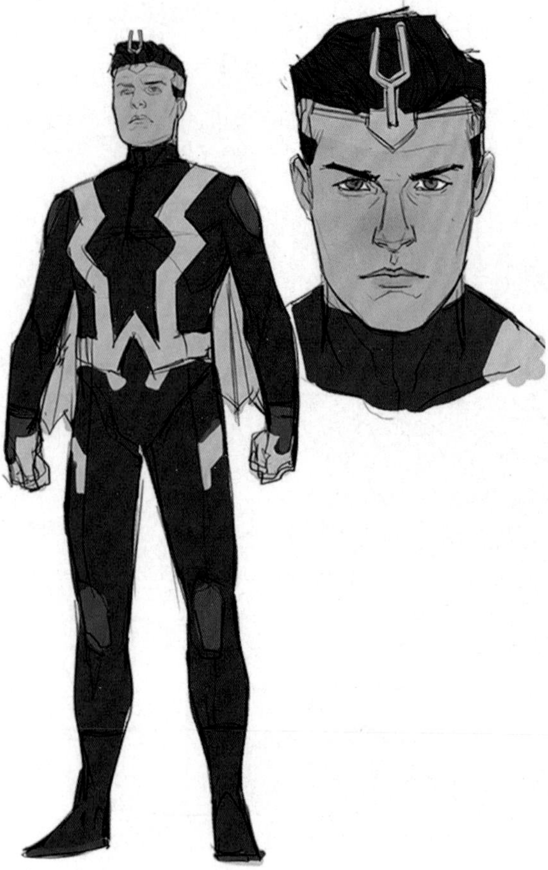

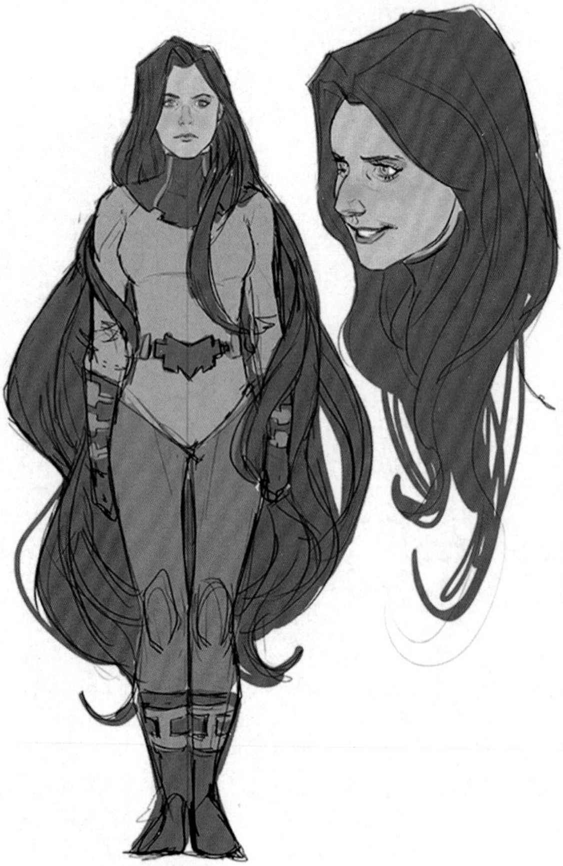

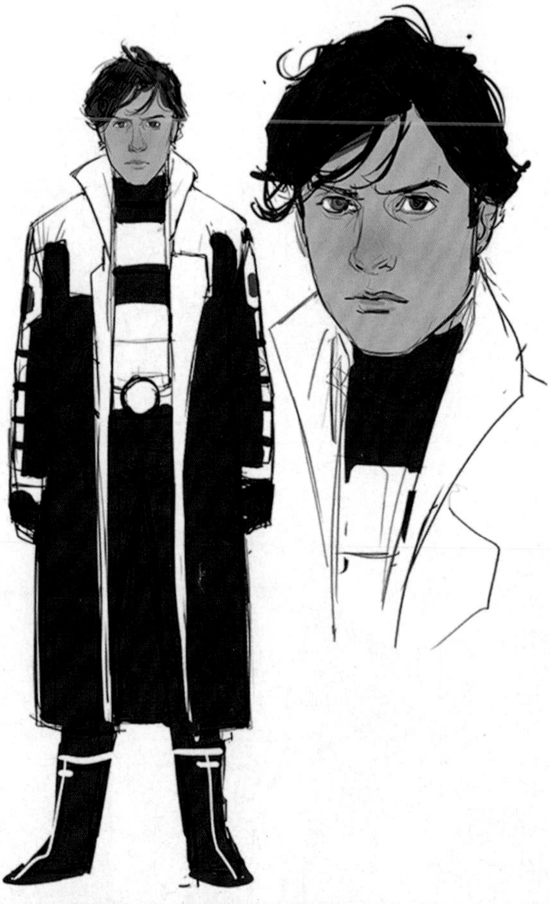